FOG ON THE TYNE

THE OFFICIAL HISTORY OF LINDISFARNE

First published in 1998 by
NORTHDOWN PUBLISHING LIMITED
PO Box 49, Bordon
Hants GU35 0AF

British Library Cataloguing-in-Publication Data
A catalogue for this book is available from the British Library

ISBN 1900711 07 9

Designed by Simon Joslin

Printed and bound in the EC

Also available from Northdown Publishing:
Rhinos, Winos & Lunatics! The Legend Of Man by Deke Leonard
Down By The Jetty – The Dr Feelgood Story by Tony Moon
The Streets Of London – The Official Biography Of Ralph McTell
by Chris Hockenhull
Drummed Out! The Sacking Of Pete Best by Spencer Leigh

Picture Credits

Photographs in this book have been reproduced courtesy of
John Anthony, Castle Communications, Michael Chapman,
Charisma / Virgin Records, Glen Colson, Maclolm Dix,
Ian Harper, Pat Hull, Ray Laidlaw / LMP, *Melody Maker*,
Mercury Records, Billy Mitchell, Jimmy Moore,
New Millennium Communications, Simon Nicol,
River City Records, Colin Thompson, Warner Brothers Records,
Barrie Wentzell, Dave Wood

While every effort has been made to trace the owners of
photographs used, this has sometimes proved impossible: such
copyright owners are invited to contact the publishers.

Acknowledgments

Thanks and deep gratitude to the following:

Ray Laidlaw and Rod Clements for being so wonderfully, patiently, 'cerebrally retentive'.

Very special thanks also to: Simon Cowe, Marty Craggs, Alan Hull, Dave Hull-Denholm, Billy Mitchell, Ian Thompson, Glen 'I've Never Seen Anything Like It Since…' Colson, John Anthony, Gus Dudgeon, Stephen Lipson, Hugh Murphy, Kenny Craddock, Bob Sargeant, Rick Blaskey, Simon Nicol, 'Uncle' Ralph McTell, Mike 'The Bike' Cartledge, Steve Hackett, David Batchelor, Steve Weltman, Chas Chandler, Sid Griffin, Michael Chapman, Rab Noakes, Alan Clark, Bert Jansch, Jeff Griffin, Tommy Duffy, Johnny Turnbull, Roy Hollingworth, John Walters, Jake Burns, Chris Rea, Barbara Dickson, Ray and Sandy Jackson.

Also To: Dave Wood, Colin Gibson, Billy Budis, Barry McKay, Peter Hamill, Brendan Healy, Mike Heatley (EMI), Dave Pegg, Roger Newell (*Bassist* magazine), Mike Waller, Rich Brunton, John Oley, Marianne Mitchelson, Marie McKidd, Michelle Dobson, Jackie Ruddick, Paul Conroy, Jimmy Moore, Bob Young, Micky Moody, Gary And Louise, Lesley Laidlaw, Gail Colson, Rick Rycroft, Frank Gibbon, Mike Elliott, Ian Welch at Northdown, Malcolm Dix, Phil Bromby for the Bickershaw programme, Chris Hart, Dave Bainbridge, Geoff Heslop, Jed Grimes.

For use of your work – Steve Sutherland (*Melody Maker*), Chris Charlesworth, Chris Welch, Caroline Boucher (*Disc & Music Echo*), *The Newcastle Evening Chronicle*, *The Journal* (Phillip Crawley and especially Dick Godfrey), Phil Sutcliffe (*Q*), Ken Kessler, Simon Jones, Sean McGhee (*Rock'n'Reel*), Geoff Wall (*Folk On Tap*), *Magic In The Air*, *Music Week*, Dave Laing & Richard Newman, Johnny Rogan, Ken Garner (*In Session Tonight*), Jerry Gilbert (*Sounds*), Michael Watts (*MM*), Michael Wale (*The Times*), Bob Randall (*NME*), Roy Carr (*NME*), Dick Meadows (*Sounds*), Keith Altham, Rosalind Russell (*Record Mirror*), Robin Denselow (*The Guardian*).

For continued enthusiasm – Frankie Marc Anthony (KLAS 99.9FM Ca, USA); Chris Groom and Julia Revell – without whom… (it's absolutely true); Reinhard Groll (keep up the great work).

For keeping the beat while I was always somewhere else – Ken Ward; Michael Heatley for leaving me alone to get on with it (thanks for the faith); Phil Allen, for 'tech support' (an understatement); Nikki for giving us Lauren; Kenny and Carol for understanding when I had to keep turning down nights out; Riddo – for being 'Riddo'…

Finally, this book is dedicated, with all my love to Lauren Jade, Richard Ian. And to Elaine – for all the patience, support, faith and especially, love – that I sometimes didn't deserve.

I hope your name is here – if not, please accept my apologies. No matter how little you felt your contribution, it was important to me…

Fog On The Tyne is for the memory of Alan Hull; Chas Chandler; Hugh Murphy and for inspiration, Gordon Clarence Hill.

The
Fog
on
&
the
Tyne
is all min

Contents

The fog on the Tyne is all mine

Hey *Mr Dream Seller*

This book was never supposed to be 'a book'…About ten years ago, it occurred to me there were an awful lot of talented musicians who had done all right for themselves in this business. So, encouraged by the support of one of my colleagues at a community enterprise project in Hartlepool, I began researching, initially with the aid of my trusty two-year-old *Music Week Directory*. Naturally, Lindisfarne had to be included in any overview of the North East. An interview was set up with Ray Laidlaw and we met backstage at Newcastle City Hall at Christmas 1988.

Ray patiently went through Lindisfarne's history – and I came away well chuffed. It soon became apparent that their story had never been fully told, and when I asked Ray for any other material he felt would be useful I was swiftly handed five bulging carrier bags of cuttings, photos and assorted ephemera…

Not realising that this was probably a ruse to get this lot in some kind of order, I then spent several weeks putting everything in sequence while compiling a diary of events. 'This is going to make a great chapter', I thought. We continued speaking via phone calls and occasional face-to-face meetings, all the time accruing more and more names and phone numbers. By 1990, I had been roped in to contribute to the band's tour programmes. It also became quite clear that a book about the band was definitely feasible. As I searched for a publisher, I continued to expand my anecdotal sources and began travelling across Britain.

Around the same time, I began working for the Virgin label. When the axe fell following the takeover by EMI, I had just instigated a two-volume CD collection of Lindisfarne and related rarities and outtakes called 'Buried Treasures'. Ironically, the man who had given me my marching orders – Virgin MD Paul Conroy – was always hugely supportive of the idea of the albums; he went back a long way with Lindisfarne, back to when he used to be a booker with the Terry King Agency. We had even talked over lunch at Kensal House about plans to celebrate Charisma's 25th Anniversary and how he was thinking of getting bands like Lindisfarne and Genesis back into some of the old clubs.

The redundancy thing was nothing personal and, eventually, I also compiled CD reissues for Jack the Lad and Charisma stablemate Bert Jansch. After Virgin, I found myself drawn further into the Lindisfarne family and in 1993 recorded the majority of the interviews for what was then called *Can't Kill The Spirit*. You will have to read much further to find out the inspiration behind that…

It is important readers realise when so many of the interviews took place. Si's were recorded over two separate occasions at the Cumberland

Arms in Tynemouth, Marty's upstairs in the Maggie Bank in North Shields and Rod's over two mammoth sessions at his house in Rothbury – one going right through the night. Ray's happened just about everywhere and anywhere else. The relevance of when these occasions took place is that what was said in the interviews relating to Alan Hull was not affected by the emotion of his passing. Nothing was tainted – in a positive sense – by rosy recollections. There are places in the text where, reading this now, some of what is contained within is either profound, endearing or funny.

I was honoured when co-manager Steve Weltman suggested I look after Lindisfarne's press and radio after Alan's death; the band are now one cornerstone of my work in press and radio. A year later, I was asked to look after press on Alan's final solo album, 'Statues And Liberties'. I relished the challenge, but was struck by the circumstances.

Now, in 1998, a second generation of road crew and technicians have come through the ranks after their fathers; even the second row of musicians, with the sons of Ray Laidlaw, Marty Craggs and Billy Mitchell putting their own contemporary stamp on music.

Fog On The Tyne – The Official History Of Lindisfarne was well on its way before I had any commitment to the band. They have always stood for honesty, and I have not been asked at any point to compromise the content of this book. Neither have I poured forth with a stream of opinionated drivel. I do not profess to be Albert Goldman. What I hope I have done is to report – as thoroughly as I can – on just what happened. I was never interested in any tabloid, sensationalist crap. It's just a great story.

Dave Ian Hill
Hartlepool, October 1998

where have you been

Chapter
ONE
LONNIE D, CLIFF AND BOB

'In early summer 1970, a tape arrived in Stratton-Smith's office and nobody knew what to make of it. So, they gave it to me and I went, "This is fucking great!" So they said "We'll send you off to Newcastle (I thought great, 'cause Mum was from there) speak to the band and do some demos."

'So I hopped on the train and, when I got into Newcastle station, a guy came and picked me up – I think it was Rod Clements – and said "Come back and meet the guys."

'So he's driving through Shields on the red road that heads out towards Tynemouth and I'm thinking "This is really weird…" Then we got to the big roundabout just before Tynemouth, turned right past the allotments and headed down Birtley Avenue until we got to number 60. Rod says to me "Have you ever been here before, John?" and I said, "Yeah – as a matter of fact, I used to live in that house over there…"

'They were called Brethren and it was me who came up with the name Lindisfarne. We'd been told there was another band called Brethren who were about to get big in America, so I said "Brethren is like a brotherhood…why don't you call yourself after the first community here in the North East – Lindisfarne? The monks at the Priory on the island were the first brethren, so there it was. I think the drummer really liked the name.'

This was how John Anthony recalled the Naming Ceremony, that essential, proud moment in the career of every band that every member claims to recall with utmost clarity just in case, one day, someone writes a book about them. In fact, what most of the band recall thinking about Anthony – who became the producer of the band's first album for the Charisma label, 'Nicely Out Of Tune' – was that he was 'potty'. Someone did, apparently mention Holy Island (or Lindisfarne, as it's known) among many other suggestions, although another was Dog Leap Stairs (whose later consolation was to be name-checked in Dire Straits 'Down To The Waterline'). There was also Two Ball Lonnen, a road name in the west end of the city – 'but that,' recalled Ray Jackson, 'sounded like an old blues singer.'

To the band, it was a bit like calling yourself Lytham St Annes or Kingston upon Hull. Still, Lindisfarne it was; a wonderful, intriguing, musical brew fermenting in a front room of a house on the North East coast of England – the same coast the monks had chosen to make their home in AD 634.

Rod Clements (born 17 November 1947 in North Shields) and Simon 'Si' Cowe (1 April 1948) first met around 1952 as infants at Kings School Tynemouth. 'Obviously, there was no musical connection,' recalls Rod, 'but we knew each other. We were part of the same gaggle of friends through school, up to the age of about 12, but I was closer to another lad called Bob Sargeant.' Bob – who would many years later gain a reputation in bands with people such as the Liverpool Scene's Andy Roberts and former Jethro Tull man Mick Abrahams as well as for his work as a producer with Madness, Haircut 100, the Beat and Breathe – would not come back into the picture until a little later. In the meantime, the first musical collaboration was to be instigated by one Ray Laidlaw.

Ray, who was also born in North Shields, on 28 May 1948, recalls that when he was 12, his cousin – who lived just over the road – was going out with a lad down the street whose little brother was learning to play guitar. It was mostly Lonnie Donegan songs, and Elvis Presley had left his mark on Tyneside as everywhere else. Geordie lads the Shadows were the first home-grown band that really had an effect on them all.

Ray got to know a lad called Giles Bavidge, 'and it turned out his neighbour was Simon Cowe.' Si recalls the time clearly. 'On my ninth or tenth birthday, I'd got an old Russian-made Spanish guitar because Giles' brother Neville had started playing skiffle. Whatever year it was, Lonnie Donegan was doing "My Old Man's A Dustman" – that's when I started playing. I learned E minor, then C, then B7th. B7th was a big stage in my career!' Ray's diary at the time recorded not only details of every visit to the movies (he remains committed to the big screen), but also reflected the excitement of being in your first band and the overwhelming impact of British rock'n'roll's earliest heroes:

> 'At last I managed to obtain a pair of drumsticks.'
> 'Today America tried to land a rocket on the moon. This was unsuccessful, but some good TV pictures are expected to be transmitted as the rocket passes.'
> 'Today, Colonel Glenn eventually made it and managed to orbit the earth three times. He was congratulated by Kennedy and Tito, among others.'
> 'Went to see The Young Ones this evening.'
> 'Giles and Simon and I are going to form a group. Simon is getting an amplifier and pick-up. Giles is getting a new guitar and I am getting some drums for Christmas.'
> 'In the evening, we took the tape recorder and guitars to my place. A great twang session.'
> 'Granda is seeing about some drums for me from a man who used to play.'
> 'I got my drums tonight. After a while Giles came up and we had our first go with the git and the drums.'

Below: St Joseph's School, North Shields, 1958. Ray Laidlaw is fourth from left, back row.

Below right: The Aristokats pictured at Camp Terrace, North Shields, August 1963. From left: Ray Laidlaw, Giles Bavidge, Rob Gray and Simon Cowe.

The group line-up was finally settled with Ray, Simon, Giles Bavidge and schoolfriend Rob Gray – who, according to Ray, learned to play bass by mathematics. 'He'd count the beats in the song. So if, for example there was 240 beats in the song, he'd know that on say, the 16th beat, he'd have to move his fingers along the fretboard. If he lost count he'd always be three beats behind everyone else.' According to Si, 'He couldn't actually play bass, so he just mimed most of the time! After a month or so, though, he *did* learn to play a few notes…'

Within days, they were faced with the prospect of potential stardom when, following an appearance by Si's mother on the popular Tyne Tees TV variety programme *The One O'Clock Show*, it was arranged for Bill Sykes, a 'man from the telly', to come and see the young stars-to-be. It was to come to nothing however, when, after the offer of a gig, Bill followed up with a phone call to Si: 'You know that gig? Well you've got to be members of the Musicians' Union and we've got to pay you a minimum of £30, so I'm afraid there's just no question…' Some

consolation came in the fact that, as Ray noted in his diary, that 'Mr Adams thought that our sound was good, but our presentation not so hot.' It was perhaps just as well; it was late January 1963 and Si had to return to boarding school at Fettes in Edinburgh.

Not that the geographic divide was going to stop the eager young Mr Cowe from continuing his musical apprenticeship: 'I started the first ever rock band at Fettes. I don't think it actually had a name, but I can remember we gave the first ever "rock" concert at the school. We did Swinging Blue Jeans, that sort of stuff, and the Headmaster actually came up to me afterwards and said, "I very much approve, Cowe. *Very* loud, but very good." I didn't expect that!

'As Fettes was a boarding school, rules were very strict, but come the weekend, on a Sunday, we actually used to escape – which was totally against the rules, you needed an "uptown chit" to do that – and do gigs in Edinburgh at funny, poky little places… We did about five. I remember I had a Burns Black Bison, with a great big tremolo arm like the Shadows were playing, 'cause they'd changed from Stratocasters – Hank had, anyway… I was really chuffed to be playing it. The only disadvantage was in the way the tremolo was set up. If you snapped a string, you were knackered, because the tension goes and the rest of the tuning goes "woo-inngg." Which happened, of course, in the first number!

'Giles and I actually wrote a song when we were 12; it was pretty naff, but imagine the Johnny Cash-type guitar "train" trundling along in E major.' In his defence, Si does point out that when he finally did write a 'proper' song – 'At Last (Number One Blues)' he was 'dead proud of it, because it was quite complicated…not just a normal blues!'

By Easter that year, the Aristokats, as they had by now called themselves, were playing regularly in and around Tynemouth while Si was away. They had even begun to consider the intricacies of increased amplification, as Ray's diary one again faithfully noted:

'While talking today Giles and I hatched an idea to remove the works from their old television and use it as an amplifier case.'

He was also quick to note that, having been 'given authority to take the telly to bits, we have been advised not to touch the works as it is dangerous to do so.' Finally, the large speaker in the bottom was linked up to Rob's amplifier 'to give him extra volume' and Ray's Dad added shelves 'in order to take the tape recorder as well as the amp.'

There was one major worry, though: Simon had made his own guitar in crafts lessons at Fettes, and no-one knew what to expect until he arrived home for the summer holidays.

Simon: 'I did woodwork lessons for one term and, at some point, had a really nice German "cello" guitar; I butchered it by smashing off the body and got the neck – 'cause I thought that was beyond me – I was sure I could make a solid body, which I did. I also made this tremolo. I didn't think it through, though; a tremolo's got to go down as well as up. The only way I could get the tremolo to do anything was by standing on the guitar with both feet, gripping the lever with both hands, while wrenching the arm up and down…which wasn't very practical for doing gigs.'

Still, the summer finished on a high when by August, Ray noted in his diary that, 'at the Gaumont, we had our own dressing room' and two weeks later, 'we were paid 30 bob each and got free food and drink.' Ultimately, like all school groups, the Aristokats drifted apart. It was especially difficult because Si's absence meant they could only play during holidays.

It was around this time that Bob Sargeant came back into the picture, with a group called the Druids. 'It was me and a chap called Pete Morton,' Bob recalled. 'We both bought guitars and Ray Laidlaw's Dad used to be my Ma's butcher and that's how it came about, with him saying, "My son's a drummer," and her saying, "My son's got a guitar," – that sort of thing.' Bob, who was lead guitarist and singer, recalls a 'residency' at Whitley Bay Boys Club, just along the coast, although 'It wasn't so much a residency – it's just that we played there six or seven times.'

When walking east from Percy Main
Or maybe take the North Tyne train
And coming South
Through green and sunny fields
You hit a place – it ain't a town
It's more a sort of a hole in the ground
A dirty hole
Called North Shields

You pass the processed fish manure
And scattered over here or there
Perhaps a corporation rubbish cart
You take a walk down Saville Street
Where if you're lucky, you might meet
A queer, or maybe even a tart

(© Simon Cowe/Giles Bavidge)

Below: Downtown Faction, circa 1967, from left: Don Whittaker, Ray, Richard Squirrel and Rod Clements.

11

Their first ever gig at the Catholic Working Men's Club in North Shields is an occasion Bob remembers clearly: 'I'd have been 15, 16 at the time and all had little Swinging Blue Jeans-type denim waistcoats, white shirts and knitted black ties. We all used to climb in the back of the butcher's van and off we went. We used to rehearse in my Gran's garage and I have a vivid memory of being in there rehearsing when President Kennedy got shot.'

For Ray, like all of them, it was the time the Beat Boom was starting: 'That was '63, '64 time. We just basically learned every song everybody did, like the Rolling Stones, the Mojos.' It was good training. The Druids had to play for long periods of time with residencies at youth clubs every other week, mostly in the North Shields, Tynemouth and Whitley Bay areas. According to Ray, 'we got reasonably proficient at it, I suppose.'

Bob Sargeant was already giving an indication of his future talents. 'Even then,' says Ray, 'he was very into sounds and used to pick up on things. He was one of the very first people I knew who was talking about this bloke called Eric Clapton.' According to Bob, the band fell apart after about a year and a half, 'more to do with people drifting away'n'stuff. It was almost like a school band, even though we didn't go to school together.'

There was also a big social element around the scene in Tynemouth, especially at the Calypso Coffee Bar in Front Street, just around the corner from where Ray Laidlaw now lives. 'We used to go *en masse*, six or seven of us – 15 sometimes – on a Sunday afternoon,' Bob recalls. 'But times changed and people wanted to play different stuff and had girlfriends – it was "he's spending more time with her than the band", that sort of thing.'

It wasn't long before Rod Clements, too, was drawn to the delights of the Calypso and its wonderful jukebox: 'I had to pass the end of Ray's street to get the bus to Tynemouth, where I had a friend called Angus Lindsay. We used to play blues records in each others' front rooms, imitating Sonny Boy Williamson, Jimmy Reed and stuff like that: he played the harp and I played acoustic guitar. Come to think of it, it was well early for us to have been doing that, 'cause that was before I was in groups'n'things. I think we had a school beat group, though.'

The fish shop at the bottom of Queen Alexandra Road was the setting for his first meeting with Ray Laidlaw, as Ray remembers clearly. 'I'd been aware of this interesting-looking chap walking round carrying an instrument case, because in those days, that was rare – people carrying guitar cases.' So the two talked of things musical and, as a result, Rod soon began frequenting the coffee bar. According to Rod 'it was never a close thing – just during the holidays' because, like Si, he was going away to school.

Rod had already formed a group called the Downtown Faction – one of several he'd got together in the 'very earliest, "messing-about-with-first-guitars, hardly-able-to-play-a-chord" days.' His debut public appearance was doing covers: '"Ginny Come Lately", "Driftin'" by the Shads. We did a prison song that was a hit in the early 1960s…not "Big House", but something like that.'

Below: Downtown Faction, 1967, possibly at St Cuthbert's College, Durham University. From left: Rod, Si, Ray, Richard.

By this time Rod had moved to bass, George Robertson played guitar, while Chris di Soren from Sunderland took the drum stool behind a singer called Richard Squirrel. Rod became the bass player 'because I increasingly fancied doing it. Even when I played guitar, I used to play the Duane Eddy tunes – "Rebel Rouser" and stuff. I wasn't into chords and didn't fancy learning all the "posh" stuff.'

The Faction played during the holidays as well as term time, at 18th birthday parties and the like. George Robertson lived 40 miles away near Bishop Auckland in Durham, and occasionally the group would travel up to each others' houses, to 'have a bit of a knockabout'. This line-up did play one gig at the Cave, just along from the Calypso in Tynemouth – a venue regularly frequented by Ray Laidlaw. 'I think that might have been our last summer holidays together, because we all had high hopes of keeping the group together and "we'll-all-go-London-and-become-pop-stars" sort of thing. Obviously, it wasn't to be.'

The Druids having broken up, Ray was looking to start a second version of the group – this time with Rod. 'Ray came up to me, having seen us at the Cave, and asked what the crack was. So I explained we'd all just left school, and he asked me if I wanted to be in the new version of the Druids.' The line-up was completed by Bob Sargeant and Pete Morton. 'They were looking for a singer,' recalls Rod, 'and were all keen on Bob doing it, but he wanted to concentrate on guitar.'

The band's influences were already reflecting a growing interest in British blues: Bob and Rod were particularly influenced by the 'Five Live Yardbirds', which they 'played to death.' For a while, they went by the name of Impact, ('If we did any gigs, it would have been three, four at the most') playing most of 'Five Live Yardbirds' and a few other songs. 'When you're young players, you go mad on an album and you learn every bloody tune on it. So if someone else can play every tune as well you've got a band.'

Very soon, the name changed to…Downtown Faction! 'We failed to turn up at a booking at a social club in Shields we'd decided wasn't for us,' Rod recalls, 'and omitted to tell anybody. So, looking for a new name, Downtown Faction had ceased to be, so I said, "Why don't we have that?"'

Above: Model T in 1967, from left, Will Browell, Bob Reynolds, Alan Green (front) and Mitch.

The search for a singer saw the return of Richard Squirrel, although this was to be relatively short-lived as his employers, detergent manufacturer Proctor and Gamble, posted him to Canada. While there, he and Rod, both devout blues aficionados, would write feverish letters to each other: 'Richard used to tell me about this amazing stuff he was hearing, all the mid-1960s psychedelic folk-rock like Paul Butterfield and Ritchie Havens, Leonard Cohen and Joni Mitchell. I remember saying "What do you think of all this new fizzidelic stuff?" – writing it like that – 'cause over in this country nobody understood what was going on.

'There was an element in the British music press that wasn't taking it seriously, and I think a bit of that had rubbed off on me. When I asked him about it and I got this long, serious letter from Richard saying that I shouldn't take the mickey out of it…"it's very serious". Oops, *sorry!*'

Bob Sargeant, on the other hand, left an impression on the others for more than just his skills as a player, as Rod recalls: 'He had this old plywood Rosetti Airstream guitar, which was as cheap as you could get but he could play it great. He wanted to improve on it, though; it wasn't a "hip" guitar to have. So he took it home, scraped all the paint off it, covered it with glue then scattered birdseed all over it! They used to say people played guitar to pull the birds, but *that* was a bit extreme!'

Soon, though, he grew tired of playing guitar and bought a Vox Continental organ. With the change of instrument came a change of band, and Bob left to join John Turnbull – later of Ian Dury and the Blockheads – and Colin Gibson, who would go on to work with Micky Moody (later of Whitesnake) in Snafu, in the Primitive Sect. 'That was short-lived. I think we did a dozen gigs and then I saw an advert for the Junco Partners saying "Organist Required". I got the gig 'cause I was the only organist who rang!'

The Downtown Faction, meanwhile, was left with a fluid line-up, with Rod and Ray at the centre and Bob Sargeant flitting in and out. A lad called John Spooner briefly filled the singer's shoes, while Billy 'Mitch' Mitchell was another mate from Shields to appear in the line-up for a few gigs. He would, in time, become very central to the extended Lindisfarne 'family'. 'But we kept a place for Richard for when he came back from Canada,' stresses Rod.

Mitch recalls this period of activity very clearly: 'When I was about 15, I used to go to the church youth club in North Shields with a lad who was mates with Will Browell. Will had played in the Wildcats with Hilton Valentine – later of the Animals – and, as he wasn't doing anything at the time, he joined our group, the Peasantville Dustmans' Choir. Why we decided to form one in the first place is a mystery, 'cause nobody could play anything: there was one guitar player and seven singers! Then more of us decided to play, so we had four guitarists – though we told one of the lads, Bob Reynolds, to buy a bass. The Church then offered to buy us a drum kit for £26 from a catalogue, and we paid them back at ten bob a week.

'We were amplified through radios and got a little spare plastic microphone: I had to be *this* close so it could pick up… Anyway, we got a bit better and then we called ourselves the Triffids, then later on, Model T.' Around this time, he became aware of Downtown Faction. 'They were really good,' Mitch recalls, 'because they had a proper drummer and a proper bass guitarist.' Each group would often check each other out as part of a mutual admiration society. 'I can't remember how, but Ray Laidlaw and I got on speaking terms. I loved the stuff they were doing, because I was into the blues, so every so often I would sing with them. I didn't want to leave my band, though, because the Faction didn't get many gigs. A few people liked that sort of stuff, but we got *loads* of gigs – because people liked what *we* were doing!'

Mitch was asked to join again after Richard Squirrel had gone to Canada, but by that time he had got a job. 'I remember Ray telling me that they were going to ask me and they were going to ask Ray Jackson from the Autumn States. I though about it and said no. Oops…'

Before Bob Sargeant joined their ranks, the Junco Partners were a major influence on Downtown Faction, as Ray Laidlaw explains. 'They were our heroes, and Rod and I used to go every week to see them. The Juncos, for my money, were the best band ever to come out of Newcastle and not make it. They were a real raunchy, soul band. They did similar material to everybody else, but they did them better – the first band I ever heard do "In The Midnight Hour".'

Rod and Ray would catch the Juncos every Wednesday night at a Whitley Bay pub called the Vic. 'It was then we realised just how important a rhythm section was to the band – they had a wonderful one in John Woods and Dave Sproats – so we set ourselves the task of getting a band together as good as that.' Still with no singer, they began advertising around the music shops in Newcastle for someone into 'rhythm and blues, Dylan stuff – which, at the time was a bit left-field, because most bands in Newcastle did soul and Tamla.'

It was now 1965-66, and the pair had felt the full force of Dylan's' first electric album, 'Highway 61 Revisited' and the power of the Butterfield Blues Band, although they were just as affected by the harmonies of the Lovin' Spoonful and the Mamas and the Papas. It was, by Ray's own admission, 'a strange amalgam.' In hindsight, such influences were to show through as the 1970s beckoned. The first response to their ad came from one Jeff Sadler who, as it turned out, was in the same class at school as an expatriate Glaswegian called Mark Knopfler. The pair had learned to play guitar together.

'Jeff's Dad was a builder,' recalls Ray, 'and he seemed immensely rich to us, although I don't know if he was!' Rod continues: 'This guy rang up my house – I think Ray was there at the time – and said he'd seen our advert. So I asked what guitar he had – always the first question – and he said, "I've got a Gretsch." "Brilliant!" I said. "And a Harmony!" So I went on, "What kind of amp have you got?" "True Voice," he says. He'd got the gig already – before we'd even *heard* him!

'So we arranged to meet up. Jeff suggested the Central Station: "I'll be driving this Bedford Dormobile Van." "You're *in*!" So we met up with him and he could play – not 'arf…' Jeff had a place to rehearse, too – his Dad's summerhouse in the garden, his Dad even playing piano for the band on a couple of occasions. Jeff Sadler was, without doubt, to prove a major asset and, in Ray Laidlaw's estimation, 'A wonderful, thoughtful and intelligent guitar player.'

Richard Squirrel returned from Canada and for a while, the line-up was settled. Another guitarist called Don Whittaker was also invited into the fold around this time. 'Don's mother owned the Cave,' recalls Si. 'It was a great place – sweaty walls and a deafening jukebox.' Apparently, Mick Taylor was a good friend of Don and would often stay at his place whenever he was in the area, 'playing with Mayall, or whoever…Don was also in Them, very briefly,' adds Si.

Rod recalls that Don was at one point Jeff's replacement when they felt the latter's commitment wasn't all it should be. Looking back, this was perhaps the first hint of things to come. However, the band did do a couple of gigs with both Jeff and Don and a tape was actually made of this line-up, 'although nobody can play it, because it's on quarter-inch four-track tape, which is now obsolete.' The period was to prove important in the musical life of Ray and Rod, as the former explained: 'It was then that we learned about experimenting with music; all about improvisation. We went right through our version of "acid rock" – all that sort of stuff. This was around the time of Hendrix – 1966 – but still all blues-based.'

This was to prove a successful mix with audiences too, and Downtown Faction became a popular draw on the coast circuit. There was, however, soon another exit from the ranks. Rod had decided to take a year off the band to concentrate on studies for his General Arts Degree at Durham University, in October 1968, striking 'a sort of 'deal' with his parents that 'if I got a degree, then I could go and do what I liked and I'd have a qualification to fall back on. They had different ambitions for me…follow in

Right: The highly-rated Jeff Sadler, circa 1967.

Opposite: Si's back room at Camp Terrace. From left: Richard, Jeff, Ray, Si (front).

Dad's footsteps and be a lawyer. I don't think my parents understood that I wanted to play guitar.' Such was always the way in rock'n'roll…

Re-enter Simon Cowe who, despite a full school life, had kept himself musically busy while at Fettes. At 16, he had to make a decision concerning his choice of A levels. Following an interview with his careers officer, Simon recalls phoning his architect father and asking 'What do I want to be?' A civil engineer, came the answer. 'Oh great, I said – I like scientific things.' However, when confirmation of his university place arrived, Simon promptly hid it – unopened – under his bedroom carpet. He was 18, and his father, believing his son had not been accepted, arranged interviews with some film units in the heart of London's film-land, around Wardour Street and Greek Street. Despite a genuine interest in photography, no work was forthcoming, according to Simon, 'because I wasn't a member of the union.'

In an extreme attempt to please his Dad, Simon decided to work on a building site. Cowe Senior had several contacts and one builder, as a favour, employed Simon as a bitumen carrier in North Shields. No sooner had he seen his first week out, when, carrying a bucket of hot bitumen up a ladder, the bucket caught the lip of the roof, spilling hot bitumen on his hand. Instinctively, Simon grabbed the scalded hand with the other – and the two fused together.

He has a clear memory of the occasion: 'At the hospital, they managed to free my hands after about two hours. I temporarily lost a layer of skin.' Luckily, there was a silver lining to this unfortunate event. With his first week's pay, Simon had also paid his first ever Insurance Stamp and 'for that one stamp,' he gleefully recalls, 'I got six months' Industrial Accident Benefit!' Thus supported, Simon went on holiday to London , catching up with several of his old school friends and playing some music together. There was even paid work as Commis Chef at the RAC Club in Pall Mall during the day and then out all night at the casinos.

When his hand finally healed, Simon returned to Tyneside and the salubrious working environment of Barbecue Express. When his father asked, in time-honoured fashion, when he was going to get a proper job, Simon's reply was clear: 'I like playing my guitar and doing rock'n'roll.' His father proceeded to find an alternative, at Turner's Photographers in Newcastle, and this did not meet with a 'negative' response. Simon did at least aspire to join a film unit and, over 18 months, learned everything he could about photography and thoroughly enjoyed his work there.

While still working at Turners, he would drive his father (who had lost his licence) up to the city each day. On one occasion, passing Ray Laidlaw at a bus stop, Simon offered a lift. 'I hadn't seen Ray for a few years and, at the time, he was an art student.' Ray mentioned Downtown Faction and that the band needed some photos: would Si be interested? Indeed he was, and the photos were duly taken.

As far as his musical introduction into the band is concerned, there is still confusion. According to Si, Rod Clements had, on two or three occasions, to visit his parents, who had retired to Majorca due to ill-health, and Si believes he stepped into his shoes. 'The band had three or four gigs booked over the two weeks that Rod would be away, so over the weekend he showed me all his bass lines. I knew the band by then, 'cos I was assistant roadie!'

This version of events is somewhat confused by time, Rod believing that while Si probably covered for him on these occasions, the invitation to join came during his last year away at university. Nonetheless, Rod recalls Si as playing bass 'more than competently'. Si on the other hand, recalls that, when Rod returned, it was a case of: 'Do you fancy rhythm guitar instead? I just tagged along.'

Around this time, as Simon recalls, he and Ray Laidlaw set up what he believes was the first rock festival in the North East. 'Ray's entrepreneurial skills were shining through even in those early days.' The blues festival, in Leazes Park, Newcastle, featured among others, Budgie Johnson's' Blues Band, the Callies, a singer named Alan Hull and, of course, Downtown Faction. Meanwhile, back at Turners, the people 'up above' had said that Simon must get his long hair cut.

'"What for?" I asked. "Because you're an assistant cameraman and you've got to look smart. One day – if you make it as a studio photographer – you might be allowed to wear a cravat and do 'casual' things like that…!"' So, on stage at Leazes Park, accompanied by a slow blues, Si's hair was indeed cut and the occasion reported in the next morning's Journal newspaper. Mr Laidlaw, ever the quotable individual, simply said, 'We are very pleased.' 'Haircut Blues', for the present, remains unreleased.

Fortunately for the band, Rod was appointed Social Secretary at his college and thanks to him, regular gigs came their way: 'I used to book the

headliners, national names like Brian Auger and Julie Driscoll, Wynder K Frogg, Fairport Convention – for 60 quid, I recall – and always used to book the Downtown Faction as support; see? When people got a bit sick of them – "Why do we always seem to have them?" – I'd get the Juncos in. As well as booking on behalf of the university, I also used to get commission off the lads!'

Rod gained his BA in English, Anthropology and Natural History in June 1969 (he also got married that spring to Kath, with whom he had shared a flat while at Durham). The line-up, which settled at Rod, Ray, Si, Jeff and Richard Squirrel, had begun recording demos even before Rod's return, 'running up and down to London to elicit the offer of a deal.'

Rod also recalls that around this time, the Downtown Faction began playing their first gigs away from the North East: 'They were through the Chrysalis agency that we got involved with, somehow. We went into the office and nobody took any notice of us...we were sitting there waiting for somebody to talk to us. I remember they were on the phone, "selling" this band as "being the scruffiest blues band you could ever wish to see...the guy's got this shabby old coat – you've never seen such a bunch of old hippies in your life! Singer stands on one leg to play the flute. They're called Jefro Toe..."'

Downtown Faction were gaining a sizeable reputation and becoming sought-after beyond Tyneside. Malcolm Dix, an agent who had the band on his books during this period, has evidence of regular bookings that show gigs such as the Locarno Ballroom, Sunderland, where the fee was £15. Another, on 18 January 1967 was followed by a second gig the next night, sharing the bill with White Ginger and the Tricity Clan, where Downtown Faction once again received the princely sum of £15. There were also gigs at the legendary Quay Club by the Tyne in Newcastle and the equally legendary Cellar Club in South Shields on 12 January 1967.

In March 1968, via a deal with Terry Ellis at the Ellis Wright (Chrysalis) Agency, the band ventured as far as Birmingham University and the London School of Economics. Rod 's letters at the time record that, in turn, their agents' fees at one point reached the dizzy heights of £2 – payable in Postal Orders, of course… In more recent years, Malcolm Dix has become much respected in the sports fraternity, at one point heading the Sports Council in the North East and facing up to the Newcastle United board around the time of Sir John Hall's arrival at St James' Park.

One recording 'test' – as they were known then – was for Island Records, with producer Guy Stevens (who worked with Free and Mott the Hoople). 'I remember him saying to us afterwards, "You sound like a band I've heard on this White Label I've just got,"' recalls Ray. 'A couple of our songs sounded just like Creedence Clearwater Revival to him. We'd never heard of them, though, at the time. "Keep working on it," he said, "It's a bit rough at the moment, but come back to me."'

The band did, however, impress engineers Mike Bobak and Geoff Gill, who offered to record them, although this was just to test their equipment in 'down time'. The test was at Morgan Studios – later known as Battery Studios – in Willesden. Ray: 'Originally there was just one little studio in the corner; now they've got the whole street...they were still building the place, at the time.' Si Cowe recalls being 'very impressed – 'cos we'd been told how expensive everything was.'

The band impressed owner Monty Babson and he offered the band a publishing deal – which Ray recalls 'wasn't up to much'. Nonetheless, for the next six months the band travelled down to Willesden eight or nine times, overnight after gigs and produced an album – although often, having driven seven or eight hours through the night, they would arrive to find someone else booked in. As Ray would later recall, 'Once we were told it was Blind Faith and another time Free.' Si's memory is of Cat Stevens getting there on one occasion, 'with no songs written at all; it was a nine-to-five thing… Scribble, scribble – we'll try this…'

There were other horror stories, too, as Rod explains: 'We used to get the morning shift – nine till one o'clock. We never had any money. Once, when the van broke down, we had to gum the radiator up with Opal Fruits – and when they finally gave out somewhere off the M1, we managed to find this place that had a Transit radiator, which they put in for us, and because we had no money we left a Fender bass. Si and I were both playing bass then, so we had a spare. So we left it with them, did the session, blagged the money off the guy at Morgan – Monty Babson – and picked the bass up on the way back!'

Such small problems were surmountable, but there was a shock in store for Rod on rejoining the band: dissent was in the air. 'I hadn't been in very long – a matter of hours I think – when I realised they wanted to have a shake-up. Richard Squirrel's head was on the chopping block and they wanted to check that out with me, because he was my friend from years ago.' The band once again chose Billy Mitchell as his replacement, but Mitch elected to stay where he was. So, while recording continued at Morgan, it was an acquaintance of Ray Laidlaw's who was approached – Raymond Lindsay Jackson.

'The first time I met Jacka,' Ray explains, 'I was at art college on Chillingham Road in Newcastle. I was going out for my lunch one day and I heard this amazing harmonica playing coming from the other end of the corridor. Because it was an old school, the sound went all the way round the walls...anyway, there he was sitting in the Common Room along with somebody with a guitar, playing this amazing harmonica. Obviously, we had similar interests. He was in a band called the Autumn States and ultimately, we nicked him with an offer he couldn't refuse.'

Jacka's love affair with the harmonica went much further back. His grandfather had taught him to play mouth-organ when he was ten years old (he was born on 12 December 1948, in North Shields) and

17

as soon as he heard Little Walter's harp on Bo Diddley's 'Pretty Thing', he was converted. During the early 1960s, he played with a group called the Zulus, finally forming the Autumn States with some school friends. After leaving school, he studied at the College of Art and Industrial Design, the same college as Ray.

He had played with the Autumn States for several years when the approach from Ray came. He was aware of the Downtown Faction and they, in turn, had checked out Jacka's group although the material he was playing with his own band was more soul-influenced than theirs. At one point, while still in the Autumn States, he had even been a candidate for a group that Rod, while still at university, had been planning with a mutual friend, Noel Johnson. 'Jacka wouldn't join and our band never got off the ground because we couldn't find a singer and a drummer,' Rod recalled in a *Sounds* interview in October 1972.

Bob Sargeant was also very aware of his talents: 'It was early on in the Juncos that I came across Ray Jackson. He was in the Autumn States, a band from Wallsend, who I think supported us at the Rex Hotel in Whitley Bay. I got quite matey with him. In fact, for some reason, I ended up getting them support gigs. I think I introduced Jacka to Ray – being a blues harmonica player – or it may have been Rod. I lost touch with Ray and then he bobbed up in Downtown Faction.'

Thus constituted, the group continued with the Morgan recordings which also featured guitarist Don Whittaker, although he was finally seduced away to London to join the Spirit of John Morgan. This should not have been a surprise, according to Si: 'Don was always saying that he was going to London – every Friday night, after a few pints.' Si also notes that one song on the Spirit Of John Morgan's first album, 'Yorkshire Blues', 'was actually written on the way back from Yorkshire in the Faction van. It was a piss-take of Buddy Guy, BB King – his hero guitarists – in a Yorkshire accent.'

With Jeff Sadler rejoining, this was a very busy period in the band's career as is illustrated by the assorted line-ups on the recordings. Included among the tracks were very early versions of Rod's 'Road To Kingdom Come' – one featuring a histrionic guitar solo – as well as other songs he'd written at university, such as 'Blues For A Dying Season'. He'd clearly found a kindred spirit in Jacka, whose singing and playing reflected the influence of Sonny Terry, Woody Guthrie and Leadbelly.

There was also the first known collective composition, the instrumental 'Jimmy's Field', as well as two Simon Cowe songs – 'Uncle Sam' and 'Far Side Of Your Wall', the latter complete with a 'distant' other-side-of-the wall chorus and a 'someone-turned-the-electric-off' ending!

Richard Squirrel and Jacka were featured lead vocalists, while Rod and Si shared bass and guitar duties. Although the band would later – quite understandably – refer to these recordings as 'not very good', there were some interesting production ideas as well as early versions of songs and more importantly, the first examples of the band's unique vocal harmonies – now Jacka was involved – as well as his very personal mandolin style.

Known to few fans and only available as acetates to the band members, the recordings would be referred to as 'The Morgan Tapes'. The sessions completed, Don Whittaker was not the only casualty; in the winter of 1969 Jeff Sadler, the man Rod had called 'the most futuristic guitarist in the world', also left for the final time.

Our Ref : MD/JAL

1st April. 1968.

M. Mervin, Esq.,
Collingwood Club,
Surtees Street,
Hartlepools, *Tel*.
Co. Durham.

Dear Mike,

    Further to our telephone conversation of Friday, 29th March, 1968, and my letter of the same date, I have much pleasure in detailing herewith list of local groups and their fees for Friday or Saturday evenings :-

"COLOURED RAIN" ....£20. 0. 0.	"PIPE DREAM" ....£25. 0. 0.
"MR. POOBAH'S CHICAGO LINE"£20. 0. 0.	"JUNCO PARTNERS" .....£25. 0. 0.
"THIS YEAR'S GIRL GROUP" ...£20. 0. 0.	"THE SECT" ....£25. 0. 0.
"NEW BLUES REVIEW".........£20. 0. 0.	"THE VILLAGE " ....£25. 0. 0.
"THE ANTIQUE SHOPPE".......£18. 0. 0.	"THE URGE".........£25. 0. 0.
"THE PLEASURE MACHINE".....£25. 0. 0.	"THE STEAM".........£18. 0. 0.
"THE DOWNTOWN FACTION".....£18. 0. 0.	"BARBED WIRE".......£18. 0. 0.
"GREGG BURMAN SOUL BAND"...£18. 0. 0.	"GEORGIA QUINTET" .....£18. 0. 0.
"THE LUSIKA STATE GROUP"...£18. 0. 0.	"THE HILTON K'S" ....£18. 0. 0.
"THE AUTUMN STATES".......£18. 0. 0.	

    I look forward to receiving your instructions with regard to bookings for the above and I will revert to you with regard to NATIONAL groups when I have received quotations from London.

    Assuring you of my close attention at all times.

        Yours sincerely,
        for DIX ENTERPRISES

        MALCOLM DIX

Chapter TWO
THE BRETHREN AND MR HULL

During 1968-69, the various members of Downtown Faction had become aware of a young 'folkie' from the opposite end of the city called Alan Hull, who had been organising something he called the Folk Arts Club at the Rex Hotel in Whitley Bay. 'What that basically meant,' according to Ray Laidlaw, 'was that you could do anything, but you couldn't bring a big sound rig in.'

By this time, the first wave of heavy metal was happening and acts like Deep Purple and Led Zeppelin were proving very popular in the North East. Bands such as Downtown Faction – who had by now renamed themselves Brethren and were performing their own 'songs with a more lightweight approach', as Ray describes them – were on a 'hiding to nothing – we couldn't get any gigs.' Something had to be done.

Born on 20 February 1945, James Alan Hull had been brought up in a building by the name of Sutton's Dwellings in Benwell, in the west end of Newcastle. 'It was a place for manual labourers,' as Alan points out. 'You couldn't get in there unless you earned lower than the minimum wage. They were set up by a Trust – there were two in Newcastle and one in London, I think. But the Dwellings were full of really friendly people.'

There was a piano at home and according to Alan's sister, he could play the top line of 'Morning' when he was three years old. 'I taught myself to get around a piano by asking my sister the chords.' He also recalls the piano was full of books: 'My father was an intelligent man – he just could not get work.'

When he was 11, he finally went off to lessons, although it wasn't long before 'I got pissed off with playing "The March Of The Tin Soldiers", so I whinged on to my mam and dad for a guitar.' He also recalls that some other possession had to be 'hocked' in order to pay for the instrument. 'What attracted me to the guitar was that I could just strum and sing along to it.' At 11, he also began attending Rutherford Grammar School: 'That was another world. The other kids' parents were doctors, lawyers…it was peculiar. The kids at the Dwellings called me a "puff" because I went to Grammar school and the Grammar-school kids called me a scruff!'

He apparently enjoyed the learning process at Rutherford, but not the discipline. 'I remember on my last day there, the headmaster said to me. "I'd like to give you your commendation – but I can't, because I wouldn't be telling the truth." So I said, "There's only two words I'd like to say to you, Mr Bennett: '*Fuck Off*!'" That's the way I left school.'

By this time he'd discovered rock'n'roll, though not by the most direct of routes. His eldest sister was into classical music and by Alan's admission, had become 'a bit of a snob', although his other sister was into pop. One particular day, Alan recalls listening to the Light Programme (the forerunner of Radio 1) on the 'wireless' – the transistor radio had yet to burst out of the East – when curiosity got the better of him: 'I was just about to turn it off, because some of this "pop" music was coming on, when I thought I'll have a listen. The record was "Rock Around The Clock" by Bill Haley and the Comets. That was *it*…

'Then it was Elvis Presley – "Hound Dog" was the first record I ever bought. Buddy Holly was the next discovery, along with Chuck Berry. It changed my life. The whole era, the late 1950s, was just incredible, astonishing: I couldn't wait to hear who was doing what next. I still liked classical, but it was the excitement of rock'n'roll. Everything for me, by then, at school was an irrelevance.'

Like so many others, he was in bands at school, 'but all we did was practice all the time and talk about it. About the sixth band, we actually did a gig, at Pendower Hall Working Men's Club.' Alan also recalls feverishly learning all Chuck Berry's songs and the 'hit parade' at the time; 'They were all based on C, A minor and G – so I knew the basic chord structure.'

The Shadows, too, were also to influence Alan, not least as role models, although he was able to claim a more direct connection than many; Hank Marvin and Bruce Welch had attended Rutherford Grammar School. 'They were two years older than me. They were regarded as heroes. I remember that Brian – Rankin, Hank's real name – got his nickname because he always had an acoustic guitar slung over his back. He used to come over to the changing rooms and show all us younger lads his guitar. So someone named him "Hank", after Hank Williams.

'The two of them were expelled from the school in the fourth year by the headmaster…weren't pulling their weight academically, I suppose…so they went to the 2I's coffee bar in London and the rest is history. Hank came back to the school the year I was leaving and the Shads had "Apache" out – so this was 1960 – and he parked his big white Roller next to the hated Bennett's Morris Minor!'

Around this time, Alan progressed through two or three locally-based bands, but 'we never broke out of the Tyneside area, which was buzzing at the time.' One was called the Klik and the other, Dean Ford & the Crestas: 'Dean Ford was a very tall handsome bloke and the women loved him. It used to cause quite a few fights in the Working Men's Club because all the middle-aged "biddies" used to fancy him like hell.' By 1965, Alan had joined the Chosen Few, a band that included his best friend, Alan 'Bumper' Brown on bass who would 'experiment in the art of living.' Sadly, Bumper is now dead.

Another member was Mickey Gallagher, who played piano and would eventually enjoy much success as a member of Ian Dury and the Blockheads, as well as with Peter Frampton and, later, the Clash. The line-up was completed by Andrew Jackman on drums and Rod Hood on vocals. The band had a manager – 'a "colourful" chap,' according to Alan – called Bill Keith,

Right: Alan in Ireland in the early 1950s.

who was well known through association with the Club A Go Go. He managed to get the band entered in a nationwide talent search, sponsored by Radio Luxembourg, and Alan clearly recalls the audition.

'One night, me and Bumper were at my house writing songs when we were told to go to the West End Boys' Club, along with the rest... We watched all these bands, one after another, then someone said "You're next". We didn't have any gear, so Bumper told the band that had just come off to leave everything on for us – and, because he was a big bloke, nobody argued! Halfway through the first song, the guy who was running it said, "Stop! – everybody else go home!" It was the bandleader Cyril Stapleton.

'He asked me if I had any more songs, and I said, "Fifty". So they emptied the hall and we did two or three more songs. Then he asked us to go to London the next day. They stopped the nationwide search there and then!' The Chosen Few duly travelled down, along with Bill Keith, and a deal was signed with Pye, a successful label with the Kinks and Donovan on their roster. Part of the deal was that the winners would appear on Radio Luxembourg – the same station that, not too many miles away, a young Raymond Laidlaw had been eagerly tuning into under the sheets in North Shields.

'We thought, "Wow!" – this is it!' Alan gleefully recalls. 'We recorded two singles for Pye, both very Beatlesque – because my fascination with the band was growing all the time – but we never completed the third because I had an argument with Cyril Stapleton during recording.' The song in question, 'This Land Is Called', was one of the Alan's earliest attempts at protest songs. 'He liked the song, but started fiddling with the words. I remember he said it should be something to the effect of, "This land ain't mine, this land is too cold" and I said "That sounds like a fuckin' *Weather Report!*"

'I was determined not to change it, I didn't care who he was...so he said, "Stop the session – everyone out!", then the "Bolshy" came out in me...so me and Bumper got thrown out. It was the end of the Chosen Few for me.' For a while, apparently, Graham Bell was drafted in as replacement although his place was ultimately taken by another guitarist and local lad, John Turnbull. As well as Mickey Gallagher, this version of the Chosen Few also included bass player Colin Gibson, who along with Turnbull, Gallagher and Bell, formed Skip Bifferty after the band's demise, recording one album for RCA in 1968. This was not, however, the last time they would cross paths with Mr Hull.

John Turnbull clearly recalls his first meeting with Alan in 1965. 'It was at his house and he was wearing a German helmet, singing at the top of his voice, playing the piano – but not in that order! I remember he had about a hundred songs, most of which ended up being recorded. They were all good songs, with great lyrics.' John too, would also come to figure very much in Alan's future.

It was around the time of his departure from the Chosen Few that Alan recalls first coming into contact with Barbara Hayes. Perhaps more than any other person, Barbara was to wield a massive influence on Alan's future. She had been working for April Music Publishing, who had handled the talent search on behalf of Luxembourg, and had got in contact with Alan soon after. 'From then on, she took over,' he recalls.

But Alan was also aware of someone else, who had been around taking photographs of several of the local bands in and around Newcastle; Dave Wood. 'He saw what was going on and thought, "There must be some money in this!"' At the time, Dave, who had been at the same school as Rod Clements, Simon Cowe and Bob Sargeant, had set up a small recording studio in the east end of the city, in Wallsend. Situated in part of an old theatre, it became the home of the NWOBHM (New Wave of British Heavy Metal) during the late 1970s, when he set up Neat Records and where it still operates to this day.

In 1967 the studio, known as Impulse, boasted a 1/2 track Ferrograph recorder and egg boxes on the wall for soundproofing. Dave Wood has his own clear memory of the time, as he recalled in *Sounds* in October 1972: 'Alan used to play with the Chosen Few at the Manhole Club in Wallsend and I owned the studio upstairs. That's how I got to know him and how mad he was. They had songs like "Today, Tonight And Tomorrow", "Big City" and "Won't Be Round You", which were pretty big, and I remember we went down to London and booked four places in a Bayswater hotel which ended up accommodating nine of us. On top of that we broke the wash basin and got thrown out.'

Left: The Klik in 1964. Mickey Gallagher plays piano while Terry Morgan and Alan Hull take centre-stage on bass and guitar. The other musicians are Kenny Anderson and John Coleman.

21

It was not long before Barbara Hayes was in Newcastle, searching out Dave Wood's studio where she had asked to meet Alan. 'Barbara had the foresight to suggest that we form our own publishing company, which became Hazy Music – which was me, Barbara and Dave. That was a saviour for me, because I knew that, whatever happened, I could have an income from the songs.' This arrangement was certainly ground-breaking – and not just for Tyneside.

'It was lucky for me and lucky for Dave that Barbara had been in publishing a long time. She was always spot-on with her royalty payments and she did all the footwork to get the dough from the record companies. She was a genuine woman. At the time, I trusted nobody. I was a young lad...I knew there was a future and I just didn't let it go. I think most people of that age on Tyneside at the time had a natural aversion to people from London.'

Alan had also tried another band with Bumper Brown called Barrabas, of which there were three versions – including one with close friend Terry Morgan, with whom Alan would later write 'Peter Brophy Don't Care'. 'We did the clubs; we tried to do something different from what was around – y'know Cream, Led Zeppelin. I liked all that, but I couldn't do it. I knew what I *could* do and what I *wanted* to do...and it wasn't *that*.

'We tried to do "progressive" music – I don't know if that is the right word – music that's not "mainstream"; not rock, certainly not folk, not heavy metal..."mind" music, I suppose. Other people have done it better since then, but it was definitely at the forefront of progressive music.' On Tyneside, according to Alan, 'people either loved it or were baffled by it.'

Hull took his inspiration from his domestic life – he was married to Pat by this time – and his work, particularly as a male nurse at St Nicholas Psychiatric Hospital in Gosforth. This experience was to prove a pivotal in informing his songwriting, and by the time he left two and a half years later he had written over one hundred songs. 'I was getting millions of ideas from schizophrenics and depressives and maniacs. My head was bursting and I was searching for some way to do it properly. I was experimenting, searching, trying to get it right – not in the lyrics, musically.'

This preoccupation with mental health left an indelible mark, as journalist Roy Carr reported in *New Musical Express* in December 1971: 'Alan, with almost fanatical dedication, felt that only by supporting mental health in its campaign to cure the afflicted can the salvation of mankind be arrived at.' Carr went on to state Alan's personal theory: 'The true reflection of a society is shown in how that society treats its mental cripples, because we're all on the brink of going under in a sea of madness. I'm fortunate, I recognise the insanity in myself. I don't write songs about it, but writing songs stops me going insane. It won't be the bomb or some virus that will destroy the world, but man's own madness.'

It is likely that Alan, like so many of his contemporaries, was also experimenting with hallucinogenic drugs during this period, almost certainly using each resulting perspective to help inform his songwriting. Eventually, according to Alan, 'things got so complicated with other people in Barrabas, I just ended up on my own with an acoustic guitar.'

It was during this period that Ray Laidlaw received a phone call from studio owner Dave Wood: 'He wanted me to come and do a session. I'd never done one in my life before, so I was really excited. So I went up and there was Alan, Bumper Brown, Graham Bell, "famous" people like that – although I didn't know they were famous at the time – and I did a couple of songs with them. One was "Lady Eleanor" (with Graham Bell on vocal); another was called "Obidiah's Grave"...I really enjoyed it.'

Wood recalls it was at this time that he became more directly involved with Alan: 'Originally he made a demo for £25 at my studio, but only paid me £10. I used to keep pestering for the rest until I realised he had no money, so I thought "if you can't beat 'em join 'em" and became his manager.' Dave also declared that, at the time, he had tapes of 280 Alan Hull songs, testament to his prolific writing. 'I find it difficult to come across a song I don't like. Alan was always a little ahead of his time – he changed my way of thinking completely and some of his early songs like "Schizoid Revolution" were frightening.'

To Alan, this felt like a natural progression, and it occurred to him the folk clubs that were springing up throughout Tyneside during the late 1960s were his best chance of exposure. 'I could do these songs on my own – like Dylan songs – stand up there in front of a microphone with my guitar and sing for an

Right: Alan and Pat's wedding day, 22 August 1966.

hour and a half. I began to get a reputation as "someone to book". I thought, "this is *great* – and I get paid for it".'

His reputation had already spread beyond the North East, as singer-songwriter Barbara Dickson recalls: 'The first time I heard of Alan Hull was when my Scots friends told me about a great singer-songwriter doing floor spots in Archie Fisher's mum's folk club in Wallsend.' Fisher was himself to draw producer Joe Boyd – the man who worked with Fairport Convention and subsequently Sandy Denny and Richard Thompson – up to Tyneside. Such was the company into which Alan was moving.

He had also begun to play further afield, appearing at the legendary Les Cousins bar in London's Greek Street, where Ralph McTell was running the 'all-nighter' in 1968. 'It was a very influential place in Soho. Jimi Hendrix, Cat Stevens, Bert Jansch, Donovan – they all played there. One day a woman called Barbara Hayes came in – to say she was "forceful" was an understatement – and said, "You must give this guy a chance." Alan played, but I remember he was very nervous. I believe that was the first time we met.'

During the summer of 1969, at Barbara's suggestion, Alan recorded a single featuring one of his songs, 'We Can Swing Together'. Inspired by a drugs bust at a Newcastle party, the song documents how the police, along with dogs, forced their way into the house and were later sued – successfully. The party was attended by several art students including Ray Jackson and future Roxy Music producer John Porter. Alan's single was produced by Hugh Murphy for Transatlantic Records, a hugely influential folk label that featured artists such as Martin Carthy and Bert Jansch.

Their A&R was run by John Whitehead, as Hugh recalls: 'I was doing a lot of stuff for Transatlantic in 1968-69 and Barbara Hayes used to do a lot of work with the label. I wasn't aware of Alan at the time, but I can recall going up to Newcastle at one point with John Whitehead and Barbara to see two bands: one was a guy called Robbie Burns. I recall getting a call from Transatlantic, who always liked to do things "on the cheap" – and I always brought things in on a budget – to do "We Can Swing Together". So we booked half a session at Trident in St Anne's Court, off Wardour Street, and did it.

'The only thing I can remember is, one of the lines was about "rolling up joints" and I said "You'd better say, 'roll-your-owns'" because you could get locked up for it then. I think it must have been recorded in an afternoon and mixed in a morning. So I had quite a lot to do with the Newcastle scene, because of Barbara and John Whitehead.' Alan clearly recalls the band drafted in by Hugh for the recording: 'It was like a who's who of the future top-notch session men; Clem Cattini on drums, Albert Lee on guitar and the "sixth Rolling Stone" – the late Ian Stewart – on piano.

'We did the track in a kind of "pop" vein, and it got lots of plays. Alan Freeman played it a lot, but it never made it. I think it opened a few doors; people were impressed by it.' Ray Laidlaw also recalls the song was already a 'local anthem'. 'It was like the old troubadours writing stories of the wars, telling a story in a song. Actually, it had just happened, he was doing it in clubs and pubs…it had never been known for anyone to sue the police and win. There were a few bands doing the song…it was a local "hit", if you like.'

It was around this time that Rod first met Alan, at a session for Robbie Burns at Impulse. 'Alan was the pianist,' Rod recalls. 'Later on, we did the first version of "Scarecrow Song".' There was even for a while a band that featured both Alan and Ray (after their session meeting at Impulse) and, although Ray was still firmly a member of Downtown Faction, the band did play live. 'They were called the Gift, around 1969,' Ray reveals. 'We did two gigs, one at the Arts Lab, which was above Mark Toney's Ice Cream Parlour in Percy Street – it's gone now – but the band never really took off.

'To be quite honest, I was trying to get Alan involved with us. I knew that we had the makings of a great band, and here was Alan floundering about…there were all sorts of ego problems. Johnny Turnbull, a wonderful lad and a great player, was basically a "hired gun" – his career's been like that ever since – and apparently wasn't going to hang around; Graham Bell, bless his little cotton socks, was totally unreliable, always has been.'

Having organised the bands from the early days, when there was just him and Rod, 'recording people's phone numbers and addresses, things like that', what struck Ray was that the Gift were 'a complete shambles. I thought, the only one with any lasting talent is Alan… We'll have him, thanks – sorry lads. I wasn't really aware of it at the time, but what I was working on was a way of combining the two.'

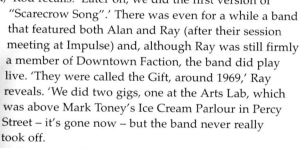

Left: Alan holds the baby while mother Sally looks on.

Alan's next decision was to prove pivotal. 'With Dave's help, we decided to set up a folk club in the cafe of the Rex Hotel on the seafront at Whitley Bay. The Rex Folk Club went on every Sunday night,' Alan explains. 'We were determined to do it right. Dave suggested an Amateur Night; we installed a PA system, charged ten bob at the door and I played every night. We built it up and up. We always had good floor singers and a main guest. I remember we had the Humblebums – Gerry Rafferty and Billy Connolly – for 30 quid, Al Stewart, "Uncle" Ralph McTell...we made more than enough to cover them.' *

The Rex was rapidly gaining a sizeable reputation on the coast, as Alan explains: 'We had people banging and knocking on the door to be let in and we had to turn them away; it was really thriving, interesting. The Rex was like an art workshop; a really good breeding ground for loads of ideas. The standard was astonishing. It was like a forward-looking, modern arts lab. We used to fill the place every night. It actually worked.'

Dave Wood was also now managing Alan, although making a living was continuing to prove difficult for a man who by now had a young family to feed: 'One thing I'll never forget was that Dave gave me ten quid a week; it doesn't sound a lot now, but in 1969...by then I was on the dole, I'd left St Nicks, and he looked at me – I had three kids, was cleaning windows for cash, and he bunged me ten quid a week. I'll *never* forget that.'

Downtown Faction had also decided on a name change; Ray can't remember who suggested Brethren. 'Yet another biblical reference. We had all this religious imagery, like the drunken old preacher in the Westerns, conning everybody; fire and brimstone and all that stuff...all that imagery came from Dylan songs...we were quite into that.'

The pieces were, indeed, all there, ready to be put into place when Alan invited Brethren to play a short spot at the Rex. 'I thought they were really good, so I booked them for three quid for the next week and made about £30 myself – a fortune then! Rod won the raffle and the prize was a Bert Jansch album. It was my own copy, but I didn't mind when I saw how much we made that night!'

'We were going through a very weird time when Alan saw us at the Rex,' recalls Si Cowe. 'Very wacky – double bass, violins, banjos. He'd heard of this band that had chucked away their amplifiers and gone "acoustic"...the drummer's sold his kit and he's playing a tambourine. "I think I'll have them on!" It was like, "What? What are these people *doing*? Never heard music like this before." So, afterwards, "Er, lads? That was interesting. I've got a few songs you might fit in with what you do. Do you want to give it a try?" So we did, the next week. Eighteen months previously, we'd been asked to do nothing but 12-bar blues. Heavy, thrash metal, psychedelic – out of the window. Acoustic's where it's at, man!'

In the wake of the burgeoning heavy rock scene, Brethren gigs were by now few and far between. 'People used to love the

Above: The Chosen Few (Alan on far right) find brief fame in an instrument ad.

Left: Alan at the Rex Folk Club, circa 1968-69.

Opposite top: From left: Bumper Brown, Alan, unidentified girl, unknown, Mickey Gallagher, Tommy Jackman, Rod Hudd.

Opposite: The Chosen Few, 1965. From left: Alan, Tommy Jackman, Mickey Gallagher, Bumper Brown, Rod Hudd.

* It was at the Rex where Ralph McTell first earned his monicker from the band. 'I was sitting in the back and this band were on in front of me. Usually, I felt I'd be alright, but this night I thought to myself, "God, how am I going to follow these guys?"

'Afterwards, we were sat round, having a few beers and they were talking about splitting up. I said, "You can't do that – you're so good." The boys have been kind enough to say that it was my enthusiasm at that point that stopped them, and we've been mates ever since. They call me "Uncle Ralph".'

gigs we *did* get, though,' Ray explained. 'There'd always been an element of folk blues in our stuff, the Woody Guthrie, Sonny Terry, Brownie McGee area from Jacka – and he knew somebody that went to a folk club, although he didn't really know what one was and we'd never been to one…so out of desperation we'd take acoustic instruments to these folk gigs. I used to place myself in the audience somewhere and clap and cheer like mad and got them all "at it!" We just tried the songs out on people.

'In those days, they were died-in-the-wool traditional clubs and they were very polite and open to let us do it. I don't know whether they liked it or not, but they certainly always gave us an opportunity.' Unwittingly, Brethren had stumbled on the 'recipe'; one born out of necessity.

The new set also included songs by Scottish singer-songwriter Rab Noakes. 'They were right for the way we felt, to put the show together. So it was really out of expediency, at first,' explains Ray. 'When we started working with Alan on a permanent basis, Rab's songs just stuck.' Noakes, who would become a great friend and associate, had come down to the North East frequently. 'He was part of the "Fife Mafia",' laughs Ray, 'along with the other Glasgow lads like Gerry Rafferty and Billy Connolly and outfits like High Speed Grass and the JSD Band, because it was like the first stop-off if you're coming out of Scotland.

'He started coming down to Tyneside and through the "folky" connections, simply because he was a soloist – the lines were blurred in those days. He used to do a weekend round the folk clubs here, which were the same places we were getting into.' Gradually, the band introduced Alan's songs into their performances, and next move seemed quite logical: why not join forces? None of the band recall actually making the decision, but like so many occasions that followed it just 'happened', it seemed natural.

Below: Studio Svengali Dave Wood, pictured circa 1969.

No-one is certain, but the first Alan Hull/Brethren gig is felt to have been at the Lampglass in Ashington, Northumberland in 1969. It's not even certain how the combination was billed, as Rod explains: 'I can't remember the first gig under that name, but I can remember one at the Poly, supporting Juicy Lucy. It was either "Brethren with Alan Hull" or "Alan Hull with Brethren". I think we did a couple up and down the country, but the way it worked was that we went on Alan's gigs if the fee warranted it and he came on ours whether it did or not!'

Alan recalls the gig as 'really terrible – but we gave it another try two months later and it was fantastic.' Ray agrees: 'I can remember the first time we did "Lady Eleanor" together and when we finished the song, I just *knew*. I said, "That's it – we've cracked it".'

Chapter
THREE
THERE YOU GO, BOYS –
SIGN THIS!

When Alan Hull joined Brethren in May 1970 there was no doubt in his mind the newly-combined band would get a deal – and very soon. Both parties had been actively searching out labels, Brethren with the help of manager Joe Robertson and Alan via Barbara Hayes and Dave Wood.

Joe Robertson had been managing the Junco Partners and another band called Gin House and, according to him, 'We would always be down at Dave's studios. He'd never stop talking about Alan Hull, and by early 1970, he was a star attraction… I had started managing Brethren, who were really hard-up and I remember Jacka virtually walked nine miles from his house to see me.' (*Sounds*, 7 October 1972)

In Alan's opinion, it was simply fortunate for Charisma – run by the hugely respected Tony Stratton-Smith – that they were the first to be approached collectively as Brethren. 'We were such a happening band that if they hadn't taken us, somebody else would've… It was just one of those things. There was a feeling that it was just a matter of time. We just *knew* we were going to happen.'

More likely, it was a combination of elements. Following the dissolution of the Nice, who were signed to the Charisma label, Newcastle-born bassist Lee Jackson was looking to form a new group – Jackson Heights – and wanted the Juncos' Charlie Harcourt as part of the line-up. In fact, according to Robertson in the same *Sounds* interview, Harcourt had already joined when he decided to go and see Stratton-Smith. One version of events is that Robertson's reaction was to use Brethren as part of Harcourt's 'transfer fee'.

As Ray Laidlaw recalls, 'I don't think he got it, but while they were talking about it he happened to have a tape of ours with him. So he put this tape on and Strat – who was probably just trying to be polite, because we weren't very good in those days – said, "They sound quite good, I'll get them a support slot at the Marquee." We duly went down and, to cut a long story short, he liked what he heard.

'The bands he had – Van der Graaf, Genesis, Rare Bird – were very diverse, but he was very moralistic: I think he felt a bit guilty about this band, the Juncos, breaking up, and thought, "Well, I've nothing to lose, I'll put a couple of singles out and see what happens." He probably thought there was something there. Strat was a journalist originally, and I think he saw something in Alan's writing – the poetry.'

Glen Colson, then Stratton-Smith's assistant, has a different recollection: 'As far as I know, it was Barbara Hayes who played

Right: Tony Stratton-Smith, Charisma Records chief and a prime mover in Lindisfarne's early fame.

Strat the tape and he said he loved the harmonica-playing. I don't think he said anything about the songs or anything else, he just said he thought he could make Jacka the next Ian Anderson. Next thing I knew, they were on at the Marquee one Sunday night.'

Ultimately, for Strat, Brethren would achieve what he had hoped for in the Koobas, a Liverpudlian group he had managed who had toured with the Beatles – and for whom Colson had been working as a roadie – and that was 'A success based on an empathy with their audience…but a far heavier writing team.' Nonetheless, Strat was later very clear in his reaction to his first taste of the band, as quoted in *Disc & Music Echo* in February 1972: 'I signed them on the strength of their songs; I thought that they really shone… I was interested in the group as a whole, with Alan making occasional solo albums.'

In *Sounds* later that year, he further admitted, '…on one hearing of the Brethren tape I realised that Ray Jackson could do for the harp what Ian Anderson had done for the flute.' According to Alan, Strat was also particularly taken by another track: 'I know that "Clear White Light" impressed him; he considered it to be a hymn – which it is. He was a deeply religious man, and when he died (July 1986) as we walked to the door of the church, "Clear White Light" was being played.' A combination of elements, indeed.

In June 1970, Brethren signed a three-year contract with Charisma. Other labels had been in the frame and Rod Clements states that, 'while those other deals were at least being talked about, there was a bit of a buzz, I think as a result of having done the Island / Abbey Road business.' Ray Laidlaw agrees. 'We were still doing recording tests on our own all through this, and when Alan had a radio show in London – *Folk On Two* – we had a test for EMI with Chris Thomas, who had worked with the Beatles as George Martin's assistant and later, everyone from the Sex Pistols to Elton John and Roxy Music.

'We did the test in the Beatles' studio – Number Four. It was an amazing feeling in there. We actually passed the test, we got offered a deal.' Alan savoured the recollection that he 'played on the very harmonium that that was used on "We Can Work It Out"' and thought Chris Thomas 'a smashing fella'. Despite the test's successful outcome, Charisma felt 'right' to the band: it was like a family, Stratton-Smith commanding much respect.

'I was a bit in awe of Strat, but he was a lovely man; I really liked him,' Rod points out. 'He was definitely a cut above most of them scuffling around the business at the time. He was a gentleman; well educated, well read; a sensitive man and a very nice man. One would have suspected a dilettante-type were it not for the fact that he was so 100 percent, wholeheartedly involved in it. When you did get talking to him, he really was deeply involved. He was a man with very broad interests; literary interests, his football interests…all part of a very complicated, very aware, sensitive man.'

Si, on the other hand, 'Didn't like Strat – for a few reasons. One was he sacked Pete Haskell, our driver, once because Pete had gone into his office to demand more money for "his lads" and Strat just sacked him like that. How can you sack somebody you're not paying? *We* paid him.'

In fact, as Si recalls, Brethren had actually signed another deal before Charisma. 'I remember reading in *Melody Maker* that Monday night at the Marquee was trial night. So we bundled all the gear in the van, got there and told Jack Barry (the owner) "We've come down from Newcastle for a trial, like it says in the paper." So he says, "No you're not, you've got to book." So we said, "It doesn't say that here." So he said we could go on at seven for half an hour. "But you're closed then," we said. "I've got bands booked all night. You can go on between 12.30 and 1 as well." So we did.

'Strat had popped in for an early tipple and saw us. What happened that night was that Jack Barry signed us to Marquee Records; straight up to the office, at the back, afterwards – "There you go boys, sign this." Strat had come and rescue us from that afterwards. Jack and Tony were good pals who saw each other every day. Jack Barry probably thought, "Strat's gonna like these – I'll nab 'em so he has to give me 100 quid to get them back…"'

On 2 July, the band made their debut at Newcastle City Hall supporting Jackson Heights, with headlining gigs of their own either side at the Mayfair and the Poly. Before the band could sign on the dotted line with Charisma, a deal needed to be struck with current managers Joe Robertson and Dave Wood. Strat had also insisted on managing the band, a normal practice at the time but, in the same circumstances now, warning bells would surely begin to ring.

'Alan had more of a career behind him and in front of him than we did at the time,' Rod Clements explains. 'He was much more of an established thing and he'd just done the "Swing Together" single…he actually had a thing going, whereas we were the young hopefuls. I think, from a pragmatic point of view, Barbara and Dave probably thought, "Great, a ready-made band for Alan" – which was quite right, because we were both sympathetic to what each other was doing and he was probably at the stage where he could have done with a band.

'Of course, we had to pay a gargantuan percentage, combining the royalty dues of Mr Wood and Mr Robertson and neither of us said, "Oh – we'll have to do something about this." I think it was actually 37 and a half per cent we were paying out at the time when the two managements combined. Fortunately, it didn't last long as it was knocked on the head by Strat.' When it came to discussing song publishing with Charisma, Alan was certainly in a stronger position. The deal that Alan had with Dave

Below: The first promotional photograph with Alan. From left: Jacka, Alan, Ray, Si, Rod.

Lindisfarne

| Representation | Open Door Management (0632) 27787 | Agency | Terry King Associates 25, Haymarket, LONDON S.W.1. Tel: 01—930—1771 |

Above: A June 1970 support date at the Marquee for Brethren, one of the less famous opening acts that month.

Below: The notorious La Chasse Club.

and Barbara was a rarity in the business at the time; to include the artist as part of the publishing operation was, according to Alan 'absolutely and totally unheard-of.'

As a result of Hayes' tenacity, she had established a situation where, in order for Charisma to discuss publishing for the band prior to signing, Charisma would have to speak to her: 'a real ball-breaker!' laughs Alan. The agreement struck with Tony Stratton-Smith was that one track per album and the B-side of any singles would belong to Charisma and the rest to Hazy Music. 'The rest of the band did their own deals – and got well shafted by another publisher – while I was sorted.'

Recording of the first album, ' Nicely Out Of Tune', began soon after the 'front-room' rehearsals in Tynemouth with John Anthony. The sleeve, along with the first logo, was designed by Ray Jackson. The title, it seems, came from the fact that the band were 'nicely out of tune' with everyone else at that time. A fair observation…

The sessions, produced by Anthony, happened between 10-14 August 1970 at Trident Studios in London's Soho, with final mixing between 1-3 September. John had been a DJ at the Speakeasy and got into production by the back door, according to one of the music papers at the time. He knew Yes and went along to one of their sessions one day, got the session together and mixed the tapes. Although he didn't get the job of producing the first album, 'a lot of people liked it' and in the spring of 1969 he got a job with the American Mercury label.

The man who hired him was Lou Reizner, who had apparently signed Rod Stewart, David Bowie and also Peter Hamill. As Hamill was a member of Van der Graaf Generator, Anthony was asked to work on their first album, 'Aerosol Grey Machine'. Hamill gave a good report to Strat, whose office was next to Mercury's, and John was asked to produce Rare Bird's first single, 'Sympathy'. It became a hit, selling one and a half million copies – a substantial start for the label.

With the Brethren album sessions came the name-change decided upon during John Anthony's stay with the band: Lindisfarne. 'John rang the record company the next morning,' Ray recalls, 'and they all thought it was wonderful, really romantic-sounding, sums up the North East; a bit of history and all that.' Alan Hull had crossed paths with John while he had worked out of Shel Talmy's office. 'So when we met, I sort of knew him and him me, I suppose, from those days. I respected him and it was mutual. I got on like a house on fire with John.'

During recording the band were booked into the Madison Hotel on Sussex Gardens, 'All in the same room! I think it was £1 for all of us, but it was bloody luxury compared to sleeping in the back of the van. I think, being the most bolshy one, I demanded we stay in a hotel…it was lovely, run by a Greek lady. That was the first time that I – certainly – began to feel we were in a rock band; staying in London, in a hotel; going round Soho, getting drinks from the record company – a couple of pints of Guinness, actually – and going to La Chasse, seeing all the roadies, who were all Geordies…' Ray Laidlaw's memories are of a hotel 'full of bands and tourists. One night, Alan came in late and had to climb in through one couple's window – right in the middle of their conjugals!'

With the band required to travel back and forwards to London due to gig commitments, Rod remembers one incident early on in the sessions that incurred the wrath of both John Anthony and Strat: 'For two reasons, we were very late indeed – like, several hours. One reason was that Alan didn't have any money to leave his wife, Pat, and had to sign on to get his dole, but that would have meant we couldn't get there at all. So we had a whip-round so that Alan could go to London – 17/6 or a pound each in the kitty. That's the kind of thing we used to do for each other.

'The other thing that went wrong was that we'd just invested in a former Co-op Funerals car, basically a London taxi – a pre-war thing, very low mileage, but very ancient. It wouldn't have passed an MOT now. It was our first journey in it, and we hadn't gone far down the road when it had drunk about a gallon of oil…it was in a hell of a state. The session was booked for three in the afternoon and we finally got there at eight in the evening.

'We got to the studio to find Si (who was living in London already – his first wife, Betsy was teaching at the London Fields Mixed Infants School) and John Anthony waiting, Si looking very embarrassed indeed and John looking very irate. More worried than anything else, because we didn't have the sense to phone – we probably didn't have the number. I doubt we got anything done that night: it may have been the first attempt at laying down the backing track to "Clear White Light".

'The next morning, we got hauled into the office and got the most almighty bollocking off Strat. Quite rightly, because apart from wasted studio time they had been worried about what had become of us; whether we'd all decided to throw in the towel and couldn't be bothered to go, or "on the hoy" in Newcastle or whatever – or whether we're lying dead splattered all over the motorway. Our motivation to him was suspect and he laid it on the line, saying it was not on, he'd invested a lot of time and money – just telling it like it was.

'I don't know about jumping up and down and thumping his fist on the desk, but he definitely made us feel very bad and we never did anything like that again.' Thus chastened, the return journey in the 'dreaded Co-op taxi' ended at the garage where it was bought, where a replacement was demanded. On the offer of a Ford Zodiac the response was 'That's more like it! ' laughs Rod. 'A real bluesmobile. I think we used the part of the advance on that and a van, too. Ian and Charlie, the roadies, used to drive that, with the gear.' Indeed, up-and-coming hopeful Chris Rea recalls their first six-wheel Ford Transit van and big PA system as 'big news for a northern band in those days'.

Gigging increased, thanks to the Terry King Agency (who employed a young booker by the name of Paul Conroy, later MD of Virgin Records) which was allied to Charisma. The band had already played their first gig outside of the North East – at Barnstaple in Devon, where they opened for Yes at the Queen's Hall. Gigs in the West Country proved a great morale booster for the band, 'because we went down so well' as Rod recalls. 'To have this extra area of the country besides our own home turf…to know you could go all that way and still crack it, with a totally strange audience…that's when we realised that we had solid ground under our feet.' *

There were a few more support gigs and, although there wasn't much money, they were given cash by Charisma to buy some new gear. It was also common practice for Si to make a little speech two or three numbers from the end of the set. 'I'd go to the mic and say "It's been very nice playing to you all here – we've had a lovely night – but there's a slight problem. It's getting quite cold, winter's coming on and the van's pretty freezing…I end up sleeping on the gear stick and I'm pretty sick of it…if there's anybody out there who has a bit of floor space and maybe a fire: we have our own sleeping bags…"'

Ray Laidlaw also remembers 'a great vicar we stayed with a few times who let us sleep in his front room.' He also remembers places like Redcar Jazz Club, 'a great gig. We supported early Fairport there; Blodwyn Pig; Cat Stevens, maybe even Jethro Tull; all those sort of people. It was on a Sunday night and you couldn't stand at the bar because of the drinking laws at the time, so you could see the lads buy a crate of beer and shove it under the table: they used to sit there and drink themselves into oblivion while the bands were on.'

Recording of 'Nicely Out Of Tune' went relatively smoothly, according to Ray. 'We went in and did the record very quick; it was mostly the songs that we'd been playing live and we had loads of ideas flying off in all directions: we always have had a very disparate sort of thing. John didn't really attempt to hold this all together. To be fair to him, there's all sorts of things on it…there was a bit of folk in what we did, a bit of blues, a bit of mainstream pop…the only thing that there's never been anything of is jazz.

'There's a little bit of soul from the sort of areas that Jacka comes from, the Marvin Gaye stuff and things like that. Our inspiration, our heroes, were the Beatles: it was always songs that were the most important thing, and they treated every song in a way it needed to be treated. They had three different writers and we had three different writers; we didn't see anything wrong in that.'

Certainly the variety on the album bore this view out. The music-hall flavour of 'Down' with its 'scratched' beginning was one intriguing track; while Rod's 'Road To Kingdom Come', written in his third year at Durham University, sounded more 'earthy'. Rod agrees with some of Ray's reference points: 'We were very much into early Dylan at the time… "Music From Big Pink"… "John Wesley Harding" was just out. That was me trying to write something like that.'

Rod also supports the disparate influences at work in the band's music at that time: 'One level (was) the international music scene that everybody knew about – the Beatles, Zappa or whoever – but it wasn't just copying them by rote…we would try anything we had as well. After a lot of unsatisfactory stuff – a lot of it didn't go anywhere – there was a yearning for something "solid"; a definite framework…some common ground or mythological framework you could relate to. That's the only reason I could explain all this biblical imagery in songs.'

In retrospect, Ray observes that all the tempos on 'Nicely Out Of Tune' were 'so flamin' slow in those

* On another visit to Devon, on the same bill as Free, Rodgers and co 'decided to pull rank.' Ray recounts. 'They were supposed to be on last, but they got fed up of waiting, so they said, "We're going on before you". It was alright, they were canny lads, but at the time they were a little more famous than we were.'

Si Cowe had been in the habit of sitting down to play his guitar. 'He had this lovely Gibson jazz guitar,' Ray explains, 'and he didn't want to spoil it by putting a strap on it. So he just sat down to play and it was quite wacky; we used to quietly promote that side of things.

'We used to start with "Eleanor" at the time,' Ray went on, 'and it was the way the thing "drips" in – first the bass, then the mandolin – well, it was really dark on stage and we were playing and playing and there was no sign of Si's parts – we couldn't hear him – and we thought, "he's taking his time"…and then one of us went over and he was asleep over his guitar! Alan was kicking his chair…' They left an impression with their performance, though because, according to Rod, 'Free must have hung about, so they came to see us at one of the Marquee gigs.'

days, I don't know why… The Band was another influence at the time and they always seemed to play everything really slow; so we thought that the only way to make it work was to do them slow…that's how we approached that album.' Si, on the other hand, felt that John Anthony was ahead of his time. 'I think he was the first of a new generation, a new breed of producers. Whereas before they had been more set in the Bill Haley-1950s, 1960s plodding-type of productions, John had new ideas and he wanted to experiment; a bit like Steve Lipson years later. We were lucky in that we got John, who was also technically able to do what we wanted. He certainly inspired us. A lovely character.'

John's own recollections appear to support the apparent spirit of experimentation; 'I recall crates of Brown Ale being consumed during the

Right: Alan's handwritten lyrics to 'Lady Elenore' (sic).

LADY ELENORE (NIGHTMARE FESTIVAL)

Banshee playing magician
Sitting lotus on the floor
Belly dancing beauty
With a power driven saw
Had my share of nightmares
Didn't think there could be much more
Then in came Roderick Usher
With the Lady Elenore

She tied my eyes with ribbon
Made of silken ghostly thread
& gazed with troubled vision
On an old four poster bed
Where Elenore had risen
To kiss the neck below my head
And bid me come along with her
To the land of the dancing dead

It's all right Lady Elenore
I'm all right where I am

She gazed with loving beauty
Like a mother to her son
Like living dieing seeing being
All rolled into one
Then all at once I heard some music
Playing in my bones
The same old song
I'd heard for years reminding me of home

sessions! I was still a neophyte, still cutting my teeth; but the songs were very well-intentioned. I think "Clear White Light" and "Lady Eleanor" really hit me; "Winter Song" would be very hard to beat – that's a classic…the crackly beginning to "Down" was my idea – I'd probably been smoking too much Red Lebanese and listening to too many Beatles albums.

'I always remember Ray Jackson saying that "the first album was a bit electronical!" I thought that was just great. I was having my bit of quirky fun…and then putting the backward count on one of them too ('Jackhammer Blues'). It was something like my sense of humour and it makes you pay attention, you know; you're into the first chorus – you're just there straight away and I like things like that in production. Possibly it was gimmicky – but for fuck's sake, it was 1970!'

'Winter Song' would, in time, certainly be regarded by many as quintessential Alan Hull, a beautiful melody married to stinging social commentary; 'Clear White Light' was certainly hugely spiritual, despite Alan's non-religious stance. The opening 'Lady Eleanor' was much inspired by the writing of Edgar Allan Poe, one of the heavier writers included in Alan's reading during his time as a psychiatric nurse; Woody Guthrie's 'Jackhammer Blues' was a nod to the particular influences of both Rod and Jacka, and a pillar of the live repertoire – as was good mate Rab Noakes' 'Turn A Deaf Ear'.

The band obviously held Rab in high regard, as Ray noted in *Sounds* in September that year: 'In his own way he's as great an artist as someone like Neil Young and his songs…well, the fact that we have never recorded somebody else's songs speaks for itself.' Alan's local hit 'We Can Swing Together' also reappeared in re-recorded form, complete with participation from the mysterious La Chasse Choir. Just were these people? Ray Laidlaw: 'La Chasse was a drinking club in Wardour Street (above a bookies and Francesco's Unisex Hair Stylist!), which was about four doors away from the Marquee. It was usually populated by roadies and Scotsmen. Y'know – people who used to like a good drink.

'It was our stamping ground; we used to go to the Marquee bar every night, the Speakeasy every night: it was sort of the nearest you could get to a Newcastle pub.' Ray also recalls that Vivian Stanshall and Keith Moon, who were good mates, would actually come in through the window at the club, having walked across the rooftops from the Who's offices a couple of streets away.

Apparently, a regular pastime with the band while frequenting these hostelries – particularly the Speakeasy – was to wait until the place had emptied and scrabble around on the floor, picking up any oose cash that had been dropped. Alan remembers crawling around on the floor with Jacka when everyone had gone 'and found 45 quid between us. I then found about five packs of Gitanes cigarettes! They were so rich, they didn't know what to do with it. That was a regular thing when we were hard up.'

Another ruse was to finish off any food that had been left on the tables; at least one very well-known musician, found face-down in his meal, would have felt the plate being removed from under him had he not been so incapacitated by drink. Ray continues: 'It was the usual thing; "we need a big chorus – let's get the lads in…" Somebody went up the road and got a couple of dozen revellers out of there and spoilt the record for us!

'It was all mates and there was probably a few famous people involved. I think Vivian Stanshall was there, because he was a regular…the Bonzos were always there… George 'Porky' Peckham, famous for the messages he used to inscribe on the middle of records he had mastered…' Paul Conroy certainly remembers being there, as he later noted on the sleeve of the band's 'Buried Treasures' collections released by Virgin in 1993.

There was also another, sort-of famous resident at Trident while Lindisfarne were there: George Harrison. 'He'd been in there for about a year, I think, recording "All Things Must Pass". I never actually saw him, he seemed to keep himself to himself. Si did, though,' Ray recalls.

'George was coming up the stairs, about four steps below me,' Si continues, 'and, being small, my first thought was, "I'm taller that George Harrison! Taller than 'God'!" This thick Scouse voice is grumbling as he's sucking his finger – "Bloody roadies…why do they cut the strings so short? Why don't they curl them round at the end?" I just nodded and mumbled back in agreement.'

JOHN ANTHONY used to be a singer with a group from Windsor called Hogsnort Rupert, a disc-jockey at London's The Pheasantry and Speakeasy, where he zapped people with a combination of soul records and freaky sounds like "Saucerful Of Secrets," and then a promotion man with American Mercury.

Now he is busy in the job that he likes best — one which he thinks of in terms of a vocation — producing.

In little more than a year he has built up a sizeable reputation with his work for the Charisma label and three or their bands — Van der Graaf, Lindisfarne and Genesis.

He has a definite line now, though: "I have to like the artist first, and that has to be a reciprocal thing. Then I go to lots of their gigs, and listen and watch how they play. After, I demo the album, and just play around and talk about ideas and structures, and usually, when I've heard the songs I've an idea how the album will change and look during full production." Probably more importantly,

however, he believes in a total involvement with the artists. "Often I go down and sing with the bands in the studio. Like, with Genesis' singer, Peter Gabriel, who lacks confidence when he goes into the studios. It helps him to build confidence in his singing. In essence it's having a love of the artist and his work, and the idea in your head of what to do with it."

He got into production by the backdoor. He knew Yes, and he went along to one of their sessions one day at Polydor, got the session together and mixed the tapes. A lot of people liked it, and in Spring 1969 he got a job with American Mercury — not a wholly successful position, apparently ("I learnt the wrong way to do things first").

JOHN ANTHONY
reciprocal thing

However, he met Van der Graaf Generator, "Who were locked away in a filing cabinet with Mercury, tucked under V." The record company then decided to close down its London office, but he got the O.K. to cut an album with Van der Graaf; just 12 hours to record and eight to mix — everything done in one or two takes. Tony Stratton-Smith, boss of the new Charisma label, liked what he did on the album and asked him to produce Rare Bird. Their first single, "Sympathy," became a hit record and sold one and a half million copies.

Like all producers he has his gripes, though. "So many bands go in under-rehearsed and don't groove with the producer. There's one right way to do an album and 400 wrong ones. That's the point of having a producer. Groups dont know what their faults are. They just go in, take a look at the console, and say, O Christ! They're lost in a deluge of technicalities."

*Its all right Lady Eleanore
I'm all all right where I am*

*Then creeping on toward me
Licking lips with tongues of fire
A host of golden demons
Screaming lust and base desire
Then when it seemed quite certain
That the screams could get no higher
I heard a voice above the rest
Screaming you're a liar*

Its all right Lady Eleanore . . . .

I'm all right in your arms . . . .

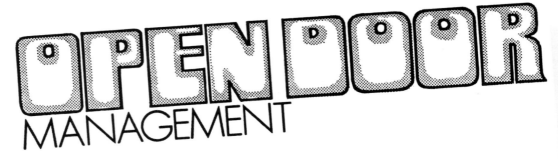

OPEN DOOR MANAGEMENT

LINDISFARNE

(Formerly Brethren)

Alan Hull – Ray Jackson – Simon Cowe – Ray Laidlaw – Rod Clements

LINDISFARNE is the inevitable result of its five members having played together in various Tyneside groups over the past six years, the last in a long line of unlucky attempts to get a totally original Newcastle group off the ground. Their story can be traced back to 1966, when Ray Laidlaw and Rod Clements formed the Downtown Faction, which was to become Newcastle's most popular blues group. Simon Cowe and Ray Jackson, both old friends of Rod and Ray, both joined in a long series of personnel changes in the group's three-year existence.

It was with the departure of their lead guitarist in December 1969 that the group decided to abandon their stale, heavy-blues style in favour of a sound which owed much to acoustic folk music but retained all the power and excitement of an electric group. Rod and Si had both been writing songs whose lyrical and musical subtleties suffered from over-amplification, and their songs proved admirably suitable to their new sound. They also began to feature some songs by Alan Hull, whom they were getting to know through their increasing involvement with the local folk scene. They changed their name to Brethren, and in May 1970, Alan joined the group. Now, for the first time, the songs of Alan, Si and Rod could be heard in their true form, undistorted by high volume or self-indulgent improvisation, while Ray Jacksons's country-blues harmonica and mandolin found a chance to express themselves. The long experience Rod and Ray, the rhythm section, have had together, has proved worthwhile by the solid foundation they provide for the group's front line.

Alan, Si and Rod have written over 300 songs between them, and must be considered among the finest writers the North has produced. All the songs featured by the group are original compositions, and a good sample can be heard on their first LP on the famous Charisma label, for whom they signed a three-year contract in June 1970.

In August they changed their name to LINDISFARNE, which is the name of an island off the coast of their native Northumberland, and it is under this name that their music will at last reach the wide audience it deserves.

Direction. Joe Robertson. David Wood.
Ground Floor Suite: 29, Arcadia, Percy Street, Newcastle upon Tyne NE1 4PZ
Telephone: (0632) 27787
Emergency Telephone: (0632) 624999 – 24 hour answerphone.

Unfortunately for John Anthony, Lindisfarne were one of several Charisma acts for which he has never received any payment: 'It got iffy at Charisma because I wasn't paid any royalties,' he subsequently recalled. 'I wasn't paid for work done. I don't get a cent on any Genesis records, or Lindisfarne. All my altruistic feeling for what Charisma was supposed to be all about disappeared; but it was pressured by the American end of the operation.

'The great thing that came out of it was, that Jac Holzman (US supremo of Elektra Records, the label that released Charisma's product over there) came in – everybody was scared of him – and said, "Hey, John, you did a great job on that Lindisfarne album…on the beginning of 'Clear White Light', can you remix it and put on a little more reverb…dub that blues song on and cut that other song off?" So on the American album, I did "Meet Me On The Corner", which became a hit later, and took off "Jackhammer Blues". Jac obviously wanted something more English. So I said okay…he'd obviously listened to the record as a professional – and you've got to say, "Fuck, this guy did the Doors, this guy did Love"…so I did it.' *

Meanwhile, Strat had been going about getting his new charges seen about town as much as possible. Rod: 'There was a short venture that he put us up for, doing the London clubs. We did the Speakeasy, the Pheasantry… A fair enough career move at the time – to put your new band from out of town in these trendy places and let the important people around town see what they're all about – but it didn't work out at all.'

Strat was also a regular at the Marquee. Chas Chandler believed that it was here that he first saw the band: 'I can't remember why I was there, but probably because I was a friendly with Tony Stratton-Smith. He had this "perch" there and I often popped in. I just thought they were a good band and when I went over to see Tony, he said he'd already signed them.' Rod also remembers Strat's regular location: 'He was always sitting at the end of the bar, next to the plate-glass window, so he could see the gig without having to deal with any of the scruffy punters.'

Certainly, on Sunday 31 May 1970, the band played the club 'with Al' as Ray's diary notes, but also returned the following Sunday, opening for American band Raven. It is this occasion that Strat clearly recalled in *Sounds* in October 1972: 'There was only about 50 people there and the group were pretty miserable. I remember encouraging them by saying that within six months they'd be turning people away.' Subsequently, they would return on 9 August (having played Plumpton – the forerunner of the Reading Festival – the day before), followed by recording the album, then 6 and 20 September, 13 and 27 October, and 3 November.

Rod recalls a more 'informal' arrangement: 'Strat's Marquee nights were a very impromptu sort of thing. We used to get shoved on at the last minute, sometimes. Once, I didn't have any bass gear with me and had to plug straight into the PA.' Nonetheless, awareness of the band was all building nicely to the album's release later that year. Glen Colson still clearly remembers the huge excitement around the band at the time of these shows: 'They were like a breath of fresh air, everyone said – but it was true. They were honest, the songs were great, they had great melodies and people were bored shitless with listening to King Crimson and all the rest of it that was going on at the time. It was very "dingy" music; the Van der Graaf thing, Genesis…it was all a bit sort of, "arranged"… These guys went down and they were like a scruffy, folky Beatles. That was the vibe, and everybody just loved it.

'I got four or five press guys down there eventually – it must have been the second or third time they played there – and they all just went crazy. No-one had heard stuff like this before. Fairport Convention were Lindisfarne's idols, but they soon overtook them because the songs were much better, not the playing. Lindisfarne became like a "popular" Fairport Convention, and I should think Fairport were well pissed off!'

Fairport's Simon Nicol well recalls meeting the band after a gig in Manchester: 'It was after a gig at UMIST or the Uni itself; I'm not sure if we shared a bill or they'd been coerced back from a separate bill…anyway, we went back to somebody's house – an after-show party for two bands in town. I didn't get to see them on that occasion, but I did meet them socially. It was just after they'd taken up that name and I'd heard of them on the grapevine as a band having a strong regional flavour.

'That's one of the great strengths of the whole Newcastle area; the fact that they cleave to it; they bind together and have an identity which I think people in more amorphous parts of the country are probably jealous of. Because they're geographically isolated, they have this turn of phrase and accent. You can always tell a Geordie, but you can't tell him much!'

* It was a connection that was to finally come up trumps some years later when John, who had put his own money as well as Trident's into the first Queen album, put in a call to Jac Holzman in California, who came over to see the band at the Marquee. No-one was interested in the band and John had sat on the tapes for a year, but Jac signed Queen the next day. 'So out of the Lindisfarne thing came a relationship which years later led to something else.'

Opposite: The earliest Lindisfarne press release.

Below: Fairport Convention, Lindisfarne's folk-rock heroes who became their friendly rivals. Simon Nicol is second left.

Nicol believes that the band had come in at just the right time, post-underground. 'What singled them out for me was the melodic nature of their work – which was the primary thing – and the fact they all sang so well. It shows just how much breadth of musicality they enjoyed. It wasn't just a case of one guy who used to play the acoustic guitar; one guy who just stood there and played harmonica; they were all throwing a lot of ideas around and I get the impression that Alan was really driven. They were a lucky band. They made great harmonies together, in a way which I can't think of any contemporary British band was able to do.

'They were gifted tunesmiths, who could come up with ear-catching tunes – particularly Alan and Simon – and then they were able to harmonise on top of that. Jacka had a lot to do with it; it wasn't Beach Boys-type pop, it was more complex. It had a really sweet note that was not heard on the underground circuit. McCartney is probably the closest to it.'

The album release was preceded in late November 1970 by the single "Clear White Light Pt II", the song which had so enraptured Strat. Called "Pt II" because Alan had already written a song with the same title, the single received great reviews and the band were beginning to get good press reaction. Reviewers were quick to pick up on the band's stated influences, with *Sounds* championing the single as 'at times the vocals were very Lennonesque. Then at times they were pure Lindisfarne, who by the way are going to have a monstrous hit on their hands.'

Melody Maker went on to say: 'Every now and then, one album manages to surface and stand apart from the anonymous mediocrity of the majority…thankfully, they defy categorisation.' Much of the heightened press was due to the enthusiasm of Glen Colson, as Ray confirms: 'He was very young – younger than us, in his late teens or early twenties – and had linked up with all the young kids who were writing on the music papers at the time. He knocked around with them all, went to the same pubs and journalists as a race are quite into staying up at night carousing – and so were we…so we all became pals.

'We were all living in London by then, dossing with friends – none of us had proper places at this stage – so were out every night, because we went to the same pubs and everything, we became the darlings of the music press because we were like them. At the time lots of musicians took themselves very seriously, and we were basically very "earthy" – the other extreme. In fact, we consciously made an effort to be a bit "slapdash" and later, in a way, it would backfire on us. Underneath, actually we were quite proud of what we did, but people began to think that we were just a band for a piss-up.'

The single wasn't a chart hit, but was immediately followed by the album itself. There were some great reviews, but it didn't sell. *Sounds'* Jerry Gilbert had this to say: 'Rarely indeed is it possible to hear a new album by a new group and decide on one hearing that every track is a potential hit single. But such is the case with Lindisfarne… The album is a straight, simple group effort with catchy, easily-memorable songs which were so typical of the early days of the Mersey boom…a happy, swinging folk sound in the old country style of Guthrie, Terry and Houston…Lindisfarne are essentially a songwriter's band – so go out, buy the album, play it right through and then put it on again.'

Meanwhile, the band gigged continually throughout November and December, including support gigs with Roy Harper at Kingston Poly and Caravan at Ewell Tech in Surrey, as well as Charisma's Christmas party at the Marquee on the 9th – 'Formal dress, bow ties or best overalls'. On 14 December, they recorded their very first session for the BBC, for Radio Two's *Nightride* programme (the Audition Panel, according to Ken Garner's excellent book *In Session Tonight*, commented 'There doesn't seem to be a lot of call for this type of ingredient in our general output.') before finally returning to Alan's old Folk Club at the Rex, to play at their Second Christmas Party on 23 December.

Lindisfarne had ended the year with, as *Melody Maker*'s Michael Watts commented, 'an album which for clarity of style bids fair to establish them as a top band for 1970.' In the same interview, it was suggested that 1971 would see a solo album from Alan before the band's second release in March. There was certainly something stirring. As much as a live act as anything else, Lindisfarne were the band everyone was looking out for.

'We were really skipping around the country,' Alan recalls of the time. 'We were definitely "doing" it, then. We'd turn up at gigs in the Midlands and there were queues – it was an underground thing… Every time we went back to them, you couldn't get in for the queues.' Jerry Gilbert, in his preview of the coming year in *Sounds* seemed to encapsulate the mood of that time, feeling that 'the pick of all the record companies looks to be Charisma, who have several of the greatest potential bands signed to them.

'I predicted several weeks back that Geordie bands would figure prominently in the changing face of music in 1971. Lindisfarne have already been strongly tipped, and purely on their songwriting strength alone it would be safe to go along with the punters. Now, with a punchy collection of catchy pop songs – a nod in the direction of early Beatledom in fact – success seems imminent.'

Chapter
FOUR
ADMISSION SIX BOB

The Lindisfarne bandwagon, once started, now seemed unstoppable, and the momentum had careered on through the holiday season. As January 1971 dawned, *Melody Maker*'s first issue of the new year broke some exciting news: 'John & Tony Smith are putting on two tours featuring Charisma artists early in the New Year. All seats will be just six shillings. First of the two will feature Van der Graaf Generator, Lindisfarne and Genesis. The second tour will apparently feature Every Which Way, Audience and either Rare Bird or Jackson Heights.'

This cut-price package tour kicked off at the Lyceum, London on 24 January, squeezing eight more dates into an already packed Lindisfarne itinerary. This already included their first session for John Peel's *Top Gear* programme on Radio 1 on 30 January, followed by *Sounds Of The Seventies* on the 19th and the BBC's *Folk On One* on 10 February. *

The idea for what became known as the Six Bob Tour had come from Strat: 'They charged the equivalent of 30p a ticket,' as Ray Laidlaw explains, 'and the idea was if it sold out every hall, they would break even. This had never been done before; put three bands on that weren't headliners and just get grass-roots reaction.'

The principle wasn't new, of course – it harked back to the package tours of the 1950s and 1960s – but it was indicative of Strat's canny eye for promotion. 'We knew all the other bands anyway,' Ray continues, 'so we all used the same gear apart from the bits and pieces that were particular, and took turns topping the bill.' All three bands shared the same tour bus, though, as Ray explains, they all had their own habits.

*Three new tracks not included on the first album were featured in these sessions, in particular Si's 'Positive Earth' (which had started life as 'Front Room Tune', 'written at 5 Camp Terrace, North Shields' according to Si and had been committed to tape during the 'NOOT' sessions), Alan's 'Psalm To A Secret' and Rod's 'Dream Within A Dream' – of which there appears to be no recorded versions other than those featured on Peel's programme.

** Around this time, Rod and Jacka played on Hamill's 'Fools Mate' solo album. 'I think we did it in one night, but it was a nice gesture. Again, it was the Charisma thing to have the exchange of artists between bands.' There was also a gig with Hamill, at the Marquee. 'He gigged the album there and had as many as he could get who'd been on the album doing the respective numbers on stage. Hugh Banton out of Van der Graaf was the keyboard player and, as Peter introduced us, Hugh did a snatch of "We Can Swing Together". We were actually quite pally.'

Below: Van der Graaf Generator, Lindisfarne's labelmates and tour companions.

Right: Lindisfarne and Genesis in Germany. From left: Steve Hackett, Tony Banks, Phil Collins, Alan, Mike Rutherford, Rod and Peter Gabriel.

'To be fair to the Genesis lads, they weren't really our sort – y'know, rough as badgers... They used to sit up the front of the tour bus with their books and their picnics and glasses of sherry, and there would be the Van der Graaf lot, rolling these enormous seven-pronged joints – it used to take all the way to Manchester to construct these things – and us lot with a couple of crates of beer. Phil (Collins) used to run around from place to place, trying a bit of everything!

'We used to play hard...that atmosphere was deliberately cultivated by Strat; he wanted us to feel like a team. There was lots of cross-pollination of ideas...we learned a lot from each other.' Rod agrees: 'It worked brilliantly, because we really did feel as though we were more part of a movement, with Strat as its figurehead. At the beginning, there was definitely a difference between the front and the back of the bus...it was great, because it did gradually merge into one thing – a gradual change in atmosphere rather than these three separate camps.

'The Van der Graaf chaps were great; they were smashing lads. We were interested in these various "recreational" pursuits, but very naïve to it all. Dave Jackson, their horn player, seemed to be the main instigator of these elaborate Rizla constructions. I remember asking if he'd show me how to make "one of those things" and his face lit up, as though it was the opportunity he'd always dreamed of. He said, "Yes, my boy. Certainly. Come and sit here..." and got all this gear out.

'They were very friendly, a bit more – it has to be said – than Genesis, actually. They were much more reserved, more serious about what they were doing. Individually, they were all canny lads, but they seemed to have a bit of a thing around them. I suppose we must have appeared that way to them as well.' **

Guitarist Steve Hackett – on his first tour with Genesis at the time – laughs at his recollection of the atmosphere on board the communal transport: 'It seemed to be three separate worlds on one coach! There would be Lindisfarne, having a good time as usual; Genesis seemingly intent on doing *The Times* crossword and then, up the front, there was drugs and pondering the meaning of the universe with Van der Graaf. I used to find either camp more preferable and more talkative in those days than my own band!'

Steve often found himself in conversation with Jacka – 'Jacko', as he continues: 'He always struck me as Lindisfarne's "diplomat", their contact with the outside world. We used to have long conversations about stuff that I can remember not one whit of...maybe as a fellow harmonica player, there was something there between us.' Steve also points out that the sheer diversity of the three bands was an attraction to the audiences, 'although, obviously, there were musical crossover points between us.'

He also recalls discussing 'the joys of Newcastle Brown versus Guinness. I'd got into drinking Newcastle Brown Ale straight out of the bottle in the days when I used to go and see the likes of Paul Butterfield and John Mayall at Eel Pie Island. Nowadays, I'm teetotal since I had problems with stomach ulcers at the end of the 1970s. I may be stone-cold sober these days, but I wasn't in those days, I can assure you!

'The Lindisfarne guys were very friendly – and that was very welcome in my early gigging days when, quite frankly, we were wondering if it was all going to work out.' Another thing Steve recalls clearly is that at the time, Genesis would go on stage incredibly nervous. 'We were painfully shy; thinking – "I hope they like us". Lindisfarne, by comparison, would fall on absolutely pissed – I really hope they don't mind me saying that – but that was part of their charm. They and their audience were at one at that point in time. No matter how "gone" they were, they always turned in a great rendition of "Lady Eleanor".

'It has that kind of naturalness to it that I used to expect from Beatles material – that sort of "comfortableness". It's something that eventually we all simplify to some degree and find out our

métier, but they'd already found that in the very early days with that song. That had a certain mystique to it.' Steve regrets not getting to know Alan a little more: 'I always thought he was a little more of an edgy character, not necessarily given to long converse. As time goes on, I'm very anxious now to conserve friendships; I consider it to be very important. I think that so much was missed out on in the early days; y'know, when you're young you're keeping your head down – just getting on with your own area of activity.

'I would love to see all the guys again and do something more with them than just share a drink. The last time I saw any of Lindisfarne was at Strat's memorial service at St Martin's In The Fields and I was talking to Jacko; I was struck by the passage of time and the feeling was almost one of the sixth form returning to pay their respects to their old headmaster – although I'm quite sure Strat would probably laugh at that! I remember "Clear White Light" being played and Keith Emerson playing extracts from "America". Strat was a man of vision, and he had the vision to sign Lindisfarne. He managed to make his passions productive.'

Alan 'loved the Six Bob Tour to death. I remember going to Sheffield City Hall – a huge place, none of these bands had played more than 300-seaters...we walked on for the soundcheck when Phil Collins – in "actor" guise – looked around at all the roadies and said, "That's it – gig's off. Too small!" I thought, "I like the cut of his jib." I'll never forget that.'

The gigs themselves gained a hugely enthusiastic response for Lindisfarne. Michael Wale, writing in *The Times* following the opening night, said: '...they are entertainers in a business that at times seems intent on boring audiences to death by pomposity and "seriousness". Who would have predicted that an audience of 1,500 Southerners would have clapped their hands in unison to the Geordie National Anthem, "Blaydon Races"?'

Melody Maker's Michael Watts appeared to see beyond the obvious bonhomie and had this to say: 'Lindisfarne are the most complete band on the Charisma label, with a flowing continuity of style and melodic strength that encompasses the best of pop and avoids its pretentiousness...the quintessence of tastefulness. And in chief writer and vocalist Alan Hull, they have a dominant figure capable of drawing together all the band's influences...'

As the tour progressed, all concerned appeared to revel in the atmosphere. Rod: 'Van der Graaf used to finish the night off and I used to play fiddle with them – the tune was the Radio 1 theme, George Martin's "Theme One" – that they did for an encore.' Then, at the end, according to Ray, there would be a jam. 'Lonnie Donegan's "Battle Of New Orleans": Phil did a verse, Peter did a verse, Peter Hamill...and Alan and Jacka.'

The band's solo gigs wound inexorably on, right through February – including Belfast – March and April, including four shows in Holland and finally to Newcastle City Hall on the 23rd. They were once again off around the country the following day, returning for a TV show in their home city on the 27t, before travelling to London once more the next day for the first of two *Sounds Of The Seventies* sessions for Radio 1. As the tour continued, they would also record sessions for the Mike Raven's *Rhythm & Blues Show* on the 12 April, with the second *Sounds Of The Seventies* on the 8 June and another *Top Gear* for John Peel on the 24th.

The first of these sessions evidenced the first public airing of Rod's new song, 'Meet Me On The Corner'* and the second the debut of Alan's 'Fog On The Tyne' – a song he claimed to have written by design, along with others such as 'Mr Inbetween' and 'We Can Swing Together', to finish the night off at folk clubs: 'Everybody used to do "Whip Jamboree" or something at the end, so the punters could bang their glasses on the table and sing along, but I thought I'd write something of my own.' Also featured was a new instrumental, 'Scotch Mist'.

To quote Ray Laidlaw from *In Session Tonight*, ' We became regulars in the BBC canteen and almost had our own coathooks.' It would not be long, as the same book notes, before several producers' shelves would be regularly raided to re-use Lindisfarne tracks throughout programming at Radio 1.

On 10 May, the band headlined at the Royal Festival Hall in London. A hugely prestigious event, the bill also included Gillian McPherson and Unicorn. In the audience with Strat that night was Texan Bob Johnson, a staff producer at CBS in the US who had just produced Bob Dylan's 'Nashville Skyline', as well as albums by Leonard Cohen and Simon & Garfunkel. According to Alan, he was there by invitation from Strat and the event had been arranged solely as a showcase for Johnson's benefit.

Strat told *Sounds* in April how the connection had come about: 'Bob heard the first album in America, played to him by his legal representative, Martin Maschat, who is also a director of Charisma in the States.' Apparently Johnson was no longer bound exclusively to CBS, and would be going into the studio with the band at the end of May. As for the show itself, the band had their own perspective, given the venue's opulence – although it says a great deal about them that they would risk such an attitude, with the knowledge of both Johnston's reputation and the reason for his attendance.

'We thought it was a hoot,' laughs Ray Laidlaw. 'A band of old rag men like us at a place like that – so we thought we'd have a bit of fun. Alan did "January Song", because we thought that would be something "serious" and "proper", and when we finished some of the audience were getting irritated, waiting for a bit of "life". So, we'd said before the show, "let's do that really daft song – 'Fog On The Tyne' – that Alan used to do in the clubs, but we'll do the same introduction as 'January Song' – so people'll think, 'Oh Christ, here's another dirge' and then we'd start singing all this stupid stuff."

'So we did it, and it brought the house down. The next night we thought we'd shove it in again and see what happens…' Johnson was completely knocked out. It was also to clear to all concerned that 'Fog On The Tyne' had to be on the album, although as Ray says 'It was never meant to be a contender, it was a one-off for that show.' The choice of producer was, given the band's stated Dylan influences, 'like a bolt out of the blue. In those days,' states Ray, 'there weren't that many big-name producers, but he was definitely one.'

* There had been an eight-track recording of the song during the sessions for the first album on 13 August the previous year, according to archive records. Rod explained the genesis of the song to *NME* on 23 October: 'I saw it as a finger-picking guitar tune. Then I thought, it'd be nice to write words for it… I already had the title, tucked away for future use.' 'Fog…' had been committed to tape as early as June. Raven's session concentrated, quite naturally, on purely blues-based tracks from the band's repertoire, plus Robert Johnson's 'Walking Blues' and 'I'm Coming Home'.

Jo Lustig

presents

an evening with

LINDISFARN[

(Charisma Recording Artists)

with special guests

GILLIAN McPHERSON

(RCA Recording Artist)

UNICORN

(Transatlantic Recording Artists)

ROYAL FESTIVAL HALL

GENERAL MANAGER: JOHN DENISON, C

MONDAY, 10th MAY, at 8 p.n

Tickets £1.00, 80p, 60p, 40p
from R.F.H. Box Office, London, S.E.
01-928 3191 and usual agents

However, there was some concern that John Anthony was now out of the picture. John himself recalls Rod's concern in particular: 'Later, when I lived in Finchley just near him, he stopped me in the street one day and said, "I hope you know that not all of us wanted Bob Johnson to do that album." The whole episode hurt, but you've got to learn from all that. What hurt more was that I wasn't told. It was a *fait accompli* – they could have put me in a fuckin' mental home when I saw that front page…' For Si, similarly, it was a case of, 'Bob Johnson was handed to us on a plate. "He's done Bob Dylan and Leonard Cohen…oh yeah, fab!" I didn't realise that John wasn't in the frame at all.'

On the other hand, Rod admitted to Bob Randall in *NME* that 'The main reason Bob got in touch with us, and took an interest, was because he sensed that – like Dylan – we're more interested in projecting the songs themselves.' Alan's reaction to Johnson's involvement was simply 'Let's get on with it!' and according to Roy Hollingworth in *Melody Maker*, Johnson's own reaction to working with the band was simply that 'he was in a position to work with whom he likes and he only works with those who have that "magic". Lindisfarne,' he said, 'have that magic.'

Johnson was a curious individual who apparently had some interesting characteristics. Glen Colson remembers 'a strange, mystical figure; meddling with drugs and being very playboy-ish. He just appeared, talking this weird sort of accent. He wouldn't have his picture taken, because he said that the Indians said that if you have your picture taken, you lost your spirit.' Rod recalls one occasion when Strat took the band and Johnson for lunch at a bistro just opposite the Charisma offices: 'He didn't eat anything. All he had was a bowl of strawberries and a glass of red wine, which was liberally replenished and he'd keep dipping the strawberries in the wine. We thought, "Strange…" Meanwhile, we thought, "Great. Pig out at the record company's expense…"'

'Looking back on it, he was probably out of it all the time; it didn't show in any bad ways, but he was very laid back – very detached. A very likeable character, actually. He had a fierce side to him – he made it very clear what he wanted in the studio, but he was one of those people you know not to mess with.'

Si 's memory is of 'the strangest character I've ever met in my life…', but he agrees with Rod, 'He was a powerful bugger. He was only little, but he radiated cool power.' As far as his approach in the studio was concerned, for Si 'It was difficult to understand what he was saying, because he said things in such a peculiar way. You understood the words – the order he put them in – but you'd have to say, "Do you mean you want me to play a bit more quietly?" "No. I mean play it off the hook." "Does that mean the beginning of the bar?" There was a lot of confusion and misunderstanding.'

The band, in their opinion, had prepared well for their second album – to be recorded at Trident again, rather than in the States as Strat had hinted to the press – and they approached the sessions with pride and confidence. After the Festival Hall show, they had retreated once again to the Scottish borders near Newcastleton, as they had done once before, to write and rehearse the new songs, but as yet had been too busy to do much preparation.

In *Sounds* on 15 May Ray told Jerry Gilbert, 'We've got Alan Hull's "January Song" and Rod Clement's "Why Can't I Be Satisfied" and there's also a couple of Simon Cowe's songs.' He went on, 'It seems pretty certain that "Meet Me On The Corner", "City Song" and "January Song" will be on the album, and there's also a selection of half a dozen old songs.' He also mentioned that there was a possibility that they would be re-recording 'Nicely Out Of Tune' for the States.

In the same interview came the first clues of the implications of the ever-increasing scale of the band's success. In the States, Elektra boss Jac Holzman was keen for Lindisfarne to tour there, but they were eager to work in Europe, after their recent success in Holland. There seemed to be no shortage of work, the problem being how to fit it all in. 'At the moment we are still at the stage where we need to play everywhere, though I dare say that we'll be able to take three months or so off later on,' explained Ray.

Rod too, looked forward to some spare time: 'I'd like to take some time off to write and rehearse regularly because it

GPO ● GREETINGS TELEGR

HD108 GTG 2.33 PM NEWCASTLEUPONTYNE T 20
GREETING LINDISFARNE THE ROYAL FESTIVAL
HALL SOUTH BANK LONDON

= GAN DOON DARZA = GREG JOHN AND ALL THE LADS AT BURMAN +

GPO ● GREETINGS ELL

M≠FE27 GTG 9.43 LONDON T 25 GREETIJGS

IDISFARNE ROYAL FESTIVAL HALL LONDONSE1 =

EST WISHES TO A GREAT GROUP STOP HOPE YOUR NEXT FESTIVAL HALL
NCERT WILL BE SOLO STOP = JO LUSTIG +

Lindisfarne Gigs Up Until September 30th 1971

Date	Venue	Fee
2/10/70	Kirklevington	£30.00
9/10/70	Locarno Sunderland	50.00
21/10/70	Revolution	20.00
22/10/70	Blaises	20.00
23/10/70	Preston	50.00
25/10/70	Durham	25.00
30/10/70	Speakeasy	20.00
31/10/70	Uxbridge	20.00
3/11/70	Marquee	15.00
7/11/70	Kingston	50.00
13/11/70	Ralph West Hall S.W.11	40.00
14/11/70	Mothers, Birmingham	20.00
18/11/70	Swansea College of Education	35.00
21/11/70	Guildford	60.00
22/11/70	Trent Polytechnic	30.00
27/11/70	Medway Tech, Chatham	45.00
28/11/70	Manchester	40.00
4/12/70	Durham	45.00
5/12/70	Ewell Tech	35.00
6/12/70	Northampton	30.00
7/12/70	Twickenham	35.00
10/12/70	Consett College	65.00
11/12/70	Leicester University	42.50
14/12/70	Night Ride	50.00
18/12/70	Blackpool	45.00
19/12/70	Huddersfield	55.00
24/12/70	Eston Teeside	50.00
26/12/70	Town Hall, Middlesborough	50.00
27/12/70	Redcar Jazz Club	40.00
30/12/70	Mayfair, Newcastle	50.00
31/12/70	Kirklevington	75.00
	1970	£1237.50

Date	Venue	Fee
1/1/71	Scarborough	
8/1/71	Newcastle Poly	£40.00
9/1/71	Golden Slipper , South Shields	80.00
12/1/71	John Peel	85.00
13/1/71	Cardiff Univ	50.00
15/1/71	Hatton Centre, Derby	75.00
16/1/71	Lanchester Poly Coventry	70.00
17/1/71	City Hall, Newcastle	60.00
19/1/71	Sound of the 70's	75.00
22/1/71	Southampton College of Ed	50.00
5/2/71	Guildford Civic Hall	40.00
6/2/71	Newcastle Univ	100.00
8/2/71	Top Rank, Cardiff	100.00
10/2/71	Folk on Friday B.B.C	50.00
12/2/71	Cardiff University	50.00
14/2/71	Angel Godalming	75.00
19/2/71	Belfast	60.00
20/2/71	Londonderry	100.00
24/2/71	Glamorgan	90.00
25/2/71	Amethyst Club Preston	100.00
26/2/71	Trent Poly	75.00
27/2/71	Kirklevington	75.00
5/3/71	Exeter University	85.00
6/3/71	Twickenham	100.00
8/3/71	University of Warwick	100.00
10/3/71	Blackpool Tech	20.00
11/3/71	Bristol	105.00
12/3/71	University of Bath	55.00
13/3/71	U.M.I.S.T Manchester	135.00
15/3/71	La Ronde, Billingham	55.00
18/3/71	East Anglia University	150.00
19/3/71	Liverpool College	130.00
20/3/71	Starlight, Boston	150.00
27/3/71	Plaza, Newbury	100.00
		100.00
		£ 2785

would be silly for a group that relies on writing to leave no opportunity for it at all; it takes away all we've got.' Ray felt that it was 'obvious we were going to need a strong producer for the next album to hold it.' Johnson's initial approach proved to be both radical and decisive. 'We rehearsed the album with all sorts of lush, vocal harmonies and great vocal arrangements – but we'd overdone it as far as he was concerned.' recalls Ray. 'So he said, "Fine. We're gonna start again".'

Johnson specifically asked Alan to sing him every song he had. 'Right, we'll have that one...don't want that one...we'll have that one...and made the whole album like that.' Rod supports this description: 'He made Alan play it like it was, stripping everything back to basics.' Roy Hollingworth recalls going down to the sessions one night: 'There was just him in the control booth, sat there – and I thought, "Is this the way the great Bob Johnson works?" He was just sat there with a great inane smile on his face.

'When there was a break in proceedings, I said, "So how are you going about doing Lindisfarne then? It's a lot different from the stuff you've been used to..." and he said, "It's wonderful. I just set the tape rolling and just let it go!" There he was, "The Jesus Of Production" you think's gonna have all of these amazing ideas, when his genius was that he pretty much let the guys do what they liked.'

Such an approach was bound to prompt questions. Rod: 'We wondered if he knew us well enough to take these kind of risks? He didn't turn up on the first morning at the studio. We'd been to lunch with him and he'd been to the Festival Hall – I don't think he'd have had any tapes or demos, because I don't think there was such things in those days. He showed up in the afternoon, then he went through the songs. Who's to say he was wrong? Not I.'

Date	Venue	Fee
2/4/71	St. John's College, Manchester	
2/4/71	Farnborough Tech.	125.00
5/4/71	Cooks Ferry Inn	90.00
7/4/71	Mushroom Club, Birmingham	100.00
8/4/71	Locarno, Sunderland	100.00
9/4/71	Club Maryland, Glasgow	200.00
10/4/71	Kirklevington	125.00
14/4/71	Exit Club, Rotterdam	100.00
16/4/71	Paradiso, Amsterdam	75.00
17/4/71	Harlem	100.00
18/4/71	Delft	80.00
23/4/71	City Hall, Newcastle	50.00
24/4/71	Manchester University	200.00
27/4/71	Newcastle T.V.	100.00
28/4/71	Sound of the 70's	50.00
30/4/71	Sheffield University	50.00
1/5/71	Arnold & Carlton College, Nottingham	175.00
5/5/71	Trinity College, Carmarthen	175.00
7/5/71	Minstrale Club, Beckenham	150.00
8/5/71	Ashington	125.00
12/5/71	Mike Raven Show	225.00
14/5/71	Didsbury College, Manchester	50.00
15/5/71	Leicester University	175.00
27/5/71	Locarno Sunderland	175.00
29/5/71	Pembroke College Oxford	250.00
30/5/71	Westcliff on Sea	150.00
5/6/71	Lawns Centre, Cottingham	150.00
8/6/71	Sound of the 70's	150.00
11/6/71	Shoreditch College, Surry	50.00
12/6/71	Starlight Boston	200.00
17/6/71	Oval Hall, Sheffield	250.00
18/6/71	Manchester Free Trade Hall	225.00
19/6/71	Newcastle City Hall	225.00
24/6/71	Top Gear	250.00
25/6/71	Kingston Poly	60.00
27/6/71	Reading Festival	250.00
30/6/71	Cardiff	350.00
		225.00
		£5680.00

One occasion during recording particularly sticks in Alan's mind: 'One of the big things Bob did was bring in a lot of California grass…we weren't averse to smoking, to relax a bit – anyway, I was a bit stoned when suddenly this big Texan face was in front of mine, telling me to come outside into Wardour Street. It wasn't a request – I mean, he carried a gun – and, as we opened the door, I remember all I could see was this blinding white and me, out of my head, in this smelly back lane.

'Then he puts this big Texan face in mine again and said words to the effect of, "I dunno what it is you got, but Dylan's got it as well – I think it's probably arrogance – and I dunno what you're doing here with these guys. What I wanna do is take you over to Nashville tonight and start the album again with my guys. Waddaya say?" I just looked into this big, florid Texan face and said, "No." Then I walked back through the door! The session just carried on as normal and I thought, "Whoops, here's another one gonna walk out…", but he said no more about it.'

All the songs mentioned in the *Sounds* piece earlier that month were recorded during the sessions, plus 'Together Forever', another Rab Noakes song from his debut album, 'Do You See The Lights?', that had so impressed the band; Alan's 'Alright On The Night', and 'Passing Ghosts' and Si's album debut, 'Uncle Sam'* , as well as Alan's 'No Time To Lose' and the 'Scotch Mist' instrumental. It is possible, however, that archive records may have incorrectly noted the date of the latter two songs.

Also included was the curiously titled 'Peter Brophy Don't Care/Light Of Philosophy', a song co-written by Alan and old Barrabas mate Terry Morgan. The title was partly inspired by the work of Belgian artist René Magritte, whose work Alan greatly admired. 'The big Texan loved it,' Alan recalled. Rod's 'Why Can't I Be Satisfied' would not make the finished album, along with several other Hull songs which would resurface later, including 'Money Game', 'Country Gentleman's Wife' and 'Dingly Dell'.

'There was one song in particular that didn't make it,' recalls Rod. 'It was called "Who's Got The Blues, Huh?". Pity, because it was Alan moving in an interesting direction, almost a Zappa-ish type of thing. It was after he got his electric guitar and he was starting to find out he could do a bluesy, electric guitar thing rather than the acoustic folk songs he was known for.

'I remember opening with it at the Marquee one night between the two albums and I remember Strat and John Anthony standing in the audience with a look of absolute *horror* on their faces. It was one of the first intimations that we didn't just want to be folky, singer-songwriterly. We wanted to be rock'n'roll, as well. This was our first attempt to stretch out and it didn't go down well *at all*…'

After three days of recording and mixing, Johnson's approach at the editing stage was, according to Si: 'Literally a scissors job on the master. There was yards and yards of this tape cut out. He chopped verses in half, chopped choruses out, cut songs in half…' For Rod, 'The pruning he did on "City Song" made perfect sense. He cut out a lot of superfluous stuff and he did impose a style on the album that possibly it wouldn't have had, otherwise.' Si agrees. 'It was because he did such a massacre, surgical-job on the album that gave it its sound. He just exuded this "do as you're told" thing.'

For Rod, the comparison with their debut was that this was 'a direct, single-minded, straight-ahead statement. There's no messing about with what the album is. You can pick any track on it and know what album it's from and how it relates to the others. If we had had our way – or even if John Anthony had done it – it would have been more like "Nicely Out Of Tune".'

What was also clear was that the album could have only one title: 'Fog On The Tyne'. Glen Colson summed up the recordings thus: 'Bob had worked with all the great artists in the world, so he wasn't phased by working with some, y'know – piss-heads from Newcastle. He wasn't scared to tell them they couldn't do this or that; they had to do exactly what he said. He was ruthless about that, but it worked. It was a great album. It sounded great – not that I think he had anything to do with the engineering quality of it – I think he was purely a performance man; he was very good at getting that out of someone.' Engineer Ken Scott's contribution would be a great source of discussion.

After completing the sessions and with seemingly no break in the gigs, Alan took off home to Newcastle for a couple of days before starting another tour – this time with Bell & Arc. He was in a positive mood when he spoke

* This song, according to Si, was written 'in the van, outside Change Is, Bob Monkhouse's club in Newcastle. I was "affiliated" with the hat-check girl there at the time, and I was waiting for her to come off duty. That's the earliest song I can remember writing. I was probably about 21.'

Date	Venue	Amount
2/7/71	Aylesbury	125.00
4/7/71	Guildford	125.00
16/7/71	Lewisham Town Hall	100.00
18/7/71	Greyhound, Croydon	110.00
7/8/71	Belfry Hotel, Sutton Coldfield	150.00
13/8/71	Kinetic Circus, Birmingham	111.00
18/8/71	Marquay, Torquay	160.00
19/8/71	Penzance	150.00
20/8/71	Queens Hall, Barnstable	150.00
21/8/71	Van Dyke, Plymouth	100.00
29/8/71	Weeley Festival	200.00
31/8/71	Top Gear BBC	50.00
4/9/71	Lee's Cliff Hall, Folkstone	150.00
5/9/71	Pavillion Hemel Hempstead	150.00
6/9/71	Quaintways, Chester	150.00
10/9/71	Marquee	126.00
11/9/71	Alex Disco, Salisbury	150.00
14/9/71	Crawley	133.00
16/9/71	Cheltenham	200.00
17/9/71	Brighton	200.00
18/9/71	Starligh Boston	250.00
20/9/71	Sound of the 70's	50.00
22/9/71	Twickehham	110.00
25/9/71	Halifax	150.00
		£3350.00

1970	1,237.50
January-March 1971.	2,785.00
April - June 1971.	5,680.00
June - September 1971.	3,350.00
TOTAL EARNINGS	£13,052.50

5% of total = £652.62½p

2½% due to J. Robertson = £326.31p

on the telephone to Roy Hollingworth: 'Johnson brought out things in Lindisfarne that we didn't know were there. He made us crisper, brighter and, as it turns out, more serious than before. We thought a lot more about what we were doing.'

When asked about his songwriting, Alan was characteristically blunt: 'I find it easier to write sad songs. When I get serious, I pick up the guitar and sing. When I get in a happy mood – Christ, I don't write about it, I go out and celebrate it with the lads.' He also spoke with great enthusiasm in the same conversation (and perhaps provoked by Johnson's comments during the 'Fog…' sessions) about a solo album he was planning. 'I've got so many songs, I'm just going to America and sing Bob Johnson the lot. He can just pick them out. It'll give me a rest, give them a rest. I see a formula like this as a good way to keep the band together for a fair amount of time…'

When this would occur appeared to depend on whether the band toured the US – although it was increasingly likely that this would happen – and the success of 'Fog On The Tyne'. As Alan admitted in the *Halifax Telegraph & Argus* following a gig in the city two weeks later, 'Bob wants me to do it in Nashville but I'm not sure yet. I've had material in hand for quite a bit. There are things I wouldn't dream of doing with a group, but I might use the London Philharmonic or session men.'

In a signpost to the future, he also admitted a disenchantment with the idea of singles, Lindisfarne's lack of success in this market illustrating that progress so far had been achieved by solid touring. 'If we get a really strong song, we may release it as a single, but generally speaking we're not interested artistically or financially in the singles market.'

Nevertheless, in early June Charisma released 'Lady Eleanor' as a single from 'Nicely Out Of Tune'. As yet, there was no release date for the new album and the huge interest in the band had to be sated. The music press gave the single excellent reviews: 'A track that's difficult, nay impossible to describe in a few lines…the enigmatic lyric is a fantasy (or could it be an hallucination?) and the group generates an atmosphere or mystique and enchantment…Lindisfarne are already ripe, already blossoming and promising delicious fruit for today, tomorrow and a decade next Thursday.'

Despite such accolades, the lead review in *Melody Maker* and even the fact that it was 'the favourite single of the wife of Radio 1 DJ Tony Blackburn' – as Alan recalled, not altogether cynically, as one might expect – it was still not a hit. Two more Radio 1 sessions were recorded, *Sounds Of The Seventies* on 6 June followed by John Peel's *Top Gear* on the 24th.

Still, the gigging went on, though the tide was about to turn with one upcoming festival appearance. Despite a very successful Reading on 27 June – with Wishbone Ash, Ralph McTell and Terry Reid among others – it was the Weeley Festival, held near the South of England resort of Clacton on 28-29 August, that was the key to unlocking the magical combination hinted at for so long.

While certain members of the band bemoaned the move from clubs to the big stages, it appeared that Lindisfarne had found their niche, with Jacka in particular rising to each occasion. The Weeley site even survived a rampage of Hell's Angels when a squad of festivalgoers formed a vigilante group and destroyed most of the Angels' prized bikes. On a bill that also included headliners the Faces, plus Rory Gallagher, the Grease Band, Loudon Wainwright III, Quintessence, Colosseum, Argent and the ubiquitous Edgar Broughton, according to *NME*, 'In terms of both performance and crowd response, Weeley was a two-band event…the Faces and Lindisfarne.

'Everyone expected Lindisfarne to do well, but nobody envisaged the wild scenes of general acceptance that greeted them halfway through their set. Indeed, if there had been time, they could have played for the remainder of the day and into the night.' Finally, the reviewer, in a touching display of honesty, also reflected: 'I'm so very pleased for all those connected with Lindisfarne in that all the dedicated hard work as opposed to superficial hype has finally paid dividends and I don't think it will be too long before they become an attraction of international repute.'

Alan recognised the significance: 'Weeley was a quarter of a million people. I remember we were just about to go on stage in front of "only" 40,000 people at another festival – Jacka was in front of me and Strat behind me – I was really nervous, shaking and Jacka said to me, "Ho'way Alan, you're not nervous, are you? They're only students, man." He got on stage and tore the fuckers apart. I think Reading was the first time he "split" the crowd: "You 15,000 on the right – shut up. You 15,000 on the left – get your arms up in the air and dey this with me…"'

Rod too, recalls the day well: 'As far as I know, Weeley was the most people, ever, in this country… as far as the eye could see, it was quite awe-inspiring. We made a habit, fortunately, of making the sun come out when we went on. Then again, it might have just seemed to happen, because there was quite a lot of boring stuff musically at the time.'

Ray agrees. 'By the time we went on at these festivals, people were suffering severe brain damage from hearing one band after another. So we just took our slap-dash, light-hearted approach…have a bit of fun. It didn't matter if there was 20,000 people there, we'll just pretend we're in a folk club. They just got up dancing – getting a bit of circulation in their legs after listening to someone like Caravan for four hours. It worked a treat.'

Weeley was certainly a turning point. As Ray put it in *NME* later that year, 'We started off being big in the North East, where we could do no wrong. It took until Weeley to establish ourselves throughout the rest of the country.'

Lindisfarne
'Lady Eleanor'

CB 153

MARKETED BY
B&C RECORDS LTD.

Melody Maker

SEPTEMBER 11, 1971   6p weekly   USA 30 cents

LINDISFARNE'S Rod Clements and Alan Hull: new album rush-released.

Jazz and folk shocks in big Radio 1 blitz

JAZZ has been slashed in a major BBC radio shake-up. OUT is Jazz Record Requests, which has been running since the end of 1964. And Humphrey Lyttelton's Best Of Jazz series has been cut by half.

Folk is also affected by the new autumn schedules. Folk On Friday has been switched to Sundays and retitled Folk On Two (see page 9).

The long-running Jazz Record Requests series, introduced on Saturdays by Steve Race at 5.50-6 p.m. on Radio Three, is being "rested" at the end of this month.

Steve Race, who has presented the request programme for many years, told the MM: "What's happened to my programme is that Radio Three has decided to give progressive pop a chance.

"There's already a great deal of it on the air elsewhere, which is why I particularly regret the loss of precious airtime for jazz."

Humphrey Lyttelton's popular The Best Of Jazz is aired from 7.03 to 8.03 on Wednesdays on Radio One and Two. From the first Wednesday in October it will be heard — still on Wednesdays — from 9.30 to 10 p.m. — a cut of half-an-hour.

The BBC's Michael Colley commented: "We are looking into ways of restoring the programme to one hour next year."

Jazz shows not affected by the autumn changes are Peter Clayton's Jazz Notes (Sundays, 11-12 midnight), Humph's Jazz Club (Sundays, 12.05 to 1.02 a.m.), Jazz In Britain (Mondays, 11 p.m.) and Charles Fox's Jazz To-day (Wednesdays, 5.55 p.m.).

FOOTNOTE: In announcing the new Radio One and Two schedules for the autumn, Douglas Muggeridge, chief of Radio One and Two, said that the emphasis on the new programmes is still on deejay personalities and comedy. "Tony Blackburn has an audience of from 10 to 14 million, Jimmy Young up to 10 million, and Pete Murray from six to seven million."

He added: "The musical explosion of the Seventies will be the middle-of-the-road rather than progressive."

● SEE PAGES 4 AND 9.

Deep Purple in depth — see page 22

Lindisfarne join Who at Oval charity

PETE TOWNSHEND this week confirmed that the Who would be headlining the Bangla Desh charity concert at London's Oval cricket ground on September 18, as exclusively reported in last week's MM. Lindisfarne are also set to appear.

Townshend regards the Oval concert as a replacement for the free concert in London which the Who had hoped to stage this summer. They could not find a suitable venue, and Pete feels this is the best replacement.

There is still a possibility that they may do a free show in the north during their tour which opens on October 18.

Meanwhile, Lindisfarne — big hits of the Weeley Festival — have been added to the bill. Manager Tony Stratton-Smith told the MM this week: "They will definitely be appearing provided the money is going to charity. The group really want to do it, even though they have a booking the same evening."

Lindisfarne's second album "Fog On The Tyne," produced by top producer Bob Johnston, will be released on Charisma on October 15 — two weeks earlier than scheduled because of the group's increasing popularity following their two hugely successful festival appearances at Reading and Weeley.

A special concert has been booked for Lindisfarne at City Hall, Newcastle — their home town — on December 4. The concert will take the form of a special party with specially invited artists performing.

Negotiations are still in hand for the Faces, though it is virtually certain they will be joining the Who and Lindisfarne at the Oval. Quintessence, too, are likely to be on the bill, and also Mott the Hoople.

Less certain to play, but still possibles are Emerson, Lake and Palmer and the Greaseband.

Guest spots are being kept open for possible appearances by George Harrison, whom co-promoter Rikki Farr has contacted in America. Farr has also been in touch with Paul McCartney's London representative for a possible appearance by McCartney's new band.

Jeff Dexter comperes the event.

Tickets are available from all branches of Harlequin and One Stop Records and Musicland or by postal application to the Oval, Kennington, S.E.11. They will also be available on the day at the same price — £1.25.

NEXT WEEK: POP POLL RESULTS!

On 11 September, Lindisfarne appeared on the front page of *Melody Maker* with the news that, even though they had a booking the same evening, they were to appear with the Who at the Oval cricket ground in aid of Bangladesh famine victims. However, Strat is quoted as saying, 'They will definitely be appearing, provided the money is going to charity.'

The same piece announced that the album would finally be released on 15 October – two weeks earlier than scheduled, because of 'the group's increasing popularity following their two hugely successful appearances at Reading and Weeley.' On a bill that also included the Faces; Quintessence and Mott the Hoople, the Oval gig was another success, while that same month the band were voted runners-up (behind Wishbone Ash) in the Brightest British New Hope category in the *Melody Maker* Poll as well as seventh in the International category. To celebrate, the band played a packed gig at the Marquee, where Rod Stewart was apparently spotted 'charging ten new pence a head to talk to chums following the Poll Winners results.... Price soon dropped to one new pee or a brandy and coke...'

The first review for 'Fog On The Tyne' appeared in *Sounds* on 25 September; well ahead of release – and what followed from Jerry Gilbert was unequivocally enthusiastic.

'"The funkiest British sound since the early Stones" was Tony Stratton-Smith's first reaction on hearing this new Lindisfarne album; but then it's not surprising he should think that because he's the group's manager. Bob Johnson's comments were almost the same, but he just happens to be the band's producer. Yet even allowing for the fact that neither of these respected gentlemen can divorce themselves sufficiently from the product to see things in perspective, they have given an assessment which is darned near the mark.

'The album is an absolute master conception, and my worst fears that Bob Johnston would kill this Geordie band's natural sense of freedom are totally unfounded.'

Each successive review agreed 'Fog On The Tyne' was a masterpiece. *Disc & Music Echo* hailed it as establishing them as the most original British group of the past two years... The secret of Lindisfarne's success seems to lie in their ability to write fine, catchy commercial melodies, instrument them sparingly yet effectively, and sing them well using a variety of lead voices and harmonies... So closely-knit are the group that it's impossible to spot the individual writers. We urge you to hear this album – ten songs to set the pace for acoustic music 1971-style.'

Perhaps unsurprisingly, *Melody Maker* – who had championed the band for so long – classed the album as 'a long time coming and well worth waiting for. It's the almost perfect blend of folk/rock, mixed with subtle melodies, occasional blues and lyrics that really mean something. If nothing else, the

* Jacka's appearance on two Stewart tracks on 'Every Picture Tells A Story' – 'Maggie May' and 'Mandolin Wind' – were actually the source of a rumour that he would be leaving the band. Matters were further confused when John Peel sat in with Stewart for an appearance on *Top Of The Pops*, 'playing' Jacka's mandolin part.

album brings out Alan Hull's undisputed talents as a song and lyrics writer…you can tell he's in a class with Paul Simon and the rest…'

Roy Carr in *NME* could only agree. 'As they say, "You've either got it mate or you ain't" and this proves beyond any doubts that these lads are possessed with the magical ingredient, "it"… Along with John Lennon's masterpiece ('Imagine'), this album has commandeered my stereo player to the exclusion of all others. Indeed, both albums have set a standard which albums of the future will have to be judged by…

'In the person of Ray "Jacka" Jackson, the band have a mandolinist/harmonica player who has given the band its individual sound. His work in Lindisfarne and on other artist's sessions – most notable being Rod Stewart's "Maggie May" * – are rapidly revealing Jackson to be one of the most original instrumentalists to have emerged in the last couple of years…and he can do a mean vocal too… A major breakthrough of a band with a purpose and a successful future.'

Finally it had all come together. Ceaseless touring had split the two albums, laying down a unique reputation for success based on live performance and in the reviews of 'Fog On The Tyne' was contained the personification of what Lindisfarne was. Hard graft, talent and entertainment, all tightly bundled up into one huge package had given Lindisfarne Britain in the palm of their hand.

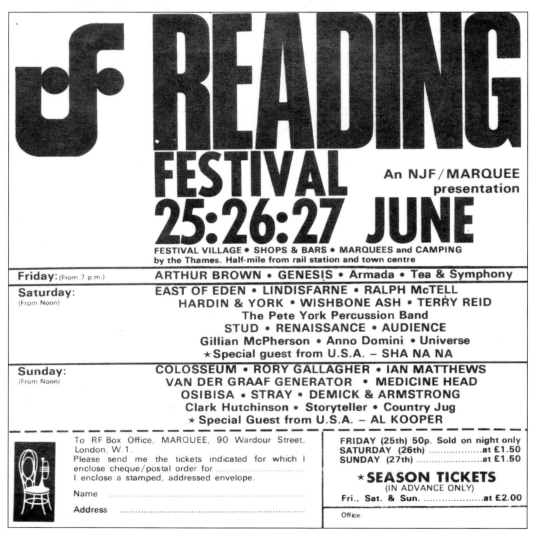

Chapter FIVE

THE MADNESS

Demand for 'Fog On The Tyne' was huge. Its first British orders were for 20,000 copies and in Newcastle two shops ordered 3,000 copies between them, selling more than 300 on the first day of release. The band decided to make a personal appearance at one of them – Windows in the centre of the city – as a thank-you to their native Tyneside for the last 12 months.

'It's the only time that I can remember getting mobbed in the street, legitimately,' recalls Ray. 'We once got mobbed by mistake – they thought we were somebody else…we hadn't been home for a long time and it was quite exciting.' By 6 November, the album had reached Number 9 in the *Sounds* chart and, in an interview with Dick Meadows, Jacka seemed to speak for everyone: 'The band will be over the moon if it gets higher still. I never realised something like this could happen so quickly.'

The apparent popular appeal of the album was perhaps best explained by long-time friend and fan of the band, Mike 'the Bike' Cartledge. A fine, hirsute Yorkshireman, Mike later hand-built a Harley he named 'Lady Eleanor' in honour of the band, beautifully air-brushed with scenes from Alan's song: 'I had access to an old fairground caravan that was slap-bang in the middle of a woodland, away from anywhere – with only the gamekeeper's cottage next to it and nothing else but trees and wildlife. The pub was about a mile and a half away and on a Friday, after work was finished, I would load up my 750 Norton Commando bike with all the necessary equipment, food and stuff – and it was away down to the caravan.

'So songs like "Alright On The Night" – "It'll be alright, we'll have a drink on a Friday night. It'll be oh so good, we'll do everything that we know we should…" Those lines, for me, just rang so true. "City Song", as well; "City streets, I see your lies, I will not play your game…" I'd had enough of the rat-race and by the weekend, I wanted to get away from it; country pubs and the good life… They were just haunting tunes: that's the top and bottom of it.' *

As the band were told that their last free night in November has been filled up with a trip to Paris for a TV show, Alan admitted to Philip Crawley in Newcastle's local daily newspaper, *The Journal*, there was still much work to be done. 'The idea is to work as much as we can until Christmas and make as much bread as possible – about £7,000-£8,000 a month at the moment. After that, we'll have a rest, then start work on our next album, which should be out by March.'

The band were also expected to start their first US tour at that time with, according to *The Journal*, Rod Stewart and the Faces. An added bonus was that 'Nicely Out Of Tune', now a year old, was still selling 500 copies a week. The album was also finally released in the US, simultaneously with 'Lady Eleanor'. Not such good news for their label came in the wake of the band's performance at the Brighton Dome. The report in *Melody Maker* said that 'the audience started dancing in the aisles and on the stage and Charisma boss Tony Stratton-Smith was told by Dome management that no further concerts would be held featuring Charisma groups.'

In response, Strat said, 'It's a pity that the people at the only place to play in Brighton are so old-fashioned. They are really out of touch with the music business today and expect an audience to react as if they were watching Dora Bryan or Ted Ray.' The final word in the piece was left to the Dome's manager who said, huffily, 'Lindisfarne behaved in a general unruly way, but the other two bands behaved correctly. We haven't banned them. We are not going to have Lindisfarne back at the Dome because they encouraged the audience to jump on stage with them.' Oh *dear…*

Following a show at the Lyceum on the 24th, with Genesis supporting, the band returned to their beloved City Hall on 4 December to throw a big Christmas party, 'complete with balloons, paper hats and all' as *The Journal* went on to say. It was a great way to end the year back home for Christmas with family and friends. BBC TV recorded the event as part of the *Sounding Off* series of shows, while not to be outdone a Tyne Tees Television documentary emphasised their North East background. Both programmes were scheduled for broadcast around March.

The show opened with a fine set from Rab Noakes, accompanied by Gerry Rafferty. The public debut of Rafferty's band, Stealers Wheel ** followed, including a couple of numbers from Humblebums days. Three Santa Clauses distributing goodies were followed by the wildly eccentric Roger Ruskin-Spear and his inventions. Ray explained the choice of the ex-Bonzos man: 'We'd seen somebody called the Times Square Two when they'd opened for the original Mothers of Invention at the City Hall. That's when we first got the idea that a gig could incorporate all sorts of stuff. Ruskin-Spear used to play a bit of sax and he had these automatons with exploding heads…'

* Mike was originally a member of a fine band of motorbike aficionados called the Hull Street Freaks, who have for many years taken every opportunity they can to get along to any Lindisfarne-related shows. There have been several occasions when the star of the show – the bike – has been special guest at various functions. Mike and his associates have also been known to take a drink or two.

** The original version of Stealers Wheel featured Rab and Gerry, but Rab left before recording began for the first album.

Right: Si at the Britannia Hotel, Holy Island, during the 'Fog On The Tyne' photo shoot.

Before wandering onstage to an 'ear-splitting welcome,' as Roy Carr reported in *New Musical Express*, Alan was brimming with excitement. 'The whole band is expanding, with Jacka being the most important part. On stage he is the link between us and the audience…he's the best singer and he's honest and you can't knock honesty. If anyone left Lindisfarne we'd die completely, we'd never be reborn.'

Launching into Rab's 'Together Forever', the set moved through 'No Time To Lose', 'January Song', 'Meet Me On The Corner', 'Alright On The Night', 'Lady Eleanor' and 'Fog On The Tyne' before a riotous night ended with 'We Can Swing Together', accompanied by old mate Kenny Craddock *** on piano and finally 'Clear White Light', for which Charlie Harcourt, now ex-Jackson Heights, added guitar. Quite a different set of circumstances from the first time Lindisfarne and Harcourt had been mentioned in the same sentence in early 1970…

The continuing success of 'Fog On The Tyne' had certainly bolstered the band's already confident mood, although they were quick to acknowledge the importance of their background. In *Disc & Music Echo*, Alan told Caroline Boucher, 'The kids in Newcastle have given us their support because we've come down to London and shit on a lot of groups that were born with silver spoons in their mouths. We were born with pickaxes in ours and we spat them right out at them.'

Alan's Lennonesque vitriol didn't stop there. 'We want to be as big as the Beatles because we've got what they had. I don't think there's any point in having ambition if you don't aim to be the best. The Beatles were the best in the world and if I want to be in the same business then I must try and better them. I honestly think that in about two years time we could produce an album of the standard of 'Abbey Road".'

Far from alienating Lindisfarne from their broader audience, comments from the last of the band to make the move South with his family seemed only to endear the outspoken Mr Hull to the populace. The same piece also spoke of Newcastle being a place that Alan could rarely go now – and he was scarcely writing, too. 'In 1969 I wrote 60 songs. That was when I was on the dole and cleaning windows occasionally. Since then, since we've been successful, I just haven't had the time. I'd like to see the group be a little more selective about their choice of work and leisure and their time for being alone because I want to see if my songwriting has developed. We've been working terribly hard and I think my songs may grow to be a reflection of that.'

Now hitting his stride, he continued: 'Great songwriters in this world are John Lennon, Dylan and Robbie Robertson of the Band. All their work reflects something that is totally real; you couldn't deny that a simple statement from Lennon is the truth, in the same way Robbie Robertson uses images and feeling that evoke the whole tradition of the East Coast of America.'

In what now seems a reference to his own need as a songwriter for the inspiration of those people and places closest to him, he continued 'I really do feel sorry for some bands that have an album coming out and say "ooh, we must write something" and scrape around and try to get something together. I can't even hate them, I just feel sorry for them.' However, he was happy to try and explain how the process worked for him, starting with a tune whose mood suggested the lyrics: 'Sometimes it comes like a flash, words and music together making a nuisance of itself in my subconscious and comes out in a rush, like vomit.'

In late October, the band had returned to the studio – this time Island – to record a single for rush release. With Bob Johnson retained as producer, Alan's 'No Time To Lose' – first committed to tape during the 'Fog On The Tyne' sessions – was recorded on the 26th along with 'Scotch Mist', written by Jacka and also around for some time. ****

'No Time To Lose' was originally intended to be included in a film called *Some Kind Of Hero*, for which both Rod and Alan were involved in writing material. 'It was one of Strat's diversification plans – getting involved in films – and it seemed a good idea at the time,' explains Ray. 'What we saw certainly wasn't very good. It became apparent as soon as they started seeing the first scenes that it was a bit amateurish: I think Alan and Rod were beginning to get cold feet. The unfortunate thing was that Alan was offered two films: one was *The Wicker Man*, which he knocked back, but it became a real cult film.' Apparently, *Some Kind Of Hero* ended up being called *Road To Kingdom Come*, according to Rod. 'It was through Strat's many connections in the media – this American

*** Ray Laidlaw had worked with Kenny at Shepherds in Gateshead. It was through him that he met Don Whittaker, who had been in Downtown Faction. 'We were all 16 at the time. Kenny was a great keyboard player and was in about three bands and we would be coming in at ten o'clock in the morning, half-asleep from doing gigs the night before, then Kenny left work to join Happy Magazine.' That band was managed by Alan Price and the drummer was Alan White, who eventually ended up in Yes, via Ginger Baker's Airforce (also with Kenny), John Lennon's Plastic Ono Band (he played on 'Imagine') and George Harrison.

**** Master versions of both tracks, dated 15 December, are also shown on the archive lists, although a 16-track version of 'Scotch Mist' was recorded as early as 1 June 1971. The December recordings are probably the tracks that Rod recalled as being their first at Island's Basing Street studios, before the next album proper.
'It was the first time we worked with the engineer, Bob Potter. I was glad though, I enjoyed those sessions. In fact, "No Time To Lose" comes as close as anything to recapturing what the band sounded like then; the live sound – all the elements – harmonicas, fiddles and mandolins over the rock'n'roll backing. I like that one. We weren't working to a demanding brief. I think we were only there for a couple of days, so we had to knock out a couple of tracks and that's all there was.'

Left: Rod, Alan and 'Lady Eleanor'.

director, who lived in London…Marvin something. Strat got me and Alan a rough draft of the script and we met him at his house in Highgate; very nice chap, nice house and proper money – seemed like a good thing to be getting in to. This was like one step along from rock'n'roll, if you like. We did the whole bit – car to pick us up in the morning, take us to the studio to see the shooting…wined and dined.

'The film was about a Vietnam draft dodger, which at the time was seen as a cool thing to do – and he comes to this country and falls in love with this girl they go to Scotland – which is where "No Time To Lose" came in. He'd taken "Road To Kingdom Come" on as the theme song because he saw the character in the song as being the character in the film; on the run, or travelling – looking for something. I wrote a song called "Some Kind Of Hero" for it, which never saw the light of day and didn't deserve to.

'I don't know whether the money changed, but it went from us having *carte blanche* to us having to go down to this guy's mews cottage and playing him our ideas and he played us his. We were looking at each other and thinking, "What's all this? Who's he and where does he fit in?" Obviously, Marvin had roped him in, and he was going to be the guy who knocked our music into shape. After an hour in his place, Alan and I made our way home and looked at each other and went, "Nah". So it was Alan's job to ring Marvin and my job to ring this Harris Rutherford II – "Composer", as his specially-printed business card stated.'

Top right: Lindisfarne at a festival 'somewhere in Europe' in 1972 – it was that kind of year!

Right: Milk and alcohol…Rod enjoys his Thanksgiving Day dinner in Middletown, Ohio, 1972.

December also found the band about as far from home on the mainland as they could get – Penzance in Cornwall. In a major interview in *Melody Maker*, with Roy Hollingworth, the band were reflective and much of the content, as much as the classic photographs taken by Barrie Wentzel, clearly showed the band's perspective and condition at that time. It begins with a clear statement from Si:

'No, we'll never work this hard again. It's killing the magic. And it's not doing us much good, either…it's tragic that we've only written four new songs since August. We had no time, we've been gigging nearly every night.' Ray accepts that they knew in October that the following months would be spent 'doing ridiculous gigs. But we knew we had to do it. We had to do it to get good, to get tight. Well, we've done it, it's taken it's toll, but it's succeeded.'

Jacka agreed: 'It's always been a shambles on stage, tuning up every minute and that. But now we've got into the part. We're so tight we could go after a residency. But imagine having a hairy night, and having to travel 200 miles the next day, and having to be capable of spewing out of a truck window at 70 mph.' Alan was wary of the response they received live. 'I wouldn't like the audiences to get more wild than they are at the moment. Christ, I come on and sing "Lady Eleanor", which is sad, and they're up there cheering already. It's mad. But I know that people love to do that, people like to get like that.'

It was Rod who returned to the subject of writing – or lack of it. 'We've been worn out and our writing has been affected,' with Alan clearly aware of what was required for the next album. 'The third album has got to be *brilliant*. Rod and myself have been pleased with what has been written. The roots to the songs have been good. But there have to be more. We'll love them, I know.' However, as Hollingworth noted, most of the songs that Alan wrote were written about three years previously – in the space of a week. 'It was just one of those weeks. He just sat down and wrote himself to death.'

But both Rod and Alan were apparently 'on the brink of a new writing phase. It's a phase that needs to come. And it needs to be exceptional.' Alan did not seem deterred: 'Southerners can't build ships, can't make fish and chips and can't write songs. The difference between London and the North is not geographical. They are totally different, the people are different. Think of most of our writers and figure out where they are from. There's only one Southerner who can write, and that's Keith Richard. The rest, well…'

Rod, however, felt that 'London can spawn good players…but they never write. It's as though some basic feeling weren't with them anymore. Southern people spend too much time being in *proper* groups. They spend too much time being it, being the good boys, being the boys who matter. There's too much of that sort of crap around… There are too many people doing second-rate things. There are too many second-rate bands. They are getting away with it somehow. An audience thinks it's enjoying itself, but give them a dose of something really good, and they'll know the difference.'

Continuing on the subject of things Northern, Alan explains, 'They make for songs. Things in London are somehow unreal. And people make it like that… I need to write my songs. If I couldn't, I'd be in a mental hospital. But I'd never be content with writing second-rate stuff.'

Rounding up the year, the band played gigs and in Edinburgh and at the Greyhound, Croydon, where Fairport – who were playing over the road at the Fairfield Halls – came over for a jam. Finally, there was a music-press report of 'such a thunderous affair at La Chasse Club in London, 'that the physical futures of certain well-known bands seemed well in doubt…there was a certain member of King Crimson and also a certain member of Lindisfarne (no names mentioned) who took life to the limit and over that).'

Strat had just returned from the US with news of possible dates with both the Beach Boys and the Kinks. There was also the news on the grapevine that the Band had also been saying good things about Lindisfarne. It had been some year.

With Christmas over, further gigs followed in January, before the release, on 4 February 1972, of 'Meet Me On The Corner' from 'Fog On The Tyne'. Actually a 'maxi-single' (as they used to be called), it came in a memorable picture sleeve of all the group in bed together at Rod's house in Finchley and the shot could only hint at the fun contained therein.

Rab Noakes is surprised that Rod didn't write more: '"Meet Me On The Corner" was such a well-crafted pop song. It's got a theme, there's a bit of mystery to it and, yes, its construction is classic: the chorus, it's got the fills in all the right places and it keeps that nice, mid-rocky tempo right the way through. It's a great little number.'

The appeal of the song that would be the only Lindisfarne track to receive a prestigious Ivor Novello songwriting award was just as irresistible to the man on the street it seemed; back to Mike Cartledge: 'I first got into the band in 1971. At the time, I was working as an apprentice at a local motorbike firm and a Lambretta scooter – of all things – came in. It had a Newcastle Brown Ale sticker stuck to it, with Lindisfarne written on it. I remember looking at it and thinking, "What's Lindisfarne?"

'We had the radio on and shortly afterwards, this record came on: it was "Meet Me On The Corner". It was the first thing of theirs I ever heard and I instantly took a liking to it. Back in those days, you got a far bigger variety in the charts and they weren't categorised: it was either a good record or a bad record. That being a good record, I went out and bought it.'

The inspired idea of the tie-up with Newcastle Brown came from Steve Weltman, then of the

Left: As cold as it looks? Another shot from the Holy Island photo shoot.

It's a monster, it's wild, it could drive a country boy mad, it's…

By DANNY HOLLOWAY

LINDISFARNE'S Ray Laidlaw

The tale of LINDISFARNE IN WONDERLAND

PICTURE FIVE Newcastle lads touring in the overwhelming, monstrous United States. The hustle and bustle can drive a country boy mad unless he relaxes, sitting on the edge of his Holiday Inn bed, watching the colourful street lights below.

And it's all happening to Lindisfarne for the first time. To them it's mesmeric, unbelievable. Last week I talked on the transatlantic phone to drummer Ray Laidlaw, in San Francisco, and asked him for his impression of the city.

"I've always had visions of San Francisco as a hippie place, with lots of mist with Clark Gable in it somewhere," Laidlaw told me. "I must have seen a dozen films about San Francisco with Clark Gable in them. So it's nice to see the place. It's like dreams coming true, you know. But I haven't seen Clark Gable."

On the first leg of their tour, Lindisfarne supported the Kinks — which they enjoyed. They didn't like New York very much — an intrusive, dehumanising place. But they were having good fun in 'Frisco.

With temperatures around 85, they've been driving around town with their bare feet hanging out the station wagon windows.

Laidlaw talked about the common ground they share with the Kinks.

"The Kinks were good enough to let us use equipment they'd borrowed. We did eight gigs with them and it was really first-class. The Kinks attract an audience who are interested in songs rather than instrumental virtuosity, and we appeal to a similar audience, so it was a really good idea being with them.

"The Kinks are really big over here, and have full houses everywhere."

Laidlaw said Lindisfarne were at first a little apprehensive about playing to American audiences. They really didn't know what formula to use. Then they realised people are the same all over, and played basically the same as they do in Britain.

One of the major problems facing British groups in America is the difference in size of venues. I asked him if he liked larger halls.

"Yeah, I do actually. There was a time when we had difficulty, but not now. We seem to get a similar atmosphere in a large auditorium as in a club. We just chat to the people and behave in the same way, and it seems to work. We've done some really big ones over here but the sound systems are so good that everybody can hear us.

"We can make little jokes or chat to the audience and you can hear every word — which isn't always as easy in England."

Laidlaw said they'd been well received so far — half-way through their five-week tour. As well as hitting most of the main cities, they're doing some medium-sized ones like Cleveland, Cincinatti and Lubbock, Texas.

One gig that they're looking forward to is the Troubadour in Los Angeles which broke Elton John and Cat Stevens.

I asked about material. Do they mind doing some of the older things, like "We Can Swing Together"?

"We change them all the time. Obviously you go off a song now and then, but you just drop it for a bit, then it comes up again. Over here we've been doing a lot of things from the first album and before, just to see how people react. We have a pretty wide scope as a band — we can go from folkie quiet things to hard rock.

"We want to try everything we are capable of, and see how American audiences react."

Are any new songs likely to come out of the tour?

"Oh, I should think there will be quite a few. It's such an experience coming here that it's bound to start things up in the little minds.

"But we're gonna have a holiday when we get back, and that should give us a chance to get some songs together. We've got some songs ready to be rehearsed already, and with the extra stuff we've got here we should be well on the way to the new album.

"Alan or Rod sometimes come along to a rehearsal with a song, and they'll sing it to us and if everybody likes it, we'll do it.

"But if one person doesn't like the song we don't do it. It's as simple as that. We'll go all through that scene when we get back where we'll sit in somebody's front room and listen to all the new songs.

"Then we'll pick out ones we want to do and go away to a friend's cottage in Scotland and learn them all. There we can be together 24 hours a day and rehearse when we want, play football, or go out and have a pint. We're friends first and a group second."

With their current single and album doing so well, I asked Laidlaw if there's any type of goal they'd like to achieve.

"We'd like to be the best group in the world and be known for being the best group in the world. We're really not happy with everything we've done recordwise. I don't know if we ever will be perfectly happy, but we want to make a brilliant album before very long.

"We know we can do it. We've got everything that's necessary. It's just a question of learning how to do it properly. The last two albums have been good in different ways, but both had short-comings. On the next one we want to eliminate those things. We'll be using Bob Johnston again as producer."

Laidlaw said he wasn't ashamed of all the hype they've had about coming out of Newcastle, because basically it was all true. They love the place and are glad they come from there. He thinks they'll always basically be a Newcastle band because that's where they started.

And so there you have it, my friends. The latest news from five Geordies touring in wonderland. Drummer Laidlaw might leave his heart in San Francisco after all. Too bad Clark Gable wasn't there to greet him.

Charisma marketing department, now co-manager of the band. 'I'd started in the business as a tea boy at NEMS, working for the Beatles. I then progressed into the PR department with Tony Barrow before going into record retail. At the time, Strat was in management with the Bonzos, the Nice and, I think, Creation.

'I used to sell tickets for Sunday night at the Lyceum, where Strat used to promote a lot of shows, and noticed that for some reason, we seemed to sell a hell of a lot of tickets for his shows. We met, Charisma started – and I got the job.' Steve had been to many gigs with the band, right across the country, 'and you just couldn't buy Newcastle Brown – and that's at a time when the band still drank it.' He took some rough designs along with him to the brewery that featured the band's faces in the gaps between the arms of the Blue Star on the label, and 'much to my amazement they said yes.'

According to Steve, in the year that the album hit along with 'Meet Me On The Corner', this unique marketing concept saw the brewery going from 'something like 50 accounts which were all in the North East of England, to over a thousand right across the country,' in the wake of each of the band's appearances. 'At the peak of the success with both albums in the chart, two hit singles – the brewery were delivering kegs of this stuff to gigs. We were *swimming* in it! About six months later, they stopped drinking it. We used to give it all away!'

With the addition of the two new tracks, 'No Time To Lose' and 'Scotch Mist', the single was a tempting buy. The song also gave the band the opportunity to play to the nation on the much maligned *Top Of The Pops* – at that time the only place to see contemporary music on television. They raided the props department at the BBC, resulting in the memorable sight of Jacka in a donkey jacket under blazing

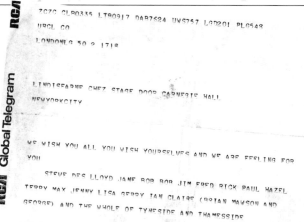

RCA Global Telegram

ZCZC CLR0335 LTR0917 OAR7624 UWS757 LGD201 PLG548

URGL CO

LONDONLG 50 2 1718

LINDISFARNE CHEZ STAGE DOOR CARNEGIE HALL

NEWYORKCITY

WE WISH YOU ALL YOU WISH YOURSELVES AND WE ARE FEELING FOR YOU

STEVE DES LLOYD JANE BOB BOB JIM FRED RICK PAUL HAZEL TERRY MAX JENNY LISA GERRY IAN CLAIRE (BRIAN MAWSON AND GEORGE) AND THE WHOLE OF TYNESIDE AND THAMESSIDE

studio lights, Alan in a Russian army uniform and Ray banging his drums with a plastic fish.

Described as 'early Dylan plus' by *Disc & Music Echo*, the single was 'launched' by two shows at London's Queen Elizabeth Hall that same night – a 'farewell' to the UK for the band, whose US dates started on 2 and 3 March with the Kinks at New York's prestigious Carnegie Hall.

Perhaps buoyed by this news, *Disc & Music Echo*'s reviewer 'left the QEH feeling more exhilarated than by any concert since the first visit of Aretha Franklin…two songs were brand new Alan Hull compositions, "Poor Old Ireland", which provided the only serious moment, and "Mandolin King", being played in public for only the second time. By the time the evening was over, a good hundred of the audience arms linked in a joyous hokey-cokey, with support group Genesis on stage joining in and the atmosphere was just as if Newcastle United had won the FA Cup.'

'Poor Old Ireland' was later the victim of a BBC policy banning any record that they feel in their opinion made inflammatory statements on the situation in Ireland at the time. 'One accepts it,' Alan commented, 'but they are wrong about it being political in implication because I am not political. It's really just a comment on a sad situation.' As far as the US dates were concerned, there was certainly some concern as to how the band would adapt to American audiences, as Alan explained: 'We're naturally concerned because most of our act is based on Northern humour,' but as he explained elsewhere, 'You don't stop being what you are just because you happen to be in New York.' Meanwhile, Charisma were left to do their job with 'Meet Me On The Corner'; Britain seemed to be primed.

'Whoosh!' was Si's over-riding memory of that first trip to the States. 'I think I worked out that from the day we left to the day we got back three months later, we had been travelling constantly at 60 miles per hour.' Originally intended as a three-week jaunt, dates were added constantly thanks to some good press from agent Bill Graham. Si continues: 'We played loads of places we'd played a month before, as we got more work. It was a real blur. We seemed to be getting limousines everywhere, "This is great. I wonder who's paying for it?" We found out, later.'

For Rod, the feeling was one of 'Spaced-outness. It definitely started to feel like, this is happening to someone else. I'm just a spectator here.' Although there were a few days off in New York and a week residency in Los Angeles at the Troubadour, it was hard work – but the band seemed to revel in it. Right from the off at Carnegie Hall, the reviews were encouraging: 'It's not that often you see genuine excitement generated by an act supporting act supporting a big name – but it happened at the Kinks' concert at Carnegie Hall this week,' raved *NME*'s US correspondent. Another US press report said that that 'Lindisfarne were a revelation', while back in Britain, *Melody Maker* felt sure that the tour would be 'a milestone for both groups'.

At the after-gig party, members of both bands were joined in a spontaneous singalong by Leslie West of Mountain. For Ray, a life-long fan of the Kinks, it certainly made good sense appearing with Davies and Co, with whom they would play eight dates. 'They attract an audience who are interested in songs rather than instrumental virtuosity, and we appeal to a similar audience.'

Below: Rubber Records' Christmas party, early 1970s. Back row, from left, Terry Morgan, Joe Sanders, Vince Gray, Pete Scott, Terry Dovey, Ray Tweedy. Middle row: Dave Wood, Lucy Roff, Brian Mawson, Brian Hulme (Prelude), Billy Mitchell. Front row: Will Browell, Ray Laidlaw, Ian Vardy (Prelude), Joe Kilner, David Pritchard, Geoff Heslop.

Although the significance of the Carnegie shows was not lost on Si, he explained that there was time for fun, too: 'We got bored, so after we'd nicked all the food from the Kinks' dressing room we went down into the big orchestra pit under the stage where there was this big room with all these orchestra instruments including five double basses… Upstairs they were playing "Louie, Louie" and we were all going "saw, saw" along with that riff. It got sort of hypnotic after a while…we were so thrilled to be doing this on these big, fancy instruments, we carried on for ten minutes.'

Dates continued to be added, including five shows in the south with Seatrain and It's A Beautiful Day as well as college work with David Bromberg. The band also appeared with Taj Mahal and at the Boarding House in San Francisco with Tim Buckley, an episode Glen Colson remembers if only because Buckley was 'killing himself with heroin…'

It was here that they managed to drink their own fee, as Ray explains. 'Fairport were on up the road and they came down to drink with us every night. They got there half an hour before we finished, so they were starting the festivities before we arrived – drinking their way through our fee. We got them back subsequently, but they'll deny it, of course…they're all pathological liars, especially that Dave Pegg!'

Glen Colson confirms that 'When our tour manager, Fred Munt, went for the bill at the end of the week, it turned out that *we* owed *them* money!' Apparently, there was more beer drunk that week than they usually sold in a year…'

The band also went down well in Illinois, while in Cleveland and Chicago the lads were disappointed the audience wasn't dancing about – until it turned out they were too stunned by the playing to do much more than gape until Lindisfarne left the stage. Then chaos broke out until the encore.

At the Troubadour, they supported Don McLean, but were thrown out because, according to Glen Colson, 'We wouldn't sign the contract with the guy who ran it. Apparently, if you play there you've got to sign a contract to go back and play there the next five times you go to LA. So Strat had said to me on the phone – because I was I charge that night – "Don't do the gig, just walk out". So we did. Don Maclean says to me, "Do you want me to come with you?" and I said, "No, 'cause we're being a bit unreasonable…" We thought we were coming back to play the stadium, or something. As it happened, I don't think they *ever* went back…'

There was also an 'interesting' gig in Lubbock, Texas; 'I couldn't get them any booze that night, because it's a dry State, so I had to get them a huge bag of grass off these guys I met on the street and they got stoned. Jacka got stoned for the first time and was playing "Yellow Rose Of Texas" on his harmonica; that was really strange… I think that was one of the only nights they went down well.' According to Glen, 'It wasn't happy work for the band; they were pretty much ignored…Elektra was a great label, but we were supporting a lot of the time, so the label didn't give a shit, really.'

Rod felt Elektra didn't really have much idea what the band meant in Britain, 'because it hadn't happened over here yet. It happened while we were over there.' Glen agrees: 'It was very different, because in the UK they were idols but in the States they were nothing. It was difficult; we got a dollar a day – we toured and toured, sometimes two flights a day.'

There were tensions too, as Glen continues, 'You tend to row with people when you're on the road that long, because it magnifies things that irritate you about them. I can remember sharing a room with Alan in New York and he'd not brought *anything*. He'd not brought a toothbrush, even though we were away for a good length of time. So I said, "What are you going to do about a toothbrush?" "Use yours!" he says. "What are you going to do for clothes?" "Wear all yours." I says, "You fuckin' won't!" So I had a huge row with him, because he hadn't brought anything with him. A bit of a liberty taker, he was. It was hard work; a lot of strain, those dates. It really turns your head when you go to America for the first time and you're only about 21.'

By 25 March 'Meet Me On The Corner' entered the Top 5 back home, while the band were at a bar in San Francisco that same week when they received the news from Charisma in London that 'Fog On The Tyne' was

93 Albert Embankment, London SE1 7TY. Telephone 01-735 7141. Cables: Oakfilm, London SE1

9th June 1972

Lindisfarne,
Charisma,
87 Brewer St.,
London W1

Dear Lindisfarne,

Thank you for appearing at Lincoln - we thoroughly enjoyed your performance which was the turning point of the festival.

We would also like to thank your Management for their co-operation.

Yours sincerely,

Stanley Baker

Stanley Baker

John Martin

John Martin

DIRECTORS: STANLEY BAKER MICHAEL DEELEY THE RT. HON. THE LORD HARLECH K.C.M.G. C.C. LEVAN JOHN MARTIN MALCOLM NIXON BARRY SPIKINGS

at Number 1 and 'Nicely Out Of Tune' had re-entered the chart at 24. It would be safe to say that Lindisfarne were probably the biggest band in Britain at that point.

Had they gone for the scheduled three weeks, they would have been back in London celebrating with everyone else in the Charisma office. 'They told us they were having a champagne party,' Alan recalls. 'Oh great…we thought. So we clubbed together all our cents and dimes together and bought one bottle of Californian wine… But you know, it didn't matter; nothing mattered, then.'

Right: A very rare shot of producer Bob Johnston at Trident Studios.

The American experience gave Alan plenty of inspiration for songs and he was sure that when he returned, he was going to say 'I'm glad America happened. Christ, I've got a *million* ideas. I can feel them building up.' But, despite the huge success of both albums, and the hit single, it seemed he would still find it difficult to find time to fully realise all that was going on in his head. There was no time to take their foot off the pedal.

A massive reception for the band was laid on by Strat: they barely had time to take it all in before yet more frenzied activity with the re-release of 'Lady Eleanor' in April. Jacka later claimed that it was not re-issued but simply, 'Pushed again – because DJs were showing more interest in it. We could have done something new, but that song is the magic we're all about.'

Whatever the reason, this time it really was a hit, cracking the Top 10. In May, the band appeared at the Montreux Jazz Festival in Switzerland (introduced as coming from Manchester) and, on 5 June, topped the bill at the massive Paris Olympia.

Expectations for the next album were high, as Alan told *NME* in May: 'Obviously we strive for perfection, like "Abbey Road" or "Sgt Pepper".' Rod told *Record Mirror* that he saw them becoming less of a folk band. 'The rock side's coming up all the time… We've always been looking round for a form to express our songs best without instrumental indulgences and we're still going to play songs as songs – it's just that they'll be rock songs rather than folk.' Si, for his part seemed adamant that, this time round, they'd 'make it our favourite numbers, rather than Bob Johnson's.' Otherwise, after the US tour, the band claimed that they were at their best and more capable than ever.

The Lincoln 'Great Western Express' Festival on May Bank Holiday proved another historic Lindisfarne landmark. As special guests on the Sunday (Ray's birthday) , the bill also included the Beach Boys, Sly and the Family Stone, Slade, Spencer Davis and labelmates Monty Python; further down the bill came the Average White Band and Focus. The band were chauffeured to the site by Si, in his Mercedes Benz 220SE. 'I bought it from an Irishman who'd put sawdust in the sump to stop the noise from the big ends. It cost me 200 quid, I made 100 mph with all the band in it, brought everyone back and the car died.'

One of the organisers was the actor Stanley Baker, who hailed their performance as 'the turning point of the festival'. With artists such as Joe Cocker, Humble Pie, the Faces, Rory Gallagher, Stone the Crows and Ry Cooder over the four days, the band's performance was certainly impressive. And the sun came out again. Si's only other memory is of 'lots of straw, lots of mud, lots of plastic sheets and lots of wet bodies.' What did he expect for £4.50 for all four days? Lincoln was the icing on the cake.

Finally, on 24 June, the front page of *Melody Maker* belonged to Lindisfarne. With the headline, 'LINDISFARNTASTIC!' came the news that, with 'Fog On The Tyne' at Number 3, 'Nicely Out Of Tune' at 26 and 'Lady Eleanor' at 10, the band would be off to Australia, Japan and Indonesia in November; followed by a second tour of the States. Recording of the next album would begin on 13 July at Island studios, with Bob Johnson.

Chapter
SIX
THE ROAD TO
KINGDOM COME

I t was now time for Lindisfarne to consider recording their third album – and, unsurprisingly given their recent hell-for-leather lifestyle, the approach to its recording couldn't have been more different from 'Fog On The Tyne'. Though they'd returned to familiar Devon surroundings to prepare, the only other similarity between the albums seemed to be the time they took to complete; three days, in this case 14-17 July 1972.

'There didn't seem to be anything like the same amount of time or care,' Rod remarks. 'It felt as though it was being rushed along.' This time, the band had gone away and worked everything out beforehand without Bob Johnston and, as Si had hinted earlier in the year, had even picked the songs themselves. Johnston, it seemed, let them get on with it, in very different fashion to previously. Rod was pleased with the way recording went: 'direct, whack-it-down, almost like playing live.'

Alan's recollections were of a 'relaxed' Bob Johnston. 'He just laid down and let the engineer, Bob Potter, get on with it. I remember him saying things like, "C'mon, I got better places to be…like the Caribbean." That didn't instil us with a lot of confidence.' What didn't help either was the band's attitude that whatever they did would sell…a view everyone around them seemed to agree with. 'We still had inventiveness,' argued Alan, 'but we weren't getting any overview of what Lindisfarne's musical future should be; we were left to our own devices.'

By way of illustration, he also recalled one occasion when he and Jacka were on the control room with Johnston and Ken Scott: 'Jacka put up a good little argument about a particular song he thought should stay – expecting Johnson to do what he wanted anyway – and he said, "Who am I to argue with you guys?".' Much had been made of Johnson sitting like 'a latter-day Henry VIII' during the previous album while the sound itself was shaped by engineer Ken Scott (who moved on to David Bowie). Now, according to Alan, Bob Potter was less involved, while Bob Johnston simply 'put one or two ideas into the mixing'.

FOG ON THE TYNE

For the first time, Si had two songs on a Lindisfarne album - 'Go Back' and the instrumental 'Plankton's Lament', a title typical of an ecological stance which would prove even more evident in the future. Rod's 'Don't Ask Me' discussed his bemusement with all that had happened to them; Alan was particularly vociferous in his praise of this song in the press. His own 'Mandolin King' had given him the opportunity to write a song for Jacka, while 'Bring Down The Government' waved his political banner as high as the level of his disgust at the way his beloved city had been torn apart by the planners on the opener, 'All Fall Down'.

Despite its serious lyric, the guitar riff in the middle of 'Bring Down The Government' had apparently been nicked from Joe Brown, resulting in much embarrassment for the band when the 1950s Brit-rocker turned up at Charisma while someone was playing the track elsewhere in the office. 'Poor Old Ireland' had been one of only two songs previously aired live and appeared to be a cry from Alan's Celtic heart. His remaining songs were 'Court In The Act', 'Wake Up Little Sister' and 'Oh, No, Not Again'.

When it was decided to augment two tracks – Alan's epic title track 'Dingly Dell'* and 'All Fall Down' - with an orchestra, the job fell to Ray's brother, Paul Laidlaw. 'I think the idea came from a "keep-it-in-the-family"-type of thing,' Rod explains. 'Paul was the only "classical" person we all knew who was good enough to tackle a job like that. I think he did a great job.' Though considerably younger than the musicians in the orchestra, Laidlaw Junior was certainly not intimidated, as Rod continues.

'He certainly didn't mess about when it came to laying it down. London session players – especially in the orchestral world, I gather – are a notorious breed to handle, especially when they're doing a pop session. They love being able to score points from the musical director – and one or two of them did try, but Paul knew his way round.' What did not appear to be evident in the songs on the album, were the 'road songs' hinted at around the time of the band's visit to the US. Was Alan, in particular, still mining songs from his treasure trove of 1968?

When the master of the album came back, Rod got quite a shock. 'There was no bass on anything: even after a bit of tweaking, it was still a bit light in that department. I remember Barbara Hayes coming to my house around that time and I put the album on saying, "We can't put this out" and she said she couldn't hear anything wrong. So I put another album on – I think it might have been Leon Russell – and I said "This is what records are supposed to sound like", because this wasn't a million miles away from what we were trying to achieve – and the bass comes pounding out. So I says, "There's plenty of bass on that!" and she says, "Yes, but that's not *folk*, dear"… A reaction like that didn't help.'

Looking back, Rod can see this was the period when things seemed to go awry. 'Everybody, myself included, was starting to lose sight of what we were all doing it for, or finding their own reasons for not working together in the same direction that we had done spontaneously before. It was becoming a bit fragmented. Like Bob Johnson sitting there going "Yeah, yeah, yeah…".'

The sleeve was to be a major departure, too. The band decided it would be plain brown recycled card, with only the band's name and title on the front – though, originally, the band hadn't even wanted their name on the British version. The final compromise was a grey sleeve with brown embossed lettering - 'a deliberately anti-packaging idea,' as Ray commented in *Sounds*.

'We were on a big conservation, Greenpeace, kick at the time,' he now explains, 'which was great, but the management should never have let us do it. They should never have let us have that grey sleeve. They should have said, "the record's fine, we're not tampering with the music…"' According to Alan, Jacka was particularly opposed to the idea. 'It was only afterwards that we discovered that all sleeves were made of recycled card.' In retrospect, the band put all the emphasis on the wrong things in marketing terms, and as Ray points out, the result was 'commercial suicide. The American sleeve was wonderful.'

* Alan's tale of 'searching for hobbits in the woods with my daughters' was actually recorded on the 21st after all the other tracks. Featuring only Alan and Rod, the song was particularly highlighted by Paul's haunting string arrangement and Rod's hallmark fretless bass. 'The volume control, the "swelling" thing, was a trick I did, sliding a note in, then fading it up at the same time just by winding the volume control up with the hand. I do it quite a lot with the Strat, now.'

Lindisfarne even had to be talked into including a poster of themselves. 'That photo was the public conception of what Lindisfarne was about,' said Ray, 'but the outside wasn't, and the first single wasn't.'** The song in question was 'All Fall Down', complete with a sleeve featuring a monstrous tower block. 'It was like, this is the album where we got "serious"; we've got to show that there's another side to us. But "All Fall Down" just wasn't "radio". Songs about what developers were doing to cities wasn't the thing to do. It's hip for bands to be into all that *now*. It wasn't *then*.'

Alan had always written songs with serious subjects as well as the boisterous stuff, as Ray notes. Some people felt the album had a certain awareness to it. After all, we were heading for the three-day week and all this unrest at the time. Alan writes about what he's interested in. He's interested in politics; he's interested in how society treats people - "Winter Song", all these things.'

Taking its title from the closing track, the 'Dingly Dell' album was previewed in late July for the benefit of the press and friends including Rab Noakes and Jacka's wife-to-be, Karen, at the recording venue, Island's Studio 2 in Basing Street, West London. As *NME* noted, the occasion wasn't a hype, it was simply a way of 'informing people what the band had been doing since "Fog On The Tyne".' Intriguingly, mention was made in the piece about 'the obvious pleasure that Bob Johnson derives from every inch of tape.'

The response was extremely positive, noting that the band's style had matured and that they had produced 'a very fine album, encompassing the full spectrum of their feelings and music.' The piece ended with the comment, 'It's just as well the Beatles aren't recording anymore, because they'd have serious rivals.' Lindisfarne, it seemed, were still on track for now.

July also saw the broadcast of their last Radio 1 session of the year, for Bob Harris. No songs from the current album were played, although 'Mandolin King' and 'Poor Old Ireland' had been featured in their Peel session, recorded back on 8 May and broadcast on 13 June.*** The final Crystal Place Garden Party of the summer saw 'Dingly Dell' performed almost in its entirety, Si so nervous he couldn't remember the song titles!

Rod now argues that, though it would have been a gamble not to play the crowd-pleasing old stuff, we'd been led to believe that we were the centre of things and everybody was looking at us to see what we were going to come up with next. So, what more natural thing to do than say "Here it is"?' *Sounds*' Jerry Gilbert felt their receiving the most vociferous ovation of the afternoon (which also featured Alan White's debut with Yes, Gary Wright's Wonderwheel and the Mahavishnu Orchestra) was a foregone conclusion. However, the new songs were well received, 'by virtue of a cleverly arranged repertoire' as Gilbert went on, 'moving from "Lady Eleanor" straight into "Plankton's Lament". From "Oh, No, Not Again",' he wrote, 'everything started to come together.'

The band had announced their biggest ever British tour and confidence was high. *Sounds*' Keith Altham suggested, 'If it were ever possible to kill a group with kindness then Lindisfarne might be the first victims. Their new album is out to rapturous reviews and their new stage act has been equally well received by reviewers and public alike.' He went on to say, 'At the moment they are the darlings of the

** According to Ray, on the Australian tour with Slade and Quo, Jim Lea – one half of Slade's writing team – told the band that, around the time of 'Dingly Dell', they got hold of a white label copy of the album. 'They all thought that "Wake Up Little Sister" was going to be the first single and they thought, "If that comes out, we're knackered."' They were just breaking then, and seriously considered holding their release back as they were looking for a Number 1.

*** During a session for Pete Drummond, recorded on 10 May, the band covered the Beatles' 'Love Me Do', while for the Peel session broadcast in February, they performed 'Dancing Jack Peel' as a nod to the 'old fella': according to Ray, 'We used to get so used to being asked for the same old songs, we took any opportunity to do something different.' This even extended to the Animals' 'Baby Can I Take You Home'.

Peel's producer John Walters was used to Barbara Hayes sticking her head round his door to ask when he was going to get 'her lads' back on. 'Me and Peely were always happy to have them on the show. They were always happy to come along even after they'd had hits, not like many others. We didn't think they were the limo-pick-you-up-and-drop-you-off crowd. Their attitude was right for the show.'

Left: Jacka, Alan, Rod, Ray and Si in Lindisfarntastic pose as featured on Melody Maker's *front page. Another photo from this session was used for the 'Dingly Dell' poster.*

Biz without a cloud on the horizon. It's almost too good to be true. Fortunately, the individuals in the group are level-headed enough not to be affected by all the rhapsodising and are probably their own best critics.'

Ray, Altham's interviewee, was in reflective mood, suggesting they'd even welcome a little constructive criticism. 'We've never really been slagged in the press, which is really a bit of a disappointment. Even the Beatles and the Stones got slagged at the height of their popularity. We've done some really shitty gigs; we have a shout about it in the dressing room and then out come the reviews that are really good and we can't understand it.'

While Ray's memory now is of 'mixed' reviews for 'Dingly Dell', Glen Colson is more blunt: 'We got such dodgy reviews. We thought it was a great album when they made it. We went along with what the band wanted, until the reviews, which said it was a piece of shit. As soon as the reviews came in, we knew it was a big mistake, although I don't really understand why. It was a shock.'

As Glen had worked so hard and closely with the band, his reaction was perhaps understandable. 'I was shattered, because I thought it was going to be my *life*. I think everybody did. Everybody thought the band were going to be millionaires and have swimming pools and things… It was very exciting being with them. They were very, very popular, and at all the colleges they were getting six and seven encores. People were saying that they were the greatest thing they'd ever seen. For those two years, they were as big as Bolan, Bowie…*all* of them.'

But now the critical tide was turning. One reviewer went so far as to say: 'Honest, I really did try to be objective (but) it all seems so utterly limp. Everything – the melodies, the singing and the playing – seems so utterly devoid of feeling. Pissed out of your brain leaning on the piano down at the Hen and Chickens, it might sound good – you might even get involved with it. But wheezing forth from your speakers, it does nothing.'

While this reviewer would possibly have disliked *anything* Lindisfarne released, such comments were disturbing. Ray believes 'Dingly Dell' was still a good album but that 'all the journalists were waiting to have a go, and then we go and do something with the sleeve they consider to be pretentious in the extreme. So they said, "Well, what's all the fuss about?"…and then on to the next big thing.' Though the album reached the Top 10, anything after 'Fog On The Tyne' was bound to be a relative disappointment. From Ray's point of view, it was a marketing failure. 'If we'd angled the album better in the way we'd presented it to people and got the first single right, the other lyrically heavier songs would have been accepted.'

Unfortunately, no-one around the band had warned Lindisfarne, and with the record company also managing the band there was no-one to argue their corner. As Ray ruefully admits, 'It was one of the drawbacks of the family atmosphere at Charisma; they were a bit naïve, they didn't really have their heads screwed on about all sorts of things.'

Above right: An unhappy-looking Alan in transit to Australia, January 1973.

Right: Robin McKidd and Rab Noakes, Lindisfarne's stalwart support act, take a refreshment break.

Perhaps they should have accepted one of the other offers to manage them – one of which came from Chas Chandler – but they declined. 'Thanks very much, but we'll do it all together with Charisma… We thought the set-up was nice and cosy, but we didn't realise the drawbacks at the time we signed.'

Despite it all, the October tour with Genesis and Rab Noakes was another great success. *Sounds* devoted its centre pages to a report of the shows at Newcastle City Hall, Stackridge filling in on the first night and Genesis returning the following night. The event brought out most of the band's family – extended or otherwise: Alan's Mam Sally, Jeff Sadler, Geoff Heslop, latterly of the Callies, and ex-manager Joe Robertson. After opening

proceedings with accompanist Robin McKidd, Rab Noakes joined the band to encore with 'Battle Of New Orleans', Stackridge grinning in appreciation from the wings. The next night, most of Plainsong turned up, as did Fairport's Simon Nicol.

The tour had begun in Dublin on the 28th with a slight stutter, the band appearing unsettled with the new material and Jacka making several references to the fact that they were nervous - 'scared shitless' was what one reviewer heard. Certainly, as the journalist went on, Jacka was not 'his usual ebullient self.' They bravely played 'Poor Old Ireland' and the title track, which although difficult to reproduce live was 'a great attempt for a song with all the subtleties of "A Day In The Life",' the review continued. Also singled out for comment was Alan's 'United States Of Mind', a song as yet unrecorded by the band.

However, the problem, as the reviewer noted, was that 'at the moment, Lindisfarne are not provoking the sort of response from the audience that they could, because of the anxiety over fresh material. It was not the audience's fault, because the help was there but was not called upon until the final number.' Perhaps, as the review closed, it was simply 'a question of balance.' Meanwhile, Chris Charlesworth, reporting on the same gig in *Melody Maker*, suggested that that the venue, a converted boxing ring, added to their problems but that it was 'a rather wooden band who scaled the stage.'

Rab Noakes, meanwhile, was the biggest surprise. Relatively unknown outside his native Scotland, he received a standing ovation and understandably has good memories of the tour: 'I'll leave the picture of the three bands on that bus to your imagination for now, but there was a motley collection of books, magazines, newspapers and beer cans available as communal reading material. On one trip, Rod was to be seen perambulating in the aisle broadcasting the question, "Is anyone not reading anything I haven't read yet?".'

Lindisfarne returned to the US in November celebrating the news that 'Lady Eleanor' had been voted Best British Single of 1972 ('Meet Me On The Corner' fifth and 'Eleanor' fourth Best International Single) by *Melody Maker*, to follow *Disc & Music Echo*'s Brightest Hope award. This time they concentrated on the East Coast and appeared on several diverse bills, including a show with the Beach Boys at the Nassau Coliseum - 'a bloody enormous venue,' as Ray describes it, another in front of a crowd of 20,000 with David Bowie in full Ziggy mode and one with Frank Zappa that didn't come off as he wouldn't move his gear to allow them to play.

The larger dates were supplemented with headlining college shows – Bob Johnston turned up at a show in Charlottesville in Virginia, a student town where author Edgar Allan Poe came from – but Rod's memory is of the tour being 'at a lower ebb than the previous one.' The fact that they had to travel most of the way in two station wagons, half the musicians in each, seemed to be one factor in diluting the 'vibe'. 'It was like slogging around. The moodiness within the band was starting to show, not so much camaraderie.'

Returning to the UK, an appearance on the BBC's *Full House* TV programme on 9 December saw them perform a song specially written about local architect William Jobling, whose work was featured in the programme, recorded at the University Theatre, Newcastle. But there would not be much respite before Lindisfarne were off again.

Left: Rod on the fiddle in New Zealand, 1973.

Five January 1973 dates in Germany preceded their first ever visit to Australia with Slade, Status Quo and Caravan, followed by dates in Japan the following month. But Ray recalls the band feeling uncomfortable: 'We sensed things weren't right and while we were away, we talked about it.' According to Ray, Alan had begun to resent being on the road so much, especially as he had three children. 'Rod was the only other one with family at the time, but for the rest of us it was like, Yahoo! Let's go for it. Alan wasn't into that.'

Travelling was inhibiting his writing: 'I couldn't see why I couldn't be sitting at home doing what I do best, which is writing songs.' His fellow band members were aware of the problem. 'A classic case,' Ray states, 'was the title track from "Dingly Dell"; it was a song from years before that we recorded for "Fog On The Tyne". There were a few other songs on the album from earlier days, too. So we felt Alan wasn't able to be as productive as he could have been.'

Rod, too, was aware that Alan was not happy. 'It was obvious to all and sundry. Increasingly, others of us were becoming dissatisfied with this or that aspect of it; we talked about it in twos or threes rather than all sitting down getting the whole thing out. I don't remember Alan being very forthcoming at all about what was bugging him. I just got the impression he'd much rather be somewhere else, not doing it…or whatever.'

Instead, Alan directed his frustration towards Charisma: 'We had a Number 1 album and they had us on a two-week tour of fishing villages. My 60 songs were used up on those albums… I just wanted to get back home, so I said, "No. I've gotta write some songs." I can't turn it on like a tap. Also, it was the money – like a sausage machine; the record company and the rest were getting their 10-15 percent straight off the top, just sitting in the office. We were having to get our clothes on, get on a plane and go on stage, getting beans.'

The warning bells had been ringing throughout the previous year, but an 'overview' was certainly missing. Chas Chandler, who by now was managing Slade, recalled discussing the problem with the band: 'On the flight out – which took about 13 hours then – they told me that it was their last tour and they were going to break up. So I spent the rest of the flight trying to persuade them to hold on to the name for a while. I said, "Stay together as businessmen, follow separate careers, but have the name Lindisfarne for ever," so they could collect their dough. I'd seen it all happen before in the Animals and I didn't want it to happen to them. But when bands decide to split up…'

One solution suggested by Strat in a lengthy and remarkable memo to the band was that Alan should take on 'a non-performing relationship that a writer like Keith Reid has with Procol Harum, or Brian Wilson with the Beach Boys'; that is, writing and/or recording but not performing live with Lindisfarne. It made a lot of sense and the band had just the person in mind for live work, as Ray pointed out. 'Billy Mitchell was suggested, because he was a great rhythm guitar player – great voice, great persona – and he could slip into that position.'

Rod suggested a 'year off, like Genesis did, and many other bands have done before and since. A bit of breathing space would have been in order for the writers to recharge their batteries.' Indeed, Alan recalls that Genesis manager Tony Smith had had a major confrontation with Strat, threatening to take them away unless he got what he wanted. 'He got it,' said Alan 'and Genesis did it right – unlike us.'

With hindsight, Glen Colson can also see the problem. 'Frankly, they didn't have a manager, because Strat was so busy doing the other stuff, so there isn't any way you can tell a band because they're badly wounded when that happens. They look upon other people in the band to blame.' However, Rod sympathised with Alan's predicament and could not see how anyone could be expected to write on the road. 'Not the way we were touring. Not that kind of writing. Some people might be able to – like if you're an out-and-out rock band – but not the kind of thing people would have expected from us.

'We were all up for keeping the thing together until the end of the Japanese bit,' Rod continued, 'but we'd already decided to knock it on the head before we went to Australia.' There were plans for a further Stateside tour, backed by direct support from a Charisma US office (as Strat had planned a switch from Elektra) and a new management company combining the talents of Strat, Who manager Peter Rudge and Ed Goodgold, manager of Sha Na Na.

For Rod, in many ways, the Australian tour in February 1973 was the high point of Lindisfarne's touring career. 'Good as the States was, when we got to Australia we were treated like the "ultimate". Each time we landed somewhere it was press conference, flash bulbs…the whole bit the whole time. Crowds of people wherever we went.'

Chas Chandler confirmed that 'the band intended to party for the whole tour! They mightn't remember me saying that much to them because they were all drunk all of the time…Geordie lads off around the world!' Then there was the time Rod and Si checked into a hotel room in Melbourne and found a whole suite full of crates of champagne, cupboards full of every kind of drink they could imagine. Naturally, they got stuck in, only to find a few days later that they had had the supply for the full tour. 'We thought *everybody* had that in their room…'

Alan recalled another occasion when the promoter took them on a tour of the McKinley's champagne factory: 'Coming back, there was this big sing-song. Who's in the middle of it? Jacka and Noddy. Next day, "Crooak".' Their fellow travellers, Caravan, were apparently lost in all of this mayhem. 'Slade and Quo were the bad lads on that tour. Caravan were into museums and things like that. We took the piss out of them mercilessly!'

After the factory tour came the longest journey, 7,000 miles from Perth to Sydney – and, as Alan explained, something had to be done to pass that time away: 'The boys hadn't been to bed – Francis Rossi, Bob Young *, Alan Hull and Noddy Holder. The first thing I saw was Bob Young with his shaving mirror looking up the hostesses' skirts – he's going, "blue, red…ooh – none at all!", all that stuff – and I was at the back with Rod, being a bit quiet, because I was tired. Then, I think, a sausage roll came flying across, then a pie, some custard; the whole plane was in uproar. Then Francis Rossi decided to take all his clothes off.'

* Still a very good friend of the band, Bob Young was Quo's tour manager, co-writer and harmonica player. He now confirms the incident aboard the plane, but denies that Francis Rossi was naked 'because he still had his socks on.' So there.

<u>MEMORANDUM</u>

TO: Alan, Si, Rod, Ray, Jacka.

FROM: Tony Stratton Smith.
----

1.   You are worried that your careers may have reached a period of stagnation.
You have completed two short tours of the U.S.A. without making a <u>decisive</u> mark.
You are immensely successful in Britain, but are sensible enough to recognise
the physical limits of that success.   All round, then, restlessness - a restlessness which could well make sharper individual differences of viewpoint
within the band about the music, and which direction offers a quick solution,
if any.   The situation is not unique; It is the time when some groups split,
which is the fools way out; or the time, often the first time, when they take
a detached, objective look at themselves, argue it out, and reunite their heads
for the next, sometimes very different, phase of their careers.

RESUME

2.   Lindisfarne have come with great flair through a 'midwifery' period.   You
have, if I may say so, been superbly supported by the people around you, in the
way of gigs, festivals, press, radio, and record marketing.   All these factors
together, created a situation in which the band could 'happen'; It did happen
because of,

        (a) Sparkling songs which, in the main, had
             the effect of making people feel good.

        (b) An indefinable, throwaway charm and
             personality - almost an anti-rock
             'amateurishness' - which was both
             refreshing and with which people
             could identify.

        (c) An unusual instrumentation, laying
             violin, mandolin, harp, guitar on a
             good, chunky rhythm sound.

        (d) An obvious and infectious enthusiasm
             for performance.

3.   Continuous performance is an attrition; time itself is an attrition.
After two years, surprise has gone and the element of 'freshness' falters.
In an ephemeral business like the making of music this is as inevitable as
that every song must end.   The heavy-instrumental bands, disguise loss of
surprise and freshness by exploring arrangement and new formulae in sound.

-2-

It is more difficult for the lighter, more fragile, songs-orientated bands.
It is easier for them to 'drift'.

4.   Similarly, the band has got by so far without real targets; a general
mood of "we're making it" was for its time sufficient.   You are now learning
that the hard part of success is not achieving it, but sustaining it.   So
now the band is viable and 'there', we have to define the targets which will
remotivate the band, and around which all future activity will be polarised.
The targets are simple: To conquer the United States and to make a lot of
money.   You have barely got your feet wet in the United States, and you are
probably anxious about it; but I tell you without reservation that both targets
can be achieved.   I never expected you to achieve much more in your first
two visits; just that you would see for yourselves, and set in motion chains
of thought.

THE PROBLEMS.

5.   What have two years of attrition, insufficient motivation in a
relatively easy climb, and the demands of success done to LINDISFARNE so far?
Possibly the following:-

        (a) The quality of the early songs has not been
        maintained.   Described coarsely, the tunes are
        not as good.   Also, the earlier songs shared two
        things lacking later.   They has a more genuine
        spiritual 'charge' which came out of life's
        eternal inner confusions - relationships, love,
        loneliness, laughter, sensibility, honesty.   And
        they had a strong story, told sensitively and with
        poetic vision.   Circa 'Dingly Dell' some of the
        writing seemed to be taking itself a little too
        seriously.   Somewhat solemnly, it was looking
        externally for its content and imagery - 'ecology',
        'government', 'law', writers need to beware of fashionable
        targets.   We therefore have to consider whether the
        pace of life on the road is harmful to the writers,
        and particularly Alan.

        (b) A 'charming amateurishness' if over-stretched can
        seem like a rather sloppy self-indulgence, a 'not-caring'
        about the audience.   A 'charming amateurishness' is
        also a 'feel' which is difficult to transfer to the States,
        at least initially.   In America, they do not have the sense
        of regional recognition we have here; the 'Geordie thing'
        means little.   Black Rock Arkansos are a relative wow!
        In America, but it would be very difficult to re-create

---

-3-

their 'hick smalltown' quality here, because it is not
part of our culture.   Just as they depend in the States
on the comic strip and the American affection for 'Main
Street U.S.A.' to give them instant identity, so do
Lindisfarne presuppose some awareness of Tyneside and
its common people in their audience.   In the States,
Lindisfarne have to be judged on songs, performances,
<u>show</u> and ability to get it on with an audience; like
any other group.   The implication is that work has to
be done, particularly on the show.'

(c) Material and arrangements may have moved in a
direction which is consciously more 'funky'.   It should
be repeated that part of Lindisfarne's uniqueness and
freshness - factors which set the group apart from the ruck -
is the unusual instrumentation.   If the sound changes
appreciably, then the group must expect to be judged by a
whole new set of criteria.   A group which trades the unique
for the possibly average must consider very carefully whether
the risk is worthwhile; also, no amount of arrangement is a
substitute for material that shines.   Violin, mandolin, harp
and guitar should still feature heavily in the 'Lindisfarne-
Sound'.

(d) One of the consequences of an initial succes is that
the group travels more to do less, in the sense of total
number of gigs accomplished.   There is also the time-consuming support work - T.V., Radio, press interviews, and etc.
It may often seem an irrational pattern of time-usage;
But what makes it really 'irrational' is if the group or
any members of the group have a diminished enthusiasm for
performance; or, for some reason, a resentment, against
continued growth.   If you're sparing with your paunches,
each one has to tell.   Again, this resentment is usually
reflected by the writers, who see the increased, sometimes
apparently pointless, demands on their time as an attack
on creative privacy.   Symptomatic of the present restlessness
was the group's insistence on a low-key sleeve and single
release vis a vis 'Dingly Dell'.   The Beatles learned years
ago, through their white album that sales are harmed badly
if you assume the audience will go along with anything.   It
will not.   The office should have fought the group on this
one.   For lack of a fight, we have reaped, together, a lowering
of morale in the sales force and a feeling of 'let-down' in
the retail trade.   As Ray Davies writes, 'Everyone's in Show
Biz, Everyone's a Star'...Nonetheless, a setback is in no
way a defeat.

-4-

RECOMMENDATIONS.

6.   These recommendations are offered as a basis for discussion only.   Apart
from the overall success of the U.K. tour, Lindisfarne's career has not
markedly gone forward, in the last four months.   But to dtop everything and
lick the wounds is no solution.   We should therefore discuss how best to re-
focus the group's personality, how to increase its projection from a (particularly
An American) stage, and how to create a more workable environment for the writers,
whose material is so vital to the future.

        (a) As a professional songwriter, and the major provider
        of material to the band, Alan should carefully consider
        whether he wishes to continue as a full-time performer.
        An alternative is that he has the kind of non-performing
        relationship that a writer like Keith Reid has with Procol
        Harum, or Brian Wilson with the Beach Boys.   The band
        would then take in an alter ego for Alan, a singer/
        instrumentalist while continuing to write, arrange,
        rehearse, perhaps record with Alan.   Alan would also,
        of course, be making solo appearances should he so wish.
        If the power of the groups projection on stage is to
        be increased, then it is important that every member is
        of a mind to do it.   But equally it is vital that the
        principal writer be given the right environment in which
        to write.   It's my opinion that Lindisfarne is one of
        the few bands in which such a critical change in the line-
        up could be managed without loss in standing, and live
        earnings.

        (b) We should not think the situation is more sluggish
        than it actually is.   Nor should we make an ill-considered
        decision which will delay overting the recovery of real
        impetus in the group's career.   America and Europe must
        be separated in our plans.   I suggest,

            a. That the five concerts in Germany in
            January, plus the Australia and Japan concerts,
            be completed.   This is vital if we're to have
            these territories to work on while the group
            lays off for its changes.

            b. After Japan, the group should lay off and
            work intensively on its show, possibly aiming
            for a short U.K. tour in May.

            c. That we attempt a definitive Lindisfarne album
            for September release (Alan could in the meanwhile
            do his solo album, to hold the position in the Spring).

On landing in Perth, they were arrested, 'banged away and told to behave ourselves,' sniggered Alan. After a little diplomacy, the party were able to do the gig next day, but that morning's tabloid front pages bore headlines like 'Pop Star Strips On Jet.' 'We were banned from Australian Airlines for ever. It was a great gig. Pity the promoter ran off with the money.'

Chas Chandler recalled the tour as an organisational catastrophe. 'I had to organise the entire road crew. The promoter was very, very inefficient. We were playing 40,000-seaters and when we got there, the stage was about a foot high, built on orange boxes. Me and our tour manager were having to literally lift almost every member of every band's road crew out of their beds...we were getting there at five and six in the morning and having to start building stages.'

The tour had actually started in New Zealand, and by the time of the second gig in Hamilton, 'we knew what to expect. It was a crazy situation.' To cap it all, according to Chas, 'it rained consistently for five days, so I had the crew out with buckets. The stages had no roof and there was 15 inches of water at one point.'

After Australia, Lindisfarne went on to Japan for their own dates. 'We arrived at one o'clock in the morning to questions like "What do you think of Japan?" and we'd only just got off the plane,' Si laughs. 'We were provided with five "friends" by the record company – I think. "I am Amy. I am your friend. I am Suki. I am your friend"...'

There was at least time to sample the famous bullet trains, and Ray recalls seeing James Brown and his entourage at one station while the band waited for the train to go to a show in Osaka. For Rod, 'It was an outrageously weird week, dashing about from place to place – from playing to a TV studio full of grannies first thing one morning until the night before we were due to come home.' On Valentine's Day, 1973, the band played their final gig at Tokyo's Shibuya Public Hall. Then came the crunch.

Si recalls the event clearly. 'Basically, I fell out with Alan – or he fell out with me, whatever. He said, "I don't fuckin' want you in the band because you're always tuning up on stage".' To put such an apparently irrational comment in context, Si adds 'It just became like a bubble about to burst – and something had to go. A lot of rash things were said by everybody in all corners and it was thought that Alan wasn't "behaving very nicely", but that wasn't the words we used at the time.

'So I said to two of them, "Alan wants me out of the band" and they said, "We're not having any of that". So Alan went over with Jacka and said "Right, we'll form another band." Then we said, "Well, *we'll* form another band."' It was over in a flash. Jacka had originally been a floating voter, as Si reveals. 'Me and Ray and Rod talked about it, but we didn't know where Jacka was. Originally he was on one side, then he jumped ship...'

Jacka's recollection is somewhat different. 'After "Dingly Dell", I found myself at odds with Si and Rod, particularly over choice of new material and direction, and I could not see myself continuing in the band with them in it. Alan and I agreed on this and decided to set about recruiting new members to form a new band, but only after the others had moved to form their band.' It transpires that, at the time, Jacka felt that another of the original band would join him and Alan.

'The biggest disappointment was that Ray, who was undecided at this point – and to some degree had played the mediator between the two camps – decided to go with Si and Rod. 'Ray and I had formed a close relationship both inside and outside the band and this came as a complete surprise.' Jacka also confirms that he did want Si out of the band. It was not the best of circumstances and Si, too, was hurt. 'It was a very nasty, tacky business,' the guitarist reflects, 'but it happens in people's lives. I was pretty bitter at the time.'

So the die was cast, with the original trio of Ray, Rod and Si on one side and Alan and Jacka on the other. The final parting came, as Alan explained, as he got into a cab with Rod on their return to London. 'When I got out, I said to him, "Is this the way it ends – not with a bang, but with a whimper?".' As Rod now recalls, the seeds of Alan's dissatisfaction were probably sown earlier on 'when we were making our brief forays into Europe in '72. 'He had this big thing about not wanting to go there, which he tried to justify in various ways like saying that they wouldn't understand his words; stuff like that. He just generally had a "down" on it.

'There was one time in Italy where he was arguing with Colin Richardson, the tour manager, threatening to get the next plane home unless "something" happened. Just generally being an unhappy man the whole time. I couldn't really see why...' In retrospect, Alan felt the split happened at the right time, but what was clear was that it was a mistake to move away to the South.

'I had a wife and three kids and we went to live in Barnet. The bairns went to school in North London and the people were smashing, but it just didn't feel right. As soon as we got there, we realised there was no reason to be there. We came straight back, after two years. We were daft; we didn't realise there were such things as trains, telephones and aeroplanes.'

As far as the band was concerned, he felt that 'If we'd carried on, we'd have become enemies. We knocked it on the head at the top. Everybody in the band was in agreement. It wasn't fun any more.'

Chapter SEVEN

WHAT'S IN A NAME?

In March 1973, Alan finally went into the studio to record the solo album that had been part of the deal struck by Barbara Hayes back in 1970. He'd already debuted four songs for a Peel session recorded in January and was evidently champing at the bit. 'I had so many songs then. A lot of them the band didn't do, for one reason or another. Because it was in the contract to do a solo album, I started writing some more.'

It also meant Alan could bring together musicians he'd wanted to work with for some time – notably Kenny Craddock, a keyboard player who'd been in a band called the Elcort. Alan hated him ''cause he was handsome and extremely talented. I used to call him fish-face. The venom was all on my side, but he came to my house one night and we've become firm friends since.' *

Musically, there was a special understanding between the two, as Kenny explained in an extensive interview with Chris Groom in October 1997: 'We became soul-mates, so when the chance to play on his album came about it was a wonderful experience.' Also invited along were Ray Laidlaw, Jacka, Colin Gibson and Johnny Turnbull, and it was clear that no animosity remained between former band-mates. 'Pipedream' was recorded in just over a week, from 19-27 March.

'We only rehearsed for a day, maybe two at the most,' Kenny continued, 'We were all much younger then and very keen; everyone on that album just wanted it to be so good.' Clearly chastened by the 'Dingly Dell' debacle, Alan turned to someone he trusted to help produce the album and found him in Mickey Sweeney, who'd worked on the road with Lindisfarne for years and, according to Alan, was 'the first full-time professional roadie in Newcastle in the mid-1960s.'

Sessions had begun with Ken Scott. 'I produced it myself, but Ken thought he was the producer. After about the fourth day, I was calling the shots and Ken met me on the stairs at Trident. "Who's the producer here, Alan?" he said. "Well everybody, really", I said. "I am", he said. "No you're not, Ken" and he walked out the door. "That's another one walked out", I thought.' Gail Colson suggested Roy Thomas Baker, who would later achieve huge international success with Queen. 'I got on great with him' Alan recalls. 'So it was produced by me, Mickey Sweeney, Roy Baker, Kenny and everyone else in the band.'**

A number of songs on 'Pipedream' had already been committed to tape by Lindisfarne – notably 'Money Game' and 'Country Gentleman's Wife', recorded during the 'Fog On The Tyne' sessions as well as featured on the Bob Harris radio session in July 1972. The latter was a fictional tale inspired by Alan's time spent working as a window cleaner in one of Newcastle's richer sectors. Interestingly, Gail Colson believes in many ways that 'Alan was at his happiest when he was cleaning windows.'

Another eventual 'Pipedream' track included in the Harris session was 'Drug Song', the clearest refugee from Alan's time as a psychiatric nurse – his most prolific writing period. 'It's one of my better songs; it has a real message and it really happened. I wrote that and 'Clear White Light' in the same night,' he explained to Steve Clarke in *New Musical Express*. 'It was the only two songs I've ever written completely under the influence.'

Also recorded was 'United States of Mind', which had been aired on the final Lindisfarne British tour. Clearly, Alan was able to indulge himself with the album; from the cover to the gatefold sleeve, which showed an array of snapshots of his wife Pat, mother Sally and close friends including Glen Colson and Dave Wood. Particularly endearing were the various shots of Alan's daughters, Rosamund, Berenice and Francesca. Mixed with these were various bizarre studio snaps depicting musicians in bare feet with trouserlegs rolled up and bass-player Colin Gibson modelling a fine Cyrano de Bergerac-style false nose. 'It seemed to go with the rolled-up trousers,' he now says.

* It was during this period that Kenny worked with Ray Laidlaw at Shepherds department store in Gateshead.

** The credit on the album is for Alan, Roy Baker and Mickey Sweeney.

Right: Mickey Sweeney manipulates the faders.

If one series of visuals were ever to personify Alan Hull, it was this combination of images. 'We just had a bloody ball. No pressure. As it says on the album sleeve. 'To Ian and Charlie: for keeping the bar open.' The bill was £1000. This was in 1972. That's 25, 30 grand, now.' The front cover of the album was a Magritte painting much admired by Alan, called *The Light of Philosophy* and not only supplied the album title but had already inspired the song, 'Peter Brophy Don't Care/Light Of Philosophy' from 'Fog On The Tyne'.

'It was all Terry Morgan's idea. He wrote most of the words – I scanned them. Terry was living with us at the time and it was his turn for the fish and chips. He came back with them wrapped in the *Sunday Times* colour supplement. Inside, there was an article on an exhibition by René Magritte and I'd never seen anything like it. It was the first time I got into surrealism. So that night, me and Terry wrote "Peter Brophy Don't Care"… "Your nose is in your pipe" – which became the cover of "Pipedream".'

It was perfect – but expensive. 'The cover cost four thousand quid,' explained Alan, 'which, for that time was a phenomenal amount. I remember Gail Colson saying, "That's highly expensive…" I just honestly didn't care. The sounds that were coming out were just great.' Another song, 'Numbers (Travelling Band)', inspired by the Six Bob Tour, was released as a single. Alan explains: 'All those games in the back of the bus. It was the first time I played scrabble, 'cause Peter Hamill was quite adept at it.

'I remember once, my wife Pat was on the bus and she spotted a fish and chip shop and she said, "I just fancy some" – and there was silence. About five minutes later, people were going, "Anybody fancy some fish and chips?" – licking their lips and getting worked up. It went round the bus like wildfire… Eventually the bus stopped and 30 mad, stoned blokes steamed into this shop, demanding fish and chips!'

For Alan, 'Pipedream' had made up for the disappointment of 'Dingly Dell'. 'I approached it with a brand-new attitude. It's a shame it's coming out as Alan Hull – it'd be great if it had been Lindisfarne as, basically, that's the way the new Lindisfarne's going.' Steve Clarke's review agreed with Alan, closing with another acknowledgement that his writing was as fine as McCartney's or Lennon's ever was: 'Alan Hull is easily one of the best songwriters currently around. Like Lennon, he has that Northern bite which makes "Pipedream" a reality.'

It was left to Roy Hollingworth in *Melody Maker* to define Alan's achievement: 'His roots may be folk, but there's nowt but a sniff of that in this collection that pulls in tunes that vary from heavy mental trips to lush, melodic love ditties… This "Pipedream" seems to find Hull in that "Clear White Light" mood with incredibly memorable music and shapely, sculptured lyrics. It's a lot prettier and softer than the stuff he's rightly famous for – but there's also an air of the sinister.

'I can't really believe that out of 12 songs, 11 of them are quite frankly brilliant, and dammit, after just one playing you'll find yourself humming them like you'd known them for years. A second play will get you picking out the lyrics (amid that Geordie half-wail) and it's then that seemingly pretty songs contain a bitter twist to them. That's quite intriguing…' Alan also pointed out in the *NME* interview that 'Pipedream' would be the 'last Alan Hull thing for as long as I can see.' He recorded two further solo sessions for Bob Harris and Peely in July and November that year, but a new band, one which would be more co-operative in its songwriting, would be next on the agenda.

It was not until April 1973 that Lindisfarne officially announced that they were to split. In the *Newcastle Journal* Rod and Alan explained that it was 'the only honest decision', Alan going on to say, 'It would have been sheer pretence to continue: we all agreed there's enough insincerity in this business without adding to it.' Alan and Jacka would retain the name and form a new six-piece band, while Rod, Si and Ray would form a group that would include old mate Billy Mitchell.

'A lot of people had to cope with a lot of disappointment,' Rod now recalls. 'Y'know when a hot air balloon comes down in a field and all the air comes out? – that's it. Back down to earth with a bump. But to us it was a big relief.' Alan now admits that he already had the Mk II band lined up. 'Originally, it was going to be the "Pipedream" band; Phil Collins on drums, Colin Gibson on bass, Johnny Turnbull*** on guitar, Kenny Craddock guitar and keyboards, me and Jacka. Now *that* would've been a band to frighten everyone.'

The first person he spoke to was Phil. 'The first band had finished and we were in the Kilt & Celt in Earl Street. Genesis weren't big then and we had a couple of beers, I told him who was going to be in the band and he said, "Great. I'll talk to Strat about it and I'll ring you later." About ten to twelve he rang. '"Thanks for the offer, but I'm going to stick with Genesis." So I said, "Phil, far be it from me – but you're making a big, big mistake"!'

Steve Hackett also recalls the approach. 'Strat was discouraging, but you could see the attraction for Phil; Lindisfarne were riding high and Genesis were struggling. As we've seen since with Phil's own stuff, he likes a simple tune – quite capable of playing in 9/8! – so it wasn't as unusual an option as it might have seemed.' This was not to be Alan's last disappointment. 'Johnny Turnbull then calls me. '"I'm staying where I am. I've got a chance with this bloke Ian Dury."'

*** Johnny had originally joined the Chosen Few when Alan left. He later toured with Lindisfarne and Genesis, along with Micky Gallagher, as a member of Bell & Arc, another Charisma signing featuring Graham Bell. Tommy Duffy had been a member of a Newcastle band called the Sect, a band Ray Laidlaw remembers from the scene around the 1960s.

Below: Phil Collins in Germany with Lindisfarne while a Genesis member. He turned down a full-time gig.

Then Colin Gibson rings up…that left me, Kenny and Jacka!'

Gibson confirms this scenario and particularly Phil Collins' potential involvement: 'I had gone to London just on chance, really, to stay with Micky Gallagher. Micky got a call from Tommy Duffy to say that there was an opening in this band of Alan's, so I said "If Johnny Turnbull does it, so will I." I had already joined Snafu, so when Johnny said yes, I left them and Tommy Duffy joined. As it turns out, that was only for about a week and Tommy ended up in Lindisfarne Mk II; I went back to Snafu when I knew Johnny wasn't doing it. By then, it was just a mish-mash. It wasn't the band it could have been, and sufficiently different from (the original) Lindisfarne.'

As Alan had retained the band name, he was contractually tied to Charisma – an obligation that must have been apparent before Rod and Alan had announced the split of the original band. The line-up was completed by Tommy Duffy on bass (who'd been working with Gary Wright's Wonderwheel along with guitarist Mick Jones, later of Foreigner); Charlie Harcourt on guitar (who'd been in the States with Kenny playing with Cat Mother) and drummer Paul Nicholls from Kenny's old band, the Elcort.

The new line-up's first offering, 'Roll On, Ruby' was recorded at Trident during early September 1973. Having learned a hard lesson with the Charisma arrangement, they had a new manager – Tony Dimitriaides, who had managed Terry Reid and went on to look after Tom Petty in the States. 'They were bitter,' notes Glen Colson, 'and we were on to other things then. They were leaving Charisma and we didn't give much to it; it wasn't going to get Lindisfarne back where they'd been, so it was just a step down, really. The "rise" was over; this was the decline.'

Charisma kept the pot boiling, nonetheless, with the release in August of *The Mocking Horse*, Alan's book of poems. On the musical front, Roy Thomas Baker was brought in to produce – or, as Alan said, 'try to keep the squabbling factions away while he got on with the job.' 'Roll On, Ruby' featured one classic Alan Hull song, 'When The War Is Over', while the Kenny Craddock-Colin Gibson writing axis came up with three songs, as did Tommy Duffy. Orchestral arrangements were contributed by Max Middleton, formerly of the Jeff Beck Group and now with Chris Rea.

'It was a horrible album to make,' according to Alan. 'People were putting their own points of view forward, not the overall picture. You can't write a book by committee, and the album was produced by committee. You've got to have a vision.' The confusion was evident on the production credit that appeared on the sleeve on the album's release: 'Produced by Roy T Baker in conjunction with Mick Sweeney and Lindisfarne.' There was also the illustration of a tree on the cover, with one broken branch falling to the ground. Just discernible on the trunk was the enigmatic inscription 'Fuck Off.'

Below: Lindisfarne MK II featured Jacka and Alan with, from left, Tommy Duffy, Paul Nichols, Kenny Craddock and Charlie Harcourt.

Still a live attraction, the band set out on the road. 'The touring wasn't so bad, they were great lads to be with, but it just wasn't happening on stage', explained Alan. ' We fell back on "Lady Eleanor", "We Can Swing Together", "Fog On The Tyne" – that got us away.' In his interview with Chris Groom, Kenny clarified the situation they found themselves in: 'Some of the things we tried (on album) didn't really work out and normally those things would have been ironed out in rehearsal or dropped before

we went out on the road, or whatever; the trouble was that Lindisfarne already had a tour lined up, with people booking tickets to see them, so we went out with what we already had.'

The band reworked some of Alan's older material to suit the new style, but Kenny agreed that, while the band played the 'hits', certain songs simply wouldn't have worked. Stiff Little Fingers guitarist and singer Jake Burns caught this version of the band in Belfast: 'The fourth of May was a hell of a day in my life. I had spent the entire afternoon shouting myself hoarse at the telly as Kevin Keegan had all but single-handedly demolished Newcastle United in the Cup Final. As if your team winning the FA Cup wasn't enough, it was also the first time I passed myself off as 18 in a pub… oh yeah, it was also the first time I saw Lindisfarne.'

As Jake explains, not many bands were 'brave enough' to play in Belfast at the time. 'We had Rory Gallagher once a year and that was about it. So I suppose you could forgive the local promoter for assuming the band's name was "Linda's Farm" – that's what it said on the tickets.' Jake had been a fan since he heard 'Fog On The Tyne', having taped his mate's copy 'as money was in short supply for a 16-year-old!' So I was expecting a low-key event – "You know, folky sort of stuff, not your Rory Gallagher everything-louder-than-everything-else, get-up-and-boogie' type of affair." *Wrong*.'

The band were, apparently, 'a revelation. I had never experienced so much warmth in one place. Almost from the word go, the place was singing, jumping and, unbelievably, smiling. I learnt a lot about audience participation that night. It doesn't have to be insincere Michael Barrymore embarrassment. It can be the most fun you can have with your clothes on.' Clearly, Lindisfarne were still a live force to be reckoned with.

Kenny believes that, while audiences were positive, the once-supportive music press gave them the hardest time: 'They tore the arse out of it – but the gigs were all to packed houses; the public reception was great.' The band toured the States for about six weeks with Little Feat and Traffic and, as Kenny explained to Chris Groom, went down well. 'The band could actually play without the audience having the preconception of how "Lindisfarne" should sound, so we got to play exactly how we wanted and without too many critics hanging around. To say we really took off there would be a bit of a sweeping statement, but we had some great nights and got to play with some good bands.'

In May 1974, a John Peel first session from this version of the band included two from the album, Alan's 'Taking Care Of Business' and Tommy Duffy's 'North Country Boy', along with two others from their next album, that would appear the following month; 'You Put The Laff On Me' from Alan and Kenny's 'In Your Head.' 'Tony got us a great deal with Warner Brothers for the second album,' explains Alan, 'but by then, the band had completely lost direction. That's not knocking anyone in that band…it's just that, together, it just didn't work.'

Alan questions whether he even had a decent song on the album, titled 'Happy Daze.' 'I don't think so – maybe "The River"***, but I wrote that years ago. By then I thought, "I'm not gonna bother with this," so I just let them get on with it!' A strange album, it was produced by Eddy Offord and recorded at Peddlers drummer Trevor Morais' house – but despite his credentials with Yes and Emerson Lake and Palmer, Offord was hardly someone best suited to the material. At one point in Lindisfarne's career, such a CV would have been the very antithesis of what the original band were about.

Kenny admitted that they had enjoyed working with Eddy but, like 'Roll On, Ruby', 'it had all become a committee thing.' Several songs were recorded in the open air, 'The River' being one: 'That was great; with two of us playing acoustic guitar, Jacka playing mandolin and the sounds of birds and the babbling brook – it all added to the ambience of the recording.' Reviews were not kind, one going as far to say that 'Happy Daze' was 'a dismal experience', with as much criticism meted out for Alan's writing contributions as the other combinations.

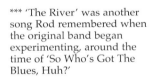

*** 'The River' was another song Rod remembered when the original band began experimenting, around the time of 'So Who's Got The Blues, Huh?'

'The whole medicine of the band was totally wrong,' Alan admitted. 'Jacka got "silliness", I became morose, Kenny became a drunk and the whole band fell to bits." It had been clear to Alan for some time that the band was doomed. 'Lindisfarne Mk II should have been strangled at birth. If I'd got the band together I'd wanted to, we'd have blown people's heads off.

'I knew within six months of the first album that it just wasn't going to work, so I just got on with it and got out as soon as I could. The new Mk II stuff didn't really deserve the name Lindisfarne.'

Left: Stiff Little Fingers, 1997. From left: Bruce Foxton, Ian McCallum, Jake Burns and Steve Grantley. While Jake witnessed Lindisfarne Mk II and later produced radio sessions with the reformed band, Ian would later enjoy musical collaborations with Alan Hull.

Both albums had a much harder, rock'n'roll feel than the earlier band and were less folk-orientated – particularly with 'Happy Daze' – but that, according to Kenny, had been the intention. 'It wasn't that Alan and Jacka particularly wanted to get away from that, but they did want to change direction and with the mixture of new musicians, that's the way it turned out.' That summer, the band appeared at Charlton Athletic Football Club, as one of the Who's 'friends' alongside Lou Reed, Humble Pie, Bad Company and Maggie Bell. In August, the band's final Bob Harris session was broadcast.

In February the following year, came the announcement that Lindisfarne had gone as far as they possibly could 'within the existing format of the band.' It went on to say that a solo album from Alan would be out in April and that Jacka planned to continue with Charlie and Tommy. Jacka went further in the Newcastle press, explaining that 'Lindisfarne are now at a stage where it does not mean what it used to. The new stuff is not what people want, so consequently we have been played down. We cannot get away from the old songs.'

Tommy felt the band should have completed the next album, as contracted: 'It would have been the definitive album by that version of the band.' They certainly had some support in the US, *Billboard* even saying 'Happy Daze' was 'the best album that came out of the name Lindisfarne'. There was even a further US tour on the cards, but realistically he was not surprised when the band folded.

Alan had been invited to write some songs for a TV play by Tom Pickard and had also been asked to take the lead role. Tommy recalls that 'Alan and Tony Dimitriaides thought that Alan's involvement in the play would lead to a solo career as both an actor and musician.' In retrospect, Ray Laidlaw believes there was substantial pressure on the band. 'They were, I think, very underrated, but they were called the wrong thing.

'If they'd been called "Alan Hull's Pipedream", or whatever, I think they would have had much more of a chance. That was record company pressure again. They wanted something with that name on it; it meant you could guarantee at least 100,000 sales, straight away.' The final Mk II gig, fittingly, was to be at Newcastle City Hall. Treated as 'a farewell party' according to *Sounds*, there was also to be guest appearances by former members currently with the 'other half' of the original band – Jack the Lad. *

As Alan finished recording 'Pipedream' at Trident, Jack the Lad entered Island studios in April 1973 to record a single with engineer John Burns, as Charisma wanted something quick. A Rod Clements song called 'One More Dance' was the choice, while three other tracks were also recorded for potential singles release.

New boy Billy Mitchell went back a long way with Ray, Rod and Si and it seemed inevitable that at some point he should be invited into the fold. His band, the Triffids – and, later, Model T – had played on the same scene as Downtown Faction. Around 1967-68, Mitch was forced to stop playing in Model T following his 21st birthday party, which he celebrated in the Rose and Crown pub, which his parents ran, opposite Tyne Tees Television studios on City Road, Newcastle.

'All the Downtown Faction lads were there; Laidlaw, Rod… My parents were away for the weekend, so I missed about a week and a half at work after that and I got the bullet.' He became a trainee supermarket manager for Fine Fare – 'a 24 hour a day job, so I had to knock the band on the head.' He sold all his gear, but after a year at Fine Fare bought an acoustic guitarand took it to a 'singaround' at the Wheatsheaf pub in New York, near North Shields, started by former Triffids Will Browell and Vince Gray. 'I hadn't heard much of this folk music and it was all rip-roaring Irish stuff – a great atmosphere,' he recalls. 'So me and Vince rehearsed a few songs, a couple of Roy Harper things – just interesting bits'n'pieces, mostly from Island Record samplers "Bumpers" and "You Can All Join In".

'We went up there and people quite liked it. It was something totally new to me. Then we became part of this big group of people who sang and played. Out of that came the Callies: Alan Morris, Vince, Will and me.' The band subsequently recorded one album in 1971 called 'On Your Side' for Rubber Records, a label operated by Dave Wood, and became a considerable draw at many of the legendary local clubs.

They played the Marquee in London, alongside fellow Geordies Hedgehog Pie and labelmate, Tony Capstick, and were also featured on a BBC North East TV programme, *The Great North Road Show*, in January 1972, playing 'Rocking Chair' from 'On Your Side', as well as Tyne Tees' *Walk Right In*.

* Following the split, Kenny, Tommy and Graham Bell recorded an album at Pete Townshend's studio. However, they could not secure a deal. 'It was bizarre,' Tommy recalls, 'We were being flown down from Newcastle to Heathrow and when we got there, we were scraping about to find enough money for the cab fare to Chiswick!' Townshend had apparently become friendly with Bell & Arc (which included both Tommy and Graham Bell) when they toured the States with the Who. 'It would never have entered my mind to ask Pete Townshend for free studio time,' Tommy recalls, but Graham did – and he got it !' Tommy subsequently became an Associate of the Royal College of Music, later being offered the post of bass tutor at Newcastle College. Now living in Brighton, he has been writing songs with Kenny Christie – whom he'd known in Newcastle – and has lately been joined by American singer Michael Dimitri. Several of their songs have been taken to Nashville by ex-Elvis Presley guitarist James Burton.

The Callies were also part of the line-up assembled at Newcastle City Hall, headlined by Alan Hull and the JSD Band, to launch 'Take Off Your Head And Listen', Rubber Records' seminal compilation of Tyneside bands**. To complete the picture, they also later appeared with Lindisfarne there, in 1972, on a bill completed by Pink Floyd alumnus Ron Geesin.

After Mitch got the sack from the supermarket, he got a job at Dunlop as a production control assistant, while still playing with the Callies at night. But when Dunlop relocated to Wrexham, he sold up and went to Canada. His wife was keen continue her career in computers, and at one of her interviews mentioned Mitch was a 'production controller'. They knew someone who had an opening and Mitch got the job. 'I didn't want it, but I got it. They thought the sun shone out of my arse, 'cause I just did everything Dunlop taught me to do... put in all their systems and it ran like clockwork!'

Having met three musicians – one from Belfast and two from Glasgow – at a bar in Vancouver, Mitch joined their group, called the Crofters, who did extremely well around the expats' clubs. After six months, he came back for a holiday at Christmas, he went to a party at Jacka's house at Longframlington in Northumberland and 'got extremely pissed. Prodigal son and all that...'

Above: The Callies, Mitch's part-time pursuit in the early 1970s.

Opposite: Mitch in a Rubber Records publicity shot.

Lindisfarne's success had been apparent to Mitch, even in Canada. He certainly recalls hearing something familiar as he walked through the Hudson Bay Company department store one day. 'At first, I thought it was Loudon Wainwright III – 'cause he sounds an awful lot like Alan – and it was something from their new album, which I hadn't heard, which was "Dingly Dell". I went straight out and bought it.'

Back at Jacka's party, 'I was in the bathroom when there's this knock on the door; it was Laidlaw. "Bugger off!" I said. So he says, "Let me in, let me in." So I let him in and he sat me on the bath and said, "I've got something to ask you. Alan's going to leave after the Japanese tour. If he does, we want you to join.' So I went back to Canada, thinking, "One day, I might be in Lindisfarne..."' In late February or early March Ray returned to Canada, as he had promised. 'He said Alan wasn't leaving. I was a bit pissed off, 'cause I was looking forward to joining.'

About five weeks later, Mitch received a phone call in the middle of the night. It was Si, as he explains: 'It was my birthday, the first of April, and straightaway he said, "Hello Si. Happy Birthday." Well remembered!' The purpose of the call was to find out if Mitch still wanted to join the band – he did, but it was to be a new band which wouldn't be called Lindisfarne 'because Alan and Jacka *are* leaving.

'So I left Canada about three days later, with my wife still heavily pregnant.' Mitch agreed to give it six months, ''cause it was like starting from scratch. We had the Lindisfarne success behind us, but we didn't know what we were going to do, what kind of music we were going to play.

'The boys took me out and bought me some guitars and a mandolin and we all bought new Vox AC30 amplifiers. Then we ran away down to Devon, to the farmhouse, which I'd heard about.' The name for the new band came from an expression Mitch's new colleagues had heard Quo use while were on tour in Australia that seemed to fit the new band perfectly – far better than original choice the Corvettes, which was 'too rock'n'roll revivalist and rather un-hip.'

There was an extremely positive feeling about Jack the Lad, as Rod explains. 'Doing nothing wasn't an option. We still had a lot to prove – I did, anyway.' He was excited by the potential. 'In terms of music – in terms of playing – the surface hadn't been scratched. This was probably my contribution to the problems Lindisfarne had in the first place; I felt we weren't being treated right as musicians because we hadn't had the chance to prove what we were capable of.'

Both the new-look Lindisfarne and Jack the Lad presented their new line-ups at a special 'Silver and Gold' party organised by Charisma where Lindisfarne received a gold disc for 'Fog On The Tyne' and silver discs for 'Nicely Out Of Tune' and 'Dingly Dell'. Meanwhile, just to confuse matters, in August Charisma released the stunningly titled 'Lindisfarne Live', a recording of the 1971 City Hall show never intended for release. The band were far from happy with this decision, particularly in terms of technical quality. The public seemed to agree. Reaching only Number 29, it fell out of the chart after only two weeks.

The new outfit's first album 'It's Jack The Lad' was recorded during November and December 1973 at Olympic Studios in Barnes. Produced by Hugh Murphy – who'd overseen Alan's 'We Can Swing Together' single in 1969 – it included a song from Mitch's Callies catalogue, the beautiful 'Turning To Winter' which he'd written while at the Dunlop factory. However, in a move that would prove to be typical, a jig was tagged on because it was getting 'too nice', as was noted by this writer in the CD issue of the album in 1992. Similarly, Rod's 'Fast Lane Driver' had a car-engine effect on it, quite naturally – immediately followed by one of an emergency siren. A mistake, but it was left on because it sounded good.

** This also featured one track each by Brethren and Alan Hull, Si's 'Positive Earth' and Alan's 'Where Is My Sixpence?'. The album ended with a shambolic version of 'We Can Swing Together' by Alan Hull with Brethren. Rather than Side A and Side B, the album had 'Rubber Top' and 'Rubber Bottom'. In *Sounds'* review in November 1971, Jerry Gilbert noted that by this time, the band had become Lindisfarne.

JACK THE LAD

'Back On The Road Again' needed the sound of a motorbike revving up. 'We searched all these sound-effect tapes and couldn't find one,' Mitch explains. 'So the tape operator says, "I've got a motorbike." So we get it all set up – the microphone down the stairs and outside – and he starts it up. It's a 125 Bantam that sounds like an electric toothbrush! We ended up using it, but slowing the tape down.'

'Promised Land ' and 'Boilermaker Blues' were two 'Doom and gloom, woe-is-me type things I'd written in Canada,' recalls Mitch, while 'A Corny Pastiche' was simply a series of tunes that that he and Will Browell used to do with the Callies; 'We thought it would be a damn good idea to do some "folk-rock" on the album.' There were also two other songs from Mitch and Vince Gray given their first airing, while Rod's 'Why Can't I Be Satisfied', originally recorded, but not released by Lindisfarne, was taken out and dusted down. Even Si contributed two songs.

'We had a lot of different musical ideas to what Hugh was used to. I think we were good for his grounding – his training. We were full of a new vitality; we were a new mixture of people and we were doing something different from anybody else – but still with a Fairport Convention base.' It seemed that the recipe for the band was, as Rod explained in the notes on the CD, 'to play a little bit of blues, a bit of folk and some of their own songs with plenty of excitement – and plenty of surprises.'

Special guest on the album was Steeleye Span's Maddy Prior, who lent her vocal to 'Song Without A Band' and Tommy Eyre – who later played with Alex Harvey and more recently with Gary Moore – was the keyboard player. 'He was always taking his keyboard apart,' laughs Mitch, 'spanners and all sorts.' Live, Jack the Lad made a conscious decision to go back to small halls and work their way back up. There were trips to Germany and Switzerland too – in the company of now-legendary road manager Fred Munt – to break the new band in before facing British audiences.

Rod has many fond memories of those early days. 'All these ideas that had been lying about that couldn't get used in Lindisfarne, for whatever reason, were now able to come to the fore. All the opportunities were there again, musically, so we made the most of it.

'It was a relief to get rid of the ego problems; the nasty vibes of those last few months and the communication problems that had grown up in the old band. It was time to get our heads down and do

omething "proper". Mitch couldn't
ave been an easier guy to get along
ith; an old mate from way back. It
as a smashing feeling.'

Rod however, would not be
ong for the second album, 'The
ld Straight Track', recorded
uring September 1974. 'The family
ing was part of it; the other thing
as, I could see the band not
etting anywhere – I'm sorry to
ay – and I seemed to be the only
ne that felt this. I don't regard it
s any credit to me now that my
eaction to that was to jump ship.'

With characteristic honesty,
od felt it was not fair to
ontinue with that attitude. He
so considered the band was
nderstaffed', particularly on
age. 'We did actually look
round for a fiddle player at the
me, but I was thinking of jacking it in by then.' With
othing lined up, he had had enough of 'bands'. 'I was starting to feel a bit
nvious of the looser way of doing things which had taken hold in the States, but
adn't happened over here.'

As suggested by the fiddler auditions, 'The Old Straight Track' was the
roduct of a definite decision to move in a folk-orientated direction – and it took
ot one but two people to fill Rod's shoes, Phil Murray and Ian 'Walter'
airbairn from Geordie favourites Hedgehog Pie. Neither had seen Jack the Lad
nd both came along to Rod's last appearance with the band, in Liverpool.
owever, Rab Noakes had been first choice, as Mitch explains. 'Ray and I went
p to his house at Strathmiglow, but he wasn't up for it. We wanted him to
lay bass…'

Mitch already knew Phil and, having taken Ray to see Hedgehog Pie in
ongbenton, near Newcastle, it was clear that he and Walter were their men.
he gig was pretty smart, so we decided to pinch both of them. Phil had
lready said yes, but Walter said he'd have to ask his mother,' as he lived at
ome at the time.

Thus constituted, the band took off to Devon again to work on some ideas
nd finally rehearsed at Pike House in Northumberland, where the sleeve
hoto for the album was taken, 'for two weeks out in the freezing cold, with
o water and no electricity and loads of beer! We got some good stuff,
hough…' With Hugh Murphy producer once again, the album drew on
orth-Eastern folklore, using both traditional and original songs. Two songs
folk historian Tommy Armstrong's powerful 'Oakey Strike Evictions' and Mitch's four-part suite
he Wurm' – were eventually singled out by the reviewers, with another track, 'Weary Whaling
round', becoming a 'live' staple, featuring Phil's doom-laden bass: 'A wonderful, dead simple, classic
ass line – as good as "Keep On Running",' according to Si.

The song, like several others, was researched at the home of the English Dance and Song Society at
ecil Sharp House. Walter apparently initially put up a lot of resistance, having, according to Mitch.
one that sort of stuff for so long in the folk-clubs in the North East…it was considered hackneyed by
hen.' Nonetheless the album was voted *Melody Maker* Folk Album of the Year and a promo film shot
ith the band in various guises, including a *West Side Story* street gang, revellers at a Medieval banquet
nd – quite naturally – as players for their beloved Newcastle United.

Hugh Murphy also had fond memories of recording 'The Old Straight Track'. 'Joan Armatrading
as recording in another studio at Olympic and I seem to remember her coming in and standing at the
ack. The first time we heard "The Troggs Tape" was at that studio and we pissed ourselves laughing.
We used to play word games as well. All those long nights in Studio Two….'

He certainly enjoyed working with the band and praised their lack of pretension. 'They were never
oo precious about it and I think that's what comes over; because it wasn't too "sacred'", or too much
rtistic angst in it. It was good fun and that's the way it should be.' It was soon clear that Mr Murray
ould be the instigator of innumerable gags – both on stage and off. It was with his arrival in Jack the
ad that the band would develop their often wacky live performances.

Above: Fan acclaim for Jack The Lad, but commercial success was harder to come by.

63, Linden Gdns,
Enfield,
Middlesex
3·7·73

Dear Rod,
        Thanks a lot for the letter
you sent me after I'd sent you
the birthday card last year.
You sent it in an O.H.M Senvelope,
remember? Anyway, in the letter
you said, and I quote :-
"Come & see us sometime" and
since Lindisfarne never did a tour
after that, I've decided to see
Jack The Lad. I'll be in the
audience at the Roundhouse on the
29th, with my friend Nick. Nick's
probably bigger than you so you'd
better be good!
        See you then,
                        Ian Long
P.S. The single's great

Right: Si and Mitch get their act together in Devon.

'Jack the Lad on the road was a lot more entertaining than we even were on stage – and we were pretty entertaining on stage,' says Si. 'Mitch is a real "yahoo"' – but multiply him by ten and you've got Phil. He's dead cool about it. He does it in a much quieter way – which is ten times funnier, sometimes.' Mitch's introduction came as early as the last night of Rod's tenure in the band, in Liverpool. 'We'd had a sort of "Goodbye Rod, Hello Phil and Walter" celebration. I was rooming with Laidlaw at the time and we must have got to bed about six in the morning.

'So I'm in bed when the phone rings. This Scouse voice went, "Is that your red van outside? Well can you shift it so we can get the bins out?" I put some clothes on and was just about to go out the door and the phone rang again. "Don't bother moving the van...it's Phil, you daft bugger!"' Thus initiated, Mitch decided he was going to room with Phil from then on. 'That's where all the plots were hatched...'

Despite outward appearances, Ray Laidlaw – 'Mr. Conscience' as Mitch refers to him – was not averse to little light relief himself. Recalling the early days of their friendship, Mitch continued: 'When Lindisfarne started taking off and making a bit of money, I was living in an attic flat in Tynemouth and he'd come home and if I wasn't in the pub already, he'd have been in there – had a few beers, bought a crate of Guinness – and when the pubs shut, he'd bring it to our house. There'd be a knock on the door – half ten, quarter to eleven – and he'd say "I'm home". Then we'd just sit and talk all night and attack this crate. Without Laidlaw none of it would have happened. He was the conscience...but he's a good raver.'

Walter, it appears, needed constant reassurance. 'A lovely bloke, but no confidence in himself,' Mitch explained. 'He was a brilliant mandolin player – but he would never admit to doing a good 'un.' Si had not met Walter until the first rehearsals. 'As soon as I heard him play, I thought, "Is this guy good, or what?" He was always good on the fiddle and mandolin, but now he's just as good on guitar. Frightening. He can turn his hand to anything.' It seems Walter also had the knack of sleeping where he fell . 'He was a big bugger – impossible to shift. We could have saved a fortune in hotel rooms,' laughs Mitch.

Glen Colson tour-managed the band for a while and could see that they had 'more of the vibe' than the Mk II Lindisfarne. 'They were a hell of a lot of fun. I wanted to show everybody in the band that I didn't side with Alan; they were all my friends as well.'

The more theatrical elements of the gigs came from Phil's time in Hedgehog Pie, according to Mitch. ' They were always full of japes, pranks, fooling about and stuff. The first line-up of Jack the Lad all took it a bit serious – me probably more than anybody...I suppose I had most to prove. I hated being

Left: Mitch in six-string action, while (below) Ray gives it some stick.

compared to Alan. When the second line-up started, all that went.' The inter-band rivalry had gone by this point, but he was always wary of Alan: 'I think he used to call us a "skiffle group".'

Si remembers one particular gig at Nottingham Boat Club where Phil excelled himself. 'We just left him on stage, doing one of his routines and all went off to the bar at the other end of the room. "Maybe another ten minutes yet…" we said. The whole places was in stitches.' Another classic was the 'mime' which involved the sculpting of an Adam and Eve statue that eventually involved the whole band and an imaginary 'appendage' that required all of them to carry it over their shoulders. You had to be there, really…

Around this time, the band also played Reading Festival, where 'The reaction was as good as any in the Lindisfarne heyday,' the press reported. It was also where Mitch had to be put to bed in the Charisma caravan, ''cause we got blitzed,' as he recalls. 'We went on stage during the JSD Band's set in these cardboard boxes; gaffa-tape braces…dancing about like lunatics. We were just having a good time. I don't think the JSD Band thought much of it.' Pictorial evidence of this sartorial interlude in Mr Mitchell's career *does* exist, but unfortunately it has been mislaid.

With the success of 'The Old Straight Track', press comparisons of Jack the Lad and Lindisfarne were rife, one particular paper printing its review in the same column as 'Happy Daze.' 'As it happened, our came out better,' says Mitch, 'but it wasn't a nice thing to do. The comparison only existed in the minds of the press. I don't think it bothered anyone else.'

Charisma, he continues, 'hated' 'The Old Straight Track' because was no single on it. 'This was when the charts were full of Mud, Gary Glitter and that. Chalk and cheese.

Obviously, we wanted success; we wanted to play and get some money so we could keep going.' Mitch believes that, after a while, very few Lindisfarne fans came to Jack the Lad gigs. 'When we first started off, we used to have them shouting for "Fog On The Tyne" – but that died, especially when "The Old Straight Track" started doing well.

'The change in line-up and approach – having the fiddle and mandolin from Walter, and Phil's type of bass playing – gave the band a totally different thing; but it was very much a live band. A lot of it was a-hundred-mile-an-hour stuff. We went on taking no prisoners.' The band began to get a lot of work in Scandinavia, where, according to Ray, were the second most popular band there and even recognised in the street.

It was while in Norway that they had a bad accident, just north of Lillehammer. One late afternoon just two dates into a 30-night tour, the van hit a patch of ice, somersaulted three times and ended up on its roof just a few yards from a sheer drop. Fortunately, a doctor had been following and all Mitch can recall is being pulled out of the back of the van upside down. He had two broken ribs. 'It was the beer kegs that did the damage when they landed on me,' he laughs. The rest of the gigs were cancelled, as Mitch recalls: 'They left me in that hospital as well, the bastards – on goat's milk cheese for a week!'

The band toured Britain the autumn of 1974 as the opening act with old friend Ralph McTell, playing to packed houses as Ralph had just hit with the single 'Streets Of London', on which Rod Clements played bass. The track had been cut in some spare studio time in October after recording a single with Bert Jansch, 'In The Bleak Midwinter', which Ralph was producing.

McTell takes up the tale: 'I'd known Prelude from a tour they'd done with me and I used them on the Bert track, so I asked them and Rod to do a recording of "Streets Of London" pretty much spontaneously after they'd all finished. So Rod says to me, "What do you want me to play like?" So I said, "You know how you played on 'Meet Me On The Corner'? That opening bit

WHAT'S IN A NAME?

ust sounds like 'Streets…' speeded up." Alan said it was really funny me telling Rod that; 'cause Rod knows, y'know? He doesn't know whether I was having a pop at him or not!'

Rod had bumped into Ralph and Bert when he had gone along to see his former band-mates at a ack the Lad gig at the Howff in Hampstead. Rod had already done one UK tour with Michael Chapman nd planned to be 'a freelance bass player. I'd had enough of groups and the mutual commitment and omplications.' He was certainly determined to plough his own furrow. 'It seemed to me that the Americans had "looser" aggregations of session men; groups of people like in New York or in Muscle Shoals – LA, Memphis – Booker T & the MGs…they all seemed to play together, but it didn't have to be group.'

Then, in a direct reference to the Lindisfarne experience, he went on, 'They didn't have to have their icture taken outside of the Houses of Parliament, doing daft things – it could be done without all of hat thing of everyone having to sign contracts together and having collective identities and images and ll this sort of stuff.' Rod was very disenchanted with the 'music industry machine', as he continued: I'm looking back on it with a great deal of hindsight, crediting my viewpoint then with more insight han I had at the time.

'I think the system – the kind of beat-group promotional system that was a very British thing from he 1960s – had outlived itself by the time Lindisfarne was happening. If you hink about it, Lindisfarne was a

*Below: The 'Jackpot'
line-up added multi-
instrumentalist
Phil Murray (second
from left) and guitar
virtuoso Walter
Fairbairn to the nucleus
of Mitch and Ray.*

* Bilzen was one of
Europe's biggest festivals at the
time and Michael was also
appearing: 'I was wandering
around on my own with my
guitar and there was a bunch of
Geordies in the back stage bar,
having a real good time I didn't
know them – so, being shy and
sensitive(!), I stayed away. Then
there was this big argument
between Lindisfarne's roadies
and the headlining bands' –
this was in the days of "We've
got a fatter roadie than you
have." I don't think the bands
themselves gave a shit who
went on last, but the roadies
did; it was all down to prestige.
'A slight kerfuffle started
up and then Lindisfarne went
on – they must have lost. In
those days, it seemed like every
song, everybody swapped
instruments and they had this
forest of microphones –
everything was miked up
separately in those days – and
the band were bloody awful.
'Course, they were well pissed
by then and they were just this
ragged mess… I was very
finicky then and hadn't come to
understand the philosophy of
the "ragged mess" yet. I just
paid no attention to them.'

fairly loose aggregation; there was Brethren, there was Downtown Faction, there was Alan. Suddenly, we were Lindisfarne and it was, "Oh – take their pictures…get them to London and get 'em signed…" This big machinery comes into play.'

Fully aware that Lindisfarne played the 'game', Rod believes that Jack the Lad simply did the same thing. 'Can anyone step into the machine? This can only happen because the machine says it's going to,' he says, rather profoundly. In retrospect, Rod feels that when he left Jack the Lad, they were probably less than pleased. Mitch was the one he felt worst about, having come over from Canada. 'Mitch does what he likes, and I love him for it. I do what I like and I suppose I hope Mitch respects that.'

Rod's Michael Chapman connection had come via Rick Kemp, who was leaving Michael's band to join Steeleye Span. 'I was very lucky to get a gig straight away. I went to see Martin Carthy, whom I vaguely knew. While we were having a drink, Rick Kemp, Chris Coates and another couple of the Steeleye gang were in the next room, unbeknown to me. After I went, Martin apparently mentioned me…'

Chapman and Clements eventually met in the Ship, a pub in Soho's Wardour Street, for a chat. 'I had this psychedelic jumper on that I'd bought in New York and my pink jeans and my bag with my bits'n'pieces in – this was the 'peg-bag'…' Michael takes up the story. When Rick mentioned Rod had been in Lindisfarne, I said, "Forget it. I once saw them play in Bilzen in Belgium and they were bloody awful!" *

'But Rick persisted. We set up this rehearsal room somewhere in Soho and in Rod walks with his bass and this peg-bag of his – 'cause he was still very hippy then – and as soon as he got this fretless bass out and played, me and Keef Hartley went, "Ooo – that'll do.".'

Rod admits he couldn't have wished for a better introduction to freelance life. 'Michael was a very individual character; a great guitar player and very strong direction. Keef was one of my heroes from years ago with John Mayall – and there I was, seemingly "holding my own".' There appeared to be plenty of resources to look after the trio, and even better, 'for every round I bought, Michael bought six. It was good crack; nice people.'

Right: Rod (right) chews the fat with, from left, Keef Hartley, Professor Sutton and Michael Chapman, 1974.

Chapter
EIGHT
THE MEETING OF THE PATHS

If Jack the Lad had any chance of making the leap in stature necessary to rival their parent band, it must have been anticipated most keenly around the time of the tour with Ralph McTell when Mitch, especially, felt they were reaching their musical peak.

'It was a great tour,' he enthused. 'We were tearing the audience apart every night, coming off with everyone on their feet and Ralph was like, "How do I follow *that*?".' The headliner graciously agrees. 'It was like what happened at the Rex with Brethren. They were a great band, wild, but not in the same way as the Saw Doctors or the Pogues – these guys could actually play. Great sound…especially the harmonies. With the inadequate PAs then, you had to do it with your own abilities. Jack the Lad did it every night.'

After a particularly good show at Leeds University, the band returned to their hotel and headed to the bar, only to be told it was closed despite the fact that they were residents. Mitch continues the story: 'There's four people in suits sat at the bar and they're being served. At that time, we did look a bit hairy, pretty raggy; but the barman wouldn't serve us.

'So Ralph comes in with his brother Bruce (who was managing him), and they're both big lads. "Not drinking, boys?" "Nah. Can't get a drink – the bar's closed." So Ralph goes, "Excuse me, I'm a resident. Can I have some drinks for my fellow residents here?" and the barman says, "I can't, Sir. The bar is closed." So Ralph went behind the bar, got out a bottle and said, "If you don't serve them, I'll smash every bottle in here. I've got loads of money, so I can afford to pay for them." So we got our drinks.'

By the time of their third and final album for Charisma, 'Rough Diamonds', Jack the Lad had established their own identity. This time, recording switched to Sound Techniques, a favoured studio of the album's producer: Fairport's Simon Nicol, fresh from working with Richard and Linda Thompson.

Simon is uncertain how his hiring came about, but assumes it was the fact he'd had his name on a couple of Fairport albums as producer. 'By then I was seen as an "independent" producer. I wasn't making money at it, but at least I was prepared to have a crack. The only person I knew was Ray Laidlaw and not that well.' He would like to think that the association came from the band, rather than 'some anonymous person in the record company.' Given Jack the Lad's stated Fairport leanings, this is a possibility, but no-one is able to confirm it one way or the other.

During recording, the band stayed at what Mitch described as 'one of the worst hotels I've stayed in my life' in Bayswater, seven to a room with Phil – who suffered from a form of asthma – adopting a unique sleeping arrangement. 'He shoved half his bed out of the window on to the balcony,' Mitch laughs 'and that's where he'd sleep, with his head and shoulders out the window and the window pulled down across him!'

'Rough Diamonds' was recorded in July 1975, and on release showed much evidence of the continued friendship between the factions. Jacka and Tommy Duffy had been along to give a friendly heckle at early gigs and Jacka had provided the sleeve's artwork; a derivation of a Jack playing card. He also provided harmonica on the opening track, 'Rocking Chair', another survivor from Mitch's Callies days.

Other highlights included the traditional 'Gentleman Soldier', a smutty tale of goings-on in a sentry box – the usual kind of fare for the band – and their classic tale of life in Arkwright Street, Mitch's 'A Letter From France'. The final track – Si's 'Jackie Lusive' – was based on a game of cards and featured a surprising guest, as Si explains. 'At the end, where there's that collage of card games, we did a line each and I remember Barbara Hayes had the most manly voice on there. Once, we were in an office somewhere and someone answered "There's a geezer called Barbara on the phone!"'

'There was a great pub up the road,' Si continues, 'that sold Ruddles County. Simon turned us on to this stuff and after a few I was ready to sing the hoose doon! I remember I put a bit in "Jacky Lusive" where it says "… will fox and addle your brain" and it came out "…box and ruddle your brain".' 'The Beachcomber', another hint at Si's ecological concerns, was 'an idea I'd had for years. It was another song we found at Cecil Sharpe House. A couple of little riffs on the mandolin, which I expanded on with the break-up with my wife that was happening at the time.'

Simon Nicol was 'a bit of a slave driver', and Mitch recalls having problems with the reggae song 'The Ballad Of Winston O'Flaherty'. 'I just could not get the rhythm guitar bit right. After an hour or two, I lost my blob and said, "well *you* fuckin' do it!" So he did…' John Kirkpatrick was brought in from Wales for some accordion on 'Gentleman Soldier', overdubbed at Morgan Studios. Simon appears to have thoroughly enjoyed making the album. 'They were such nice, outgoing chaps with people like Walter, who I hadn't met before – it's just that it was terribly expensive keeping him lubricated, straight into the Carlsberg Specials at half ten in the morning. That pinned my ears back a bit.'

In his opinion, the band's real asset was Phil Murray. 'It was his downright enthusiasm. He loved being in a band, being in the

tudio, and he just loved his guitar – he was infatuated with it. That was a bit of a bind though, as it never did sound as good to us as it did to him!' However, Simon was not entirely comfortable during the sessions. 'Twenty years ago, I was even less socially graced; I'm not a natural mixer. To be a good producer, you have to be all things to all people, try and understand what everyone's thinking, measure their moods and co-ordinate things so people make their best performance at the same time, together. It was more important then, because we were dealing with eight-track machines.'

One track he particularly enjoyed was 'Captain Grant'. 'The rhythm section on that really *swings*. Obviously, Mitch enjoyed himself. All the voices on the end of "Jacky Lusive" were good fun too.' The addition of Jacka was no surprise, either. 'Ray Jackson was so close to the band that I think it was inevitable he would get roped in. He was noted once for his two-tone shoes – correspondents footwear!'

Jack the Lad became almost as frequent visitors to the BBC studios as Lindisfarne: 'We did God knows how many Peel sessions,' Mitch recalls. * The significance of the sole Bob Harris session recorded on 2 October, did not become apparent until much later, as BBC producer Jeff Griffin explained: 'In the 1980s, I was first phoned and then visited by two policemen from the Avon and Somerset Constabulary who were part of the team investigating the behaviour of the Surrey force some years before, at the time of the Guildford bombings. They showed me a photograph of Jack the Lad with a couple of girls in it and asked me if I thought it had been taken in our Maida Vale studio. I said that as far as I could see it had not – the background did not look like the studio as I remembered it.

'I then asked them what importance was attached to the photo and they told me that one of the girls in the photo was Carole Richardson, who had been imprisoned for the bombings. She had always maintained she had been at a Jack the Lad concert in south London and had produced the photo to prove it. The group themselves could not positively identify the venue but did agree that it had been taken at one of the two places and their concert had indeed been on 5 October – the night of the bombings! Carole Richardson was released in October 1989…'

Another historic, though certainly considerably more flippant chapter in Jack the Lad's career was their appearance on the *Old Grey Whistle Test* along with bluesman Freddie King. To the astonishment of both TV crew and blues veteran, this was this occasion when the nation was introduced to Jack the Lad's 'Morris Miner's Dance' – a live favourite, complete with shovels, miner's lamps and 'dorty workin' clays' (soiled working apparel).

'The origin is from the Shiremoor Marras,' Mitch explains. 'They actually did a sort of miner's dance, entertaining at old people's homes and over-60s clubs and that. They were great. So we nicked it. Most people were bemused by it.'

A *Whistle Test* appearance was a major plus for any band at that time, and highly prestigious. 'We'd spent three or four years trying to get on the only rock'n'roll programme on the telly and we go on and o a fuckin' dance!' There was, however, method in their madness. 'We thought people would notice it was different. I remember you worked from two ends of the studio, Freddie King at one end…they just swung the cameras round and it was our turn. I'm still waiting to see it on *Sounds Of The Seventies…*'

Rab Noakes also toured colleges with the band during the winter of 1975, around the time of the release of 'Home Sweet Home', a non-album Rod Clements song, backed with 'Big Ocean Liner', written by Alan Price's cousin, Dave.

'Mike Elliott was also on the tour,' Rab recalls. 'It was fairly substantial – 30-odd dates in a 12-seater transit. Little Feat's "Sailin' Shoes" was the album played more often than any other, and Fairport's "Full House"… Mitchell was a stormer on that tour. That was a nice time; I recall that tour with fondness. It wasn't as smart as the '72 Lindisfarne-Genesis one, but it was great fun.'

Elsewhere, while Jack the Lad were involved with 'Rough Diamonds', Alan had released his second solo album, 'Squire', taking advantage of a clause Tony Dimitriaides had included in Lindisfarne's Warner Brothers contract. 'I was ready for it then, but the band had broken up with massive debts that were all on my neck. I took them all on because the rest of them didn't have any money – so I had a budget to bring "Squire" in on, so I could pay off the debts.'

Most of the songs came from a Tom Pickard play that Alan had been involved with while in the Mk II band. 'Tom – a great poet, great Socialist, great friend – rang me up and said, "I've got this play, *Second City Firsts*, for BBC2 – do you want to write the music for it?" "Be proud to," I said. "Give me the script, come round and we'll talk about it."' Moreover, having cast the whole play, the director wanted to cast Alan in the main part. 'So I said, "I can't act." So he says, "Can you read?" "I dunno. Just about." So he says, "Well, you can act." So I got the job…'

The idea for the title track was also inspired by Pickard. 'It's a great song and the album sort of came out of that,' Alan explained. Derek Taylor was in the driving seat at Warners at the time, and stories of the former Beatles PR man are rife in the music business. Alan, naturally, had his own: 'There was one day when Tony Dimitriaides was there with a guy I think was setting up Dark Horse Records for George Harrison. We had a very nice meal and then, all of a sudden, the place went quiet and Derek says, "Hello, George – sit next to Alan." It's George Harrison, of course, and he says "Hello, Squire", which I thought was a nice start. He then proceeded to talk to me as if I'd been at school with him.

'He'd just got back from a tour of the States with Shankar and we started talking music straight away. Here was George Harrison talking to me about songwriting. So I said, "George, I'm having

* Jack the Lad actually recorded eight Peel sessions between May 1973 and September 1976. There was also the Bob Harris recording in October 1974, as well as *Sounds On Sunday*.

terrible problems trying to get a rhyme for this word." "Pfah!" he says. "Every word has its rhyme." So said to try "orange", and left him thinking about it. Anyway, we all went back to the office and Derek played some of the album and George said, "You sound a bit like John." So I say, "Well actually, there's track on the other side where I sound a bit like *you!*" We spent all day together… I know what the rhyme is, anyway; it's "budgerigar"…'

The album was not a massive success, although there was praise for songs such as the title track an 'One More Bottle Of Wine', also a single and arguably a classic. There was also a cover of the rock'n'ro song 'Ain't Nothin' Shakin' (But The Leaves On The Trees)', featuring guitarist Micky Moody, a friend the album's bassist, Colin Gibson, who had played with him in Snafu.

Moody, who would go on to form Whitesnake with David Coverdale, recalls Lindisfarne coming to see Snafu whenever they played the Newcastle area and believes he was invited to play on 'Squire' after a show at Hammersmith Odeon attended by Alan. 'He was obviously impressed and asked Colin and me to play on the track. We played live, with no overdubs: it was a rock'n'roller with manic overtones!' Alan was clearly happy at their contribution, noting on the sleeve credits, 'Thanks Snafu… Tight as shite.'

A single, 'Crazy Woman', was recorded after the release of the album and, as Alan explained, this was Warners' attempt at a 'commercial' single. 'It was Derek Taylor's idea,' Alan told the Lindisfarne fan magazine *Magic In The Air* in early 1995. 'They were really behind me and we got this commercial producer, Peter Swettenham, in. It was a great song, but it didn't do anything.'

Alan played some live solo dates, but was wary of getting on stage on his own. Glen Colson worke with him, even managing him for a while. 'We drove around the country on this tour, but we didn't pu many people. We'd booked a lot of smaller halls, but it wasn't successful. We had Tom Robinson supporting, in his band Café Society.' Glen had at one time also been attempting to get Alan involved part of another set-up, 'an English Crosby, Stills and Nash with Rab Noakes and Gerry Rafferty. I couldn't bring it together. It was my dream to form a supergroup, because I said to Alan, "You can't do it by yourself, you're only drawing a hundred people."'

Rab also remembers another occasion at Alan's home in Whickham when they all discussed Glen's proposal of a band consisting of Alan, Rab and Nick Lowe. 'At that time, there wasn't a lot going on for me, so I should have been game to have leapt into something like that. Nick was just out of Brinsley Schwarz and Rockpile was yet to come, but it just sort of evaporated…'

Ultimately Warners decided against taking up the option on another album. Reviews had been fair but perhaps best personified by the redoubtable Steve Clarke who felt that, while 'Squire' 'did not enhance Alan's reputation as one of the country's best straight working-class hero songwriters, it certainly does nothing to decrease it.'

Alan was simply left reflecting on what could have been. '"Squire" should have been done proper! Again, it was my fault, but it got me out on the road on my own. The album was rushed. I needed to g money to pay the Mk II debts off, because I had bank managers, tax and VAT men on to me, so I took the money out of the advance. That's why it was rushed and cheap.'

Derek Taylor did however give Alan a present. 'It was a book called *I Did It My Way* by T Dan Sm – "Dan The Plan" of the album.' A local politician in Newcastle, Smith had been at the centre of investigation for corruption.

'Inside this book, Derek had written, "Let's put a realistic price on this, Alan – six million pounds!" He'd had to drop me from Warners and he sent me this letter, apologising and wishing me well.'

Where to now? Alan returned to his home on the banks of the Tyne, to consider his options and one morning woke up with a sudden realisation. It was almost a year since the Warners contract had lapsed and he hadn't written a single song. 'I thought, "Christ, I haven't got a recording contract – I'm not even on the dole. I'd better get my career sorted out."' It was the incentive – along with much plain talking from Pat – that he needed to get back to it. In the summer of 1976, Alan once again went into Dave Woods' studio to put down some demos. 'I recorded six songs that I'd written in about ten days. There was "I Wish You Well", "Easy And Free"….'

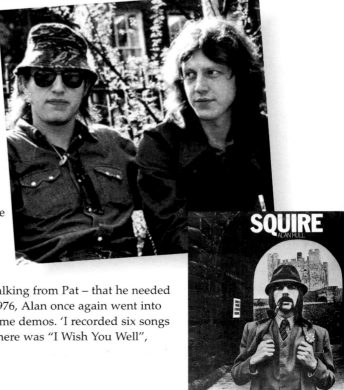

So, via the ever-reliable Barbara Hayes once again, Alan took himself off to London to meet Abe Hock, who had handled people such as Stevie Wonder and Dory Previn, as well as helping get Led Zeppelin's SwanSong label off the ground. 'He said, "Look, I'll manage you." He had heard the tapes and liked them. He said, "You need a recording contract. We'll phone you tomorrow and I'll have one for you." And he did.' The deal was with Elton John's Rocket label. It seemed Alan was ready for the fray once more.

Jack the Lad, meanwhile, were approaching their fourth album. Their severing of the Charisma link was more a case of the band saying goodbye to them than the other way round, as Mitch explains. 'We felt that they weren't really behind the band at that time and we needed somebody with a bit of faith.' The band first secured new management, with the help of Barbara Hayes, signing with Arnakata who handled Be Bop Deluxe, the Strawbs and the Tourists (with Annie Lennox and Dave Stewart). 'It seemed like everything was falling into place,' Mitch continues. 'It just seemed right. A bit of interest and a bit of push.'

Mitch is full of praise for Barbara's talents. 'She was a gold prospector, you know? – "I'll just go and dig up there and see what I can find" – she signed everybody up: Pete Scott, Hully, Robbie Burns and me. Anybody who could put words on paper and play a guitar, she had them. That's fair enough. I've got nothing bad to say about her. She tried very hard, she got us that deal and they got us with United Artists.'

For 'Jackpot', the producer's mantle fell to Tom Allom who would later gain a sizeable reputation with a whole host of heavy rock clients, including Judas Priest. The band had rehearsed in Devon once again and went into Wessex Studios to record the album during the summer of 1976. By this time, Mitch was doing most of the writing, for reasons which would soon become apparent. 'It came out a lot different to the stuff I'd been doing before; I don't know why, but I loved the way it was done in the studio.' Compared to the previous two albums, the production values were considerably higher this time. 'There was still the "Captain Grant" folky feel about it, but we got carried away with intricate productions.'

He was full of praise for Tom Allom, too. 'Tom was great, He'd go to the far ends of a fart to get something. He had some great ideas. The first thing we did was a set of tunes and "Trinidad", which I thought was the best thing we'd ever done. The sound difference from the Charisma stuff was amazing.'

One of Mitch's main memories was a song called 'We'll Give You The Roll', which he apparently wrote with Kiki Dee in mind. 'Tom got some brass players in and, because it was my song and we couldn't read the parts, I had to explain what I wanted. The four of them are sat there, reading the paper, so I'm going, "I want bap, bap, da, da – like 'Getaway' – Georgie Fame, you know?" They were only the Blue Flames… "Oh shit…" But it worked out great.'

Mitch also recalls that the original engineer, Bill Price, was pulled away from the sessions for a band called the Sex Pistols. Former Herd man Andy Bown (now a fully paid-up member of Status Quo) played piano. 'He knew what we wanted and we got it,' laughs Mitch. Rosalind Russell in *Record Mirror* felt the band were trying hard to marry folk and rock, but that ultimately 'Jackpot' fell 'between two stools.' She reserved her praise for 'Trinidad' – 'the only Geordie reggae song I've ever heard' – and 'The Tender', with which the band were going to 'wipe the floor with live audiences.'

Also on board 'Jackpot' was Jacka, who had recently signed a singles deal with EMI. Mitch admits he was asked to join on a permanent basis, but Jacka had his sights set elsewhere. 'I thoroughly enjoyed playing with them, but I wouldn't have wanted to join them while they were playing that type of music. I didn't want to keep playing folk music of the type that Lindisfarne did,' he told Newcastle's *Out Now* magazine. 'Jack the Lad's material was a little far removed from the direction I was taking. I was writing totally different stuff and I'd got used to my own independence.'

Very little of the recording, however, included Si. His marriage was deteriorating and rehearsals in Devon had been fraught with problems, especially as the other half of the equation was one of the band's roadies. Finally, Mitch was the one who had to suggest to Si that 'enough was enough'. Si's exit was particularly sad, as much of the writing had been shared by him and Mitch and Si's own musical ideas and idiosyncrasies were a major part of Jack the Lad. As it turned out, Si would actually take perhaps the most intriguing career route of all the various former Lindisfarne members.

Despite the deal with EMI, signed in March 1976, it seemed clear that Jacka was finding times hard and his future seemed 'a little uncertain', as *Out Now* reported in a interview at the time. Initially, Jacka had contacted Warners, as he had worked with them before, but they weren't willing to do anything.

'Basically,' he explained, 'they'd lost quite a bit on the last Lindisfarne album because they gave us an advance of £30,000, but only sold about 1,500 copies. They were a bit put out.' He vainly attempted other routes, but soon realised he was getting nowhere.

Jacka then linked up with John Brewer, a manager from London. 'He seemed to be doing all right, but I was a bit wary. He had a big flash office and a Rolls-Royce, but he had no artists on his books who were doing anything: Noel Redding was the only name I recognised.' Nonetheless, Brewer took him around all the record companies, but could not manage to clinch a deal. Jacka already had songs written, so his reaction was to go into Impulse to record some demos, as he explained in the article. 'I'd written about ten songs at the time, but I still couldn't get a deal. As a last attempt, I tried Barry McKay of Oz Records, but I didn't really know what he could do.'

It was Barry who had secured Jacka a publishing deal with Chappell Music in 1975 and also negotiated the recording deal with EMI for three singles and an option on an album. Unfortunately, the advance – 'which should have lasted a couple of months' – was soon consumed trying to get a band on the road. Captain Whizzo consisted of Colin Mason on drums, Jimmy Wylie on bass and guitarist Robert Barton, plus Jacka and Charlie. A tour was announced in the national music press for May and June, but only three local dates materialised. *

Jacka admitted in *Out Now* that he had got the wrong people and the band 'didn't last five minutes.' It was not until June that the first single was recorded, and even then things moved very slowly. The single, 'Take Some Time'/'Working On', was produced by Muff Winwood, formerly of the Spencer Davis Group, who'd heard Jacka's demos when he was doing the rounds of the record companies. 'There were three songs he liked at that particular time and he said, "We'll go in the studio tomorrow." That was good enough for me.' Muff also gave Jacka the confidence to record his own songs, clearly a daunting prospect given the talents in his 'old band'.

The single, however, was stillborn and no further material surfaced. EMI's apparent lack of commitment to Jacka's product soon became a legal issue and in a landmark case, Jacka – with huge support from manager McKay – took the giant label to court and won. McKay, a shrewd and confident individual, had also approached Rod Stewart's management about Jacka's possible involvement in Rod's imminent tour. Rod apparently wanted to reproduce songs like 'Maggie May' and 'Mandolin Wind' as they had been on record, but was looking for someone who could also play guitar and piano, so no further progress was made. **

At the end of the day, Jacka was determined to get his solo career off the ground and Barry was equally determined to help him achieve that. After the Mk II band had folded, Jacka had continued to write with Charlie Harcourt, but as he admitted in the *Out Now* interview, he only played mandolin and harmonic and found it hard to accompany himself. After touring as duo around the folk clubs and the Captain Whizzo episode, Jacka and Charlie finally formed a band, Harcourt's Heroes, playing American R&B.

'I wanted to get back to the music I used to go and see when I was 17 or 18, down at the Club A Go Go. My idols were John Lee Hooker and Jimmy Reed. I found I had an affinity with that style of music; found I could play harmonica in the blues style very well,' he said in the interview. 'I wanted to get bac to that style of music after I left Lindisfarne because I wasn't doing as much musically as I could have been doing. I was more of a frontman than a musician.'

The rest of the band were Colin Mason from the aborted Captain Whizzo band and sax player/vocalist Marty Craggs: both were from Newcastle, Manchester-born bassist Barry Spence the only 'outsider', although he had often appeared on the local club circuit.

Right: Promotional shots of Jacka and Bob Barton for the latter's 'Benwell Lad' single.

Marty, a veteran of several Tyneside bands, recalls one occasion, many years before, passing the Downtown Faction van somewhere on the road. 'I said to Neil Perry – the sax player with the Juncos – "Quick, get your sax out." So we worked out this quick harmony, "nee-nah, nee-nah." Then we opened the side door of our van and the two of us went "nee-nah, nee-nah", like a police siren. Just one of those daft things you do.'

The Heroes' policy of playing the local clubs and pubs was a calculated attempt at establishing a firm local base, rather than rushing into the big time. 'The pubs and clubs are the real place to play,' said Jacka at the time, plainly as keen to return to soaking up that atmosphere of his formative years as were the rest of his former Lindisfarne colleagues. The reality was that with nationwide tours, a lot of people had to be paid. However, Jacka reckoned that the band 'were making as much money as I ever did in the second Lindisfarne.'

They also understood, however, that a move outside the area had to be made at some point. Marty Craggs can recall several demos at Impulse, as well as recordings made at Chappell Studios in London, but nothing came of it. Meanwhile, the band's residencies at the Rex at Whitley Bay and the Newton Park Hotel, Heaton, were always packed out. 'Jacka was really going for it,' recalls Marty. 'He was really serious about the band.' Most of Harcourt's Heroes were also featured in a 1976 BBC TV special with a live studio audience called *Sounds Like Ray Jackson*, multi-instrumentalist Jim Hornsby being brought in to play banjo, dobro and pedal steel guitar.

Also around this time, Jacka was commissioned by producer Malcolm Gerrie – later of *The Tube*, *The White Room*, etc – to write theme tunes for Tyne Tees children's television programmes including *Razzmatazz*, *Lynn's Look-In*, *Check It Out*, *Mad About* and many more. The previous year, Jacka had also been involved in a TV series called *Troubadour*. The connection came through an old Downtown Faction roadie who had also been at art college and later a journalist at the BBC.

'The idea was to have songs on a minstrel-type basis and they thought mandolin and harmonica would be nice instruments to use. My friend asked me to help and write some of the subject material. That was the hardest part because trying to write songs about a one-way system or a new shopping arcade was a killer. It was quite a challenge, but not very interesting. I needed the money and it was better than cleaning windows.'

Rod had been busy too, since his first tour with Michael Chapman in 1974. He had already been rehearsing with Ralph's band when 'Streets…' had been a surprise hit and, although Ralph had done the subsequent tour (with Jack the Lad) solo, the planned band tour went ahead in early 1975. Shortly after, old mate Rab Noakes invited Rod to join a band he had put together around the time of his 'Never Too Late' album that year. Rab had drafted in Charlie Harcourt, whom he had known from the Mk II band and the drummer was Pick Withers, later of Dire Straits. He and Rod made a formidable rhythm section.

'Not long before, I'd been out for a drink with Rab, Joe Egan and a couple of the other lads from Stealers Wheel,' explained Rod. 'Rab gave me a copy of the album, which had "Drunk Again" on it. I went home, played it and thought, "this is my next job." At the first rehearsals it was obvious that Rab had given everyone a copy

Left to right:- Marty Craggs, Colin Mason, Ray Jackson, Barry Spence, Charlie Harcourt.

HARCOURT'S HEROES.

Few people can have failed to notice that lurking somewhere in the depths of the North-East is a group of gentlemen going under the name of Harcourt's Heroes. Spare pieces of wall and assorted hoardings announce their local appearances in beautiful shades of day-glo and it would be an extremely unlucky person that has so far missed out on the opportunity of seeing what is fast becoming the area's fave rave. Over the past three months, every night has been gig night for Harcourt's Heroes, allowing them to develop their extremly tasty music and catch a loyal following at the same time.

So, who are Harcourt's Heroes? The 'Harcourt' in the name refers of course to Charlie Harcourt, for many years a familiar figure to Geordie rock afficianados. During the latter part of the sixties Charlie worked with The Junco Partners - a name that is almost as much a part of local folklore as The Animals or Lindisfarne. After the termination of The Juncos Charlie found himself doing a short stint with ex-Nice man, Lee Jackson's Jackson Heights and it was Lee who prompted a sharp turn in Charlie's career. Lee put Charlie in touch with manager Mike Jeffries, who was involved with a touring package of soul duo Jimmy and Bella and the now almost forgotten classic American band, Cat Mother and the All Night Newsboys. Charlie became one of Jimmy and Bella's

---

* Formerly of Beckett (with Terry Wilson-Slesser, who went on to Back Street Crawler with Paul Kossoff), Robert Barton released a single in 1975, called 'Benwell Lad', dedicated to Alan Hull. Jacka and featuring both Alan and Jacka. During the early 1990s, Robert accompanied Bert Jansch on tour.

** Jacka had originally played on a Long John Baldry album called 'It Ain't Easy'. Baldry had seen him with Lindisfarne at the Marquee when they first went to London. 'He asked me afterwards if I'd like to do a session with an acoustic slide player called Sam Lee, who was in his band. One side of the album was to be produced by Rod Stewart and the other by Elton John, who were both in Steampacket with Baldry.' Rod Stewart then heard Jacka play mandolin and a few months later, asked him to play on 'Every Picture Tells A Story'. Jacka was paid £15 for the two tracks: the album topped the transatlantic charts.

of the album – everybody had learned it – because he said, "Shall we try so-an'-so?" and everybody knew it. It was brilliant.'

After rehearsals in Tynemouth, Noakes and band went out on tour with labelmates Greenslade – a strange combination but, as Rab pointed out, 'Warners bankrolled it. We were very well looked after in that respect. That was quite a nice little outing, with some nutty bits of behaviour.'

On one occasion at Manchester Free Trade Hall, 'We were sitting in this room at the foot of the stairs that went up to the stage while Greenslade were still on. There's this bit near the end of the set when this massive gong went off. All of a sudden, Rod let out this almighty excited yell, as he's running back down the stairs to us: "The roadie plays the gong – it's the fuckin' *roadie* who plays the gong!".'

Right: Jack the Lad in festive mode at Reading. Ray stands behind Mitch with the cutout while Walter, Phil and Si express satisfaction.

The same band played live on the *Old Grey Whistle Test*, direct from Studio A in Glasgow, on a Scottish special that also included the Sensational Alex Harvey Band – the historic performance of 'Delilah' as featured on *Sounds Of The Seventies* – and studio interviews with Nazareth's Dan McCafferty and Gallagher and Lyle. During the summer of 1975, Rod and Pick found time to play on one track from Prelude's album, 'Owlcreek Incident', before Rod took off on tour once again to Germany with Michael Chapman.

That same summer, Rod was also invited to produce Bert Jansch's third album for Charisma, 'A Rare Conundrum', and was delighted – as he explained in his notes for Bert's 'Three Chord Trick' in 1992 – 'to find myself presiding over a return to the more familiar side of Bert, with an emphasis on acoustic sounds, traditionally-inspired material and plenty of guitar.' The nucleus of the band was Bert, Rod and Pick, with contributions from Ralph on harmonica, fiddle player Mike Piggot and Rod's old mate from Newcastle, Dave Bainbridge – who been working with Prelude – on Fender Rhodes piano.

In November the band played three weeks of gigs in Denmark and Sweden, Martin Jenkins of Hedgehog Pie filling in for Mike Piggot. It was in Stockholm where Rod first met Marie McKidd, a Swedish girl married to Robin McKidd of Scottish band High Speed Grass and a good friend of Rab Noakes. Robin had backed Rab on the 1972 Lindisfarne-Genesis tour, while Rod and Pick had also done a couple of gigs with High Speed Grass around that time.

Right: Jack the Lad plus special guest rock the Hortense Festival in Norway : from left, Walter, Jacka and Mitch.

'I had been speaking to Robin on the phone while he was away touring,' explains Marie. 'He told me that some very great friends of his were coming over and said I should check them out, so I went along.' Later, some time after Marie's divorce from Robin, Rod and Marie met again and have been together ever since. Bert recalls that 'Scandinavia was really the only time we actually got together; where it worked, as a "band".' It seemed clear that since leaving Jack the Lad Rod had established a very fine musical reputation for himself.

As previously hinted, Si had matrimonial problems which led to his departure from the ranks after playing on just two 'Jackpot' tracks. The parties concerned tried to work things out during the course of three traumatic days at the rehearsal cottage in Devon, as Si recalls: 'We were upstairs trying to "work our thing out, man" and the band would be woken up in the middle of the night by the sound of windows breaking and people being thrown downstairs…terrible, awful.' It was a disturbing time for Si. 'The most harrowing portion of my life. I hate even thinking about it.'

Having split from both the group and his wife, Si linked up with Rod and Bert. 'It was like hero worship. At school in 1966, me and my mate Neil Rennie just used to dote on Bert and Davey Graham: "Dylan? Forget it!" So sitting with him and suggesting "Three Chord Trick" was a real feather in the hat.' Si played a few gigs with Bert and Rod, including Newcastle Poly, and was delighted to be along. 'I found a fuzz-box, so it was "wee-inngg…" and Bert's playing the opposite – very short, acoustic-sounding, "sproing-y" stuff. It was great.'

The relationship didn't last, as Bert was looking for something different in the studio. 'Rod came over and said not to worry. Exactly the same thing had happened to the guitarist before me. "It's very difficult when you're playing guitar with Bert Jansch," he said. I got on fine, personally, with Bert.' As Rod moved on to Bert's album, Si – still living in London – began hanging out at the various music venues in Islington, looking for work. One day, he was at one such venue, just down the road from the Hope & Anchor, he noticed an advert for something called the 7:84 Theatre Group. They were looking for a guitarist/singer and Si phoned them up the next day.

'I said, "What's 7:84 mean?" and they explained that 7 percent of the population owned 84 percent of the wealth. "Interesting," I thought. "That's not very fair, is it?" ' So Si joined what was a Socialist theatre group, funded by the Arts Council, which wrote contemporary plays, 'taking them round to working-class people who wouldn't normally be able to afford to – or be interested in – going to see plays.' At 27, Si admitted he still didn't know what 'Socialist' meant, but soon began a crash course which, he now says 'totally politicised' him.

The group also included several other interesting individuals, including fellow Geordie Jim Barclay, actress Harriet Walter and Colm Meaney – who many years later became Chief O'Brien, the new 'Scotty' in Star Trek: The Next Generation.

There was also a bassist called Gareth Williams and Si can recall being in a pub with him when he commented on an accappella song he had heard the Swingle Singers perform on Radio 4. 'For the next couple of months on the road, he would get members of the band and do things like "Da Doo Ron Ron"- vocals only, into the mic!' Gareth later founded the Flying Pickets, whose chart-topping success was based on just such a style.

Also in the group was Mike O'Neill, Si's best mate, who had come down to London from Lancashire with Georgie Fame and played piano with the group. Mike had enjoyed a hit single, 'Entry Of The Gladiators', as 'Nero' of Nero and the Gladiators, during the 1960s. '7:84 could be fuckin' boring sometimes – meetings every day, meetings about meetings,' Si admits, 'but it was also amazingly enjoyable. It was a great group feeling with 7:84. It was the kind of thing I'd felt with Lindisfarne and Jack the Lad.' Si was obviously very much at home with them.

During the first half of 1976, ex-members of the original Lindisfarne were approached by Andy Hudson, Director of the Newcastle Festival, about the possibility of putting together a reunion that summer. 'It was Jacka who said "No",' explained Alan. 'His advice was coming from Barry McKay and Barry was right. He'd said if Lindisfarne were getting back together again, don't do it for the festival, do it at the City Hall. I respected Jacka for his decision. He was perfectly right and I thought well, if one person doesn't want to do it then none of us can. Then Barry got back and said, "Why don't we do it at Christmas?"'

All the animosity of the break-up had gone, according to Ray. 'That only lasted about three weeks anyway. We had the same circle of friends, so we were bound to run into each other. Jacka was playing with Jack the Lad and I was playing on Alan's stuff and it carried on like that.' Word on the proposed show soon got out and, in November, the press announced that the original members of the band would be re-forming for two shows, at Newcastle City Hall on 22 and 23 December. It was also stressed that this was not a permanent reunion.

'On the night we all got back together,' Alan explained, 'we had all agreed on the phone to meet in some pub where nobody knows us. It was just a chat to see if it fitted in with everyone's diary,' he went on. 'So there the five of us were, somewhere on the South of the Tyne in a pub, thinking no-one would know us and we were fuckin' nearly mobbed! Faces turning round, people asking for autographs. I think it was Rod who said that it was the first time the five of us had sat down with nobody else since '72! We got on so well. We decided there and then to do it – as a one-off.'

There was naturally huge interest from TV and the BBC planned both a documentary and a recording of the shows, Metro Radio broadcasting live with repeats later. Such was the response that a third show had to be added at 6pm on the second day. The band met for rehearsals at Alan's house in Whickham to re-learn the old songs, as he recalls. 'We had to put some of the old records on to remember some of them and everybody said, "Hey, that's fuckin' great, that, innit?" It was back to the joyousness of it.'

For Si, 'There was absolutely no bad feeling left whatsoever. I hadn't seen the lads for three years. It was like, "Alright Alan? Alright Jacka?" – just like that. There was no void of emotion; it was, "Gannin' for a pint, then?"' The last days of 1972 were clearly back in perspective. 'People said things they didn't really mean. A fuse blew, it was reconnected. It took three years when we all went off and did different things and, by the end of that time, it was just nowt.'

Alan found the occasion strange. 'Everybody had done lots of good things; Jacka did a lot of good things, Jack the Lad did; Rod had been with everybody, being Rod – I'd been "Pipedreaming"... it was all very good, but it wasn't Lindisfarne.' As December approached, the various members returned to Tyneside from commitments elsewhere. Ray had just completed a Jack the Lad tour in October with Spl Enz, while the same month, Rod had recorded 'Tequila Sunset' for Ralph's 'Right Side Up' album, followed in November by a three-week Scandinavian tour with Bert's band; Jacka was busy with Harcourt's Heroes and Si continued his work with 7:84.

Rehearsals began at the disused Pavilion cinema on Newcastle's Westgate Road. Speaking to the Newcastle Journal, Ray spoke of the feeling they got began when playing again: 'We tried to analyse it, but we couldn't. It will be magic on stage together again.'

'I was nervous at the show,' Si explained. 'We all were. I just remember Ray coming round afterwards with the big handshakes – "well done, well done, well done!" – which seemed a bit strange, because we knew each other too well to shake hands with each other.' The *New Musical Express* review the show (albeit under a picture of the Mk II band) was ecstatic. 'How can you be objective about mass hysteria? All the misgivings were immediately removed when they took the stage; there was enough energy in the air to carry them through anything.'

The high points of the first half, as the review went on, were Alan's 'Winter Song' and 'Scotch Mist' 'After the interval, all hell broke loose. "Lady Eleanor" brought the house to their feet.; they stayed the and the gig was transformed into an occasion, with the band indulging in all manner of buffoonery.' Th included Si having his hair shorn of about two feet and then thrown to the audience and Jacka launchi into his harmonica solo, complete with impersonations of a London bus and James Hunt winning the World Motor Racing Championship! By the end, *NME* went on, 'there was no alternative but to smile, stamp your feet and sing along with them.'

Having given their all, the band finally left the stage. No encore was planned and they began to wa and change in their dressing rooms. The house lights were turned on, but still the audience stood their ground stamping and applauding. Not one person left the hall, despite a BBC man's attempt to tell the there was no more.

Finally the band hurriedly dressed again, having had a brief conference to decide what to do – and to tumultuous response, sang an unrehearsed, five-part harmony version of 'White Christmas'. The audience went bananas. 'We did it, it was wonderful – a few quid in the back pocket – and had a great time. Bye-bye – and off we went again,' says Ray, succinctly. That was that.

After the Christmas shows, Si went back to 7:84 and Ray returned to Jack the Lad, who were still very much in demand. Certainly, as Mitch pointed out, they had not been worried about Ray's involvement in the reunion, and Ray himself confirms that at this point he was still very much committed to Jack. Unfortunately, despite continued live work, United Artists pulled out. The band we contracted for another album, but it was not to be.

'It was a funny relationship with the management company,' states Mitch. 'I could never really figu it out. I think "Jackpot" sold reasonably well, but I was never one for the business side of it.' However retrospect, Mitch feels they went too far with the album. 'I think we all felt we had to go for something here. I liked it, but it didn't work.' A single from the album, a cover of Andy Fairweather-Low's 'Eigh Ton Crazy', seemed to capture the spirit of the band but, by the spring of 1977, Jack the Lad had come the end of the road.

The lack of a hit single was one vital part, but it was all the more disappointing as Jack the Lad ha long since come out from under the shadow of the 'old' band. In fact, they had remained together lon than the both the original and Mk II bands, producing a greater amount of studio material. Following one final show in Newcastle at the Mayfair Ballroom, the last performance came just down the road o Teesside, at Redcar's Coatham Bowl.

Alan, meanwhile, had been recording tracks for his solo album deal with Rocket and Ray had bee recording with the band, along with Kenny Craddock, Peter Kirtley, Colin Gibson and another drumm Terry Popple, who had been in Snafu with Colin. 'At the same time,' Alan recalled, 'Kenny had a ban called Radiator and they wanted me in because they wanted the songs and a proper frontman.'

Kenny had drawn together the same group of musicians that were playing on Alan's sessions and when his band began playing live and using Alan's songs, a Radiator album started to become more

ely. 'I remember I scared the shit out of this MD at Rocket,' Alan explains. 'He said I had to have a
oducer and the guy I wanted was Jimmy Horowitz; but even though Jimmy and I got on great, he
asn't allowed to do it because of personal reasons. So I was landed with Norman Smith – who
gineered the Beatles and Pink Floyd – and he was there as producer on the first day of recording at
ident, with a great engineer called Peter Kelsey.'

The first song recorded was 'Dancing On The Judgement Day'. 'Me and the boys downstairs –
vallop, wallop, wallop" – and I'm saying to Peter, "Cop a lug to this"…and this guy, Norman Smith, is
:ting in the corner and we said, "What do you think?" He just looked at us as if to say, "Who are you?"
 I said, "We think it's fine" and we just carried on. He never turned up the next day. Another
oducer walks out the door!'

As Radiator continued to play more shows, Alan admitted working with the band
as giving him the buzz for playing live again – but all was not
itirely comfortable. 'There was a lot of pressure on me as the
ontman, because it was the first time I hadn't had Jacka with me; but I
ally didn't mind – I enjoyed it. The band was cookin' – really good. I
ways thought that Radiator would be like a British version of Steely
an.' In May, both Radiator and Harcourt's Heroes appeared together at
e City Hall. *

Rod, meanwhile, was as busy as ever. The tangled web that included
alph, Bert, Rab and Michael had been very good to him. After the
ndisfarne shows at Christmas, he returned to Scandinavia with Michael
napman in January 1977. They travelled in 'Hartley's Ark', a Transit pick-
 with an ornate wood panel at the back constructed by drummer Keef
artley. 'He wanted to be a builder and a rock'n'roller at the same time,'
ughs Rod.

Chapman's memories are bleaker. 'That was the oddest tour in the
orld. Minus 28 degrees was the warmest day. We got one of the roadies to
rive us to Russia and we couldn't get in.'

* In the summer of 1977,
Radiator finally called it a day.
'It was a brilliant band,' Alan
recalled. 'I tell you, on stage,
with two drummers was
great. It just couldn't last
though. It was a big band and
couldn't get enough gigs to
make it self-sufficient. It got
great reviews in *NME* but it
just couldn't sustain itself.'

*Left: Ticket queues for the
Christmas concerts were
enormoous.*

*Below: Onstage at the
City Hall.*

91

As a result of all this activity with Michael, the trio returned for some festivals in the summer. Michael had utmost respect for Rod. 'Then as now, I still think he's an amazing musician. There's a bass line on "Northern Lights" that Rod played on my "Man Who Hated Mornings" album which is really simple, but I can't find it; which is a tribute to the man's playing. Whatever it takes to be a good musician, Rod Clements has got it.'

Bert, too, held Rod in high regard. 'He's solid and original as a player; he has a unique style. When I first met him, I didn't know he played everything, I just knew he played bass. As an all-rounder, he's great.'

During June-July 1977, the suggestion arose that Lindisfarne should return to the City Hall once again in December. This time, according to Ray, 'We thought that if we were going to do it again, let's put the tin lid on it. We never did a decent live album the first time round, so we'll record it this year; the band at its best, at the best gig in the world for it – sounding the way it should.'

Promoted by Barry McKay, four shows were announced: 21-24 December, but were to be sold by postal application only. The reason for this particular move was that 50 per cent of the tickets for the previous year's shows were sold to fans outside the North East.

Below: Ray, Rod, Si and Jacka in action, Christmas 1976. As the press advert (right) shows, other musical forces were also at work…

METRO RADIO
In association with BARRY McKAY
Present:

THE LAST CHANCE DANCE
LINDISFARNE
CHRISTMAS CONCER
With JACKA, SI, RAY, ROD and ALAN

NEWCASTLE CITY HALL
December 22 and 23, 1976

Tickets are available by postal application and are limited to
tickets per application.

Area seats ....
Balcony seats .... £3, £2.75 and £2.50
..... £3, £2.75, £2.50 and £2.25

Crossed cheques and postal orders only, made payable to M.
Associates Ltd., should be sent, together with a stamped
addressed envelope, to Lindisfarne '76, M.B.M. Associates Ltd.,
Box 1LT, Newcastle upon Tyne, NE99 1LT.
Please note: Tickets are NOT available from MET
RADIO, OZ RECORDS or the CITY HALL.

CITY HALL, NEWCASTLE, SUNDAY, DEC.
Doors Open 7.15 p.m.

THE ANARCHY IN THE U.K. TOUR
SEX PISTOLS
from the U.S.A.

JOHNNY THUNDER &
THE NEW YORK DOLLS
DAMNED   **THE CLASH**

Tickets on sale from CITY HALL BOX OFFICE
Tel. 20007. Open 10.30-5.30 p.m. daily

* In fact, Jacka finally left Harcourt's Heroes in November 1977. Keyboard player Mike Waller, who only played five gigs while Jacka was in the band and left music college on the strength of the work with Harcourt's Heroes, confirms that they continued until June 1978, with John 'Hutch' Hutchinson taking Jacka's place. During the 1980s, according to Mike, 'Jacka still enjoyed playing the Lindisfarne Social Club with a band of his choice about once a year. He always included Charlie H and Barry Spence and would chose some great older material including "You Send Me", "When A Man Loves A Woman", "Drift Away" and "Hey Babe".'

The band were approached with offers of substantial guarantees to play a full British tour, but declined. It emerged that they had received a similar approach prior to the '76 shows, which they had also refused as they felt such an idea would detract from the main reasons for getting back together at the City Hall. Following the announcement, interest was intense and several labels had come forward with offers. It started to become clear that these should be given serious consideration, but this was kept under wraps.

Meanwhile, as plans went ahead for the shows, a further date was added, making an unprecedented five consecutive performances. Banners went up outside the City Hall announcing the 'Lindisfarne Occupation'. The music press hinted at chances of a permanent reunion following the success of the previous year's shows, but in the *Sunday Sun* on 11 December the question of the band reforming permanently was vehemently denied, Alan stating that such a reunion 'would be like Ena Sharples going back to *Coronation Street* after five years in repertory.' Meanwhile, Radiator's album 'Isn't It Strange' was prepared for release on Elton John's Rocket label.

Following the demise of Jack the Lad, Ray had moved on to Radiator, but by the summer, he had knocked his involvement with them on the head. Jacka, on the other hand said, 'There is no way the band will get together again. I am quite adamant I would not be part of a reformed Lindisfarne.'

He went on to confirm his commitment to Harcourt's Heroes, stating that 'I have stuck it out for a long time with my own career, done a lot of groundwork and I think I'm going to crack it next year. A re-formation would be purely a nostalgia thing and I think Christmas concerts are enough to satisfy that. We split up in 1972 because we were not creating any more.' *

On Christmas Eve, as the Island Mobile stood outside recording, old mate Mike Elliott, acting as Santa, introduced the band to a huge applause and, as this writer noted in the 1996 CD reissue, 'It was to be a very special night indeed. When you listen to the opening bars of "Lady Eleanor", there is no doubt that this is the beginning of something wonderful.'

All the vital ingredients that combine to make Lindisfarne's unique musical recipe were thrown into the pot: Rod's homage to Dylan, 'Road To Kingdom Come'; Si's curiously quirky 'Uncle Sam'; Alan's truly moving 'Winter Song' – perhaps the epitome of his brilliant knack of combining social commentary and melody. Then there was Jacka's amazing blues harp, nodding firmly in the direction of his idols in Chicago and the Mississippi delta, and then, the stark jazz overtones of Rod's bass on 'Dingly Dell' .

Along for the party too, were the Killingworth Sword Dancers, who contributed a unique 'performance' during 'We Can Swing Together', while another highlight was the inclusion of a live brass section for 'All Fall Down'. The shows were another great success – and the recording a very fine live document of the band.

Right: Jack the Lad's final gig at Redgar Bowl, 1977. The unfamiliar face (right) is drummer Eric Green.

Chapter NINE

BACK – AND FOURTH

In January 1978, Lindisfarne quietly disappeared to Surrey Sound Studios to see what they would sound like with new songs 'because we hadn't done anything new,' explained Ray. 'It was a traumatic period – we didn't know if we were going to like it.' Alan recalled of the time: 'When something's not working, it's not working; but when something's *nearly* working, you can work on it – that's what we did at Surrey Sound.'

Inside the studio, where the Police had recorded, the band cut four tracks*, 'two of which were really good,' as Ray recalls. These were 'Juke Box Gypsy' and 'Woman', both written by Alan. With Barry McKay now their manager, Lindisfarne decided to shop around for a deal, and it was crucial that, if a permanent reunion were to happen, it had to based on new, quality material.

Time was booked for the band to go into Rockfield Studios in Monmouth, Wales, having clinched a deal with Gus Dudgeon, who had produced all the classic Elton John material. Gus loved the quality of the tape and, as a bonus, had wanted to produce the band since he first heard 'Lady Eleanor'. 'Because we hadn't worked together for such a long time,' Ray explained, 'we got Gus in because he would be someone at the helm and would pull all the bits together.'

Before starting work with Dudgeon, the band put down four tracks themselves during the month of rehearsals at Rockfield. These were two songs from Si – 'Stick Together'** and 'See How They Run' – one co-written by Jacka and Charlie Harcourt, 'When It Gets The Hardest', and Alan's anthem in honour of the Jarrow March, 'Marshall Riley's Army'.

'There was no trepidation for me, going into that album,' Si explains. 'I'd done a lot of writing with 7:84 and I think out of five productions I did with them, a lot of other people in the 7:84 band and in the cast learned a lot from my experience as a songwriter. So I had come out of what was for me a very intense songwriting period.'

In Gus Dudgeon, the band were working with a perfectionist. 'I remember he took two days just trying to get a snare sound,' Ray recalls. 'He had me up the wall! We tried about 15 different snare drums and God knows how many different heads. Now you could just sample it, but then, everything had to be miked up.'

Right: With producer Gus Dudgeon (foreground) at his studio, The Mill, Cookham.

As Lindisfarne finished rehearsing one day around 5.30pm with Gus due to arrive at six, Alan took out his songbook and sat down behind the piano. 'Laidlaw says, "What's this one here?" So I said, "Nah. It's not right. It's not a proper song – it's not even finished." As I started, Jacka and Si wandered in and, when it came to the chorus, they just automatically joined in with the Lindisfarne "sweet and sour" harmonies. Just as that happened, the door opened and there was Gus Dudgeon. "Carry on," he says. We finished the song and then he said, "Hello, I'm Gus. That's the single – we'll do that tomorrow" – and we did.'

Gus Dudgeon confirms the event. 'There have only been two occasions for me when the hit song has been written during the sessions; once was with Chris Rea with "Fool (If You Think It's Over)" and the first time, when Alan Hull wrote "Run For Home" while I was driving to the sessions.'

Rick Blaskey, marketing manager at their new label, Phonogram, remembers the period well. 'My first meeting with McKay was memorable. I was utterly won over by his total and utter – but quiet – confidence and conviction in his band. In his mind, they had it all together, they would deliver on all sides; it was simply a question of making sure the record company reflected and represented the band with the same commitment, enthusiasm, determination and attitude.'

The album was completed before the record deal was signed, allowing the band to launch their new single on the wave of publicity their permanent reunion inspired. On 18 April came the unique announcement 'Lindisfarne are back together again and their new single is out tomorrow' – and 'Run For Home'/'Stick Together' duly followed. 'The first thing people knew about it was on the telly on the Friday night; on the Saturday, it was in the shops. People around the area had heard, but not *that* many.'

In the midst of the punk explosion, the success of 'Run For Home' was remarkable. Finally entering the Top 10, the single remained in the charts for 16 weeks – longer than anyone else except John Travolta and Boney M! – selling 250,000 copies by September and winning a silver disc. 'It was the perfect song,' Ray insists. 'Its lyric stirred something in everyone – no matter where you were from, or where you were returning to.'

Lindisfarne learned a lot from Dudgeon, though the fact that he was a slow, meticulous worker did occasionally rub them up the wrong way. The band needed that type of approach at the time, as Ray went on: 'We'd never worked together for three years and we'd never really made a "proper" record, to be honest.

'The first three weren't made the way they are now; we just went in and whacked them down. With Gus, it was very much the methodical way, which we weren't used to, and we got very frustrated – it was, "Right, this bit doesn't involve me, so I'll go down to the shops in Reading," or something like that and when you came back, four or five hours later it didn't sound any different. *He* knew, but I certainly couldn't tell.'

Manager McKay had encouraged Rick Blaskey to arrange a press conference to launch the album, titled 'Back And Fourth' and Rick's memory is of being urged by Barry to think of the band much as the Beatles were perceived, 'with very separate personalities, persona and roles'. Meeting them all individually for the first time bore out Barry's claim. 'How such disparate individuals could create such musical harmony is purely down to *chemistry*!'

All the songs bar two were Alan Hull's, the exceptions Jacka and Charlie's 'King's Cross Blues' and 'Warm Feeling'; this latter instantly became a live favourite. Reviews of the May tour were extremely encouraging, the *Newcastle Evening Chronicle* noting the new material played at the City Hall evidenced 'a sharper, bluesy feel to Lindisfarne.' Ray's description of the album at the time reflected the deliberate attempt to make an American-sounding record: 'a Geordie version of Fleetwood Mac'.

* One of the other songs, 'Reunion', surfaced much later on one of Virgin's two rarities collections, 'Buried Treasures'. 'Everybody was writing songs,' recalls Alan of the time. 'We even did one together. Si had this little tune from the 7:84 Theatre Group, so we said, "That's all right, that. Let's work on it." We all put our penn'orth in.'

** This song was written with David Edgar while Si was with 7:84. 'It was felt,' Si explained, 'that after "Reunion", that it was nice, but it's sort of, "patting-yourself-on-the-back" song, saying, "Oh here we are; back together again"; a bit obvious. It was a bit Abba.' Si also recalls Edgar was not at all pleased with what had happened to the song. 'David really was an absolute genius; very professional. But he was pissed off that I'd changed the song without asking him. Unfortunately, when everyone was asked for their songs, I ventured "Stick Together" – but there was only two verses. So I went to the bedroom and wrote the last verse, which he thought was crap, of course. So we split the royalties.'

When subsequently released in the US, *Concert News* in St Louis agreed it was 'just right for the American market…they never lose that raw-edged Newcastle sound that so much characterises Lindisfarne.' The same reviewer highlighted 'Marshal Riley's Army' as 'the best song, classic Alan Hull. It's pure vintage Lindisfarne, the only track produced by themselves, and nostalgia for the group's past flows from the hard-hitting lyrics almost spat out.'

At a Hammersmith Odeon show in August, Robin Smith in *Record Mirror* said, 'Could they handle a gig at the prestigious Hammy O? Yes, Lindisfarne pulled 'em in. "Juke Box Gypsy" featured a gypsy flashing a G-string. It would have been nice had she not looked like somebody's grandmother… "Make Me Want To Stay" was a North East equivalent of an Elton John song… There was a well-timed blow between the eyes with "Lady Eleanor" and nostalgia really broke out of its cage with "We Can Swing Together", as the misty-eyed crowd jerked up and down. Quite a neet.'

In the midst of a predominantly punk and new wave line-up, the band also returned to Reading Festival, scene of one of their greatest triumphs, third on the bill under the Motors and Status Quo. Lindisfarne had planned to descend on their old friends from a hot air balloon, as Ray explains: 'Phonogram had this balloon they used for advertising and it was in *The Sun* that we planned to drop in on the festival from this. Sticky Micky was the pilot, I remember; Micky Glue was his name. I think it was too windy on the day, or something. We had every intention of doing it. We'll have a bash at anything.'

September brought a second single as 'Juke Box Gypsy' was released, coupled with 'When It Gets The Hardest', a Jackson/Harcourt song which had been part of Harcourt's Heroes live set. Rick Blaskey had begged to differ. '"Warm Feeling" had the continuity of harmony, melody and quality of "Run For Home" and would therefore hit the same market,' he explained. 'Everyone seemed to disagree, without anyone expressing the same conviction for "Juke Box Gypsy"… I lost the vote – but they tried to appease me by putting my good friend, Emma Jacobs (daughter of David) on the sleeve!'

However, the song was not without controversy and part of the lyric had to be changed to keep Auntie Beeb happy, transposing the line 'One more poke and she can do it all night' with '(Your magic medicine feels so fine)/You can be my dream any old time.' Just back from Rotterdam, where Lindisfarne had played to 100,000 people, Barry McKay said, 'The new lyrics mean the same thing, Alan has no objections to altering a few words.' The things you do for airplay…

With the release in November of 'Magic In The Air' – the double live recording of the 1977 reunion shows – the band set off on another British tour, consisting of 39 dates. Several days off were incorporated into the tour, another lesson learned from first time around. *Sounds'* Phil Sutcliffe said that 'Magic in the Air' '…in no way betrays its title; great songs, atmosphere, as if 2,000 people are trying to elbow their way out of your speakers, those immortal spine-tingling harmonies…'

Record Mirror recounted that 'The Famous Five are joined by a cast of thousands, packed like elephants in a broom cupboard' and that the album was 'an irresistible piece of unabashed fun and serious melody. The band are as long-lasting and reliable as Marks & Spencer underwear.' A single, 'Brand New Day', recorded with Gus Dudgeon in October, was also released to coincide with the album.

Support on the tour came from Mike Elliott and Chris Rea, who had just completed his debut album 'Whatever Happened To Benny Santini?', also produced by Dudgeon. *** The first date of the tour, at Oxford Poly, was broadcast as part of TV's *Rock Goes To College* series and the following night, at Bridlington, Mike Cartledge was in the audience again to see the return of his heroes.

'Mike Elliott was doing the fill-in after Chris Rea and he came on in his father Christmas suit and started telling gags. Now, someone in the band had one of these "laughing bags" and they had a microphone backstage; every time Mike was trying to do one of his gags, they would put this up to the mic. Everybody was creased up. So, towards the end of their set, during "Clear White Light", Mike appeared back on stage, still in his suit, with a load of custard pies and they ended up having a pie fight on stage. Everybody was covered in this stuff… then they all just linked arms and sang "White Christmas". That was the icing on the cake.'

Chris Rea also clearly remembers the shows. 'I still have many, many happy memories of that tour. Because we went on first, we were in the stage-door pub by nine, pissed by 10.15 – they always wanted a curry, so by 11.30, I was full of everything and keeling over!' Chris recalled in 1994. 'This I regret. I would have loved, now, to have sat with Hully – who could drink all night, easy – and talked songs and lyrics, because he truly is one of the boys who had "it". As talented as any of the American league of that time and in the Grand Prix of Formula 1 songwriters, he is up there with the rest. I've often stopped half-way through a certain line, while writing, and thought, "What would Hully think?"'

*** Chris had been well aware of Lindisfarne during their formative years: 'I first remember the band, before I had bought a guitar. When I think back, I can remember them giving me the idea that this "music stuff" was something to have a go at. It was, I think, the fact that they were musical, that is, the songs were great.

'There was a lot of bull and dross around at this time; the scene was exploding with all kinds of "let's be a serious progressive rock band" types of things, most of which were just opportunities for big egos trying to be rich and famous and hiding behind a wall of volume and talentless mush. Lindisfarne were different to these meandering headaches that sent you rushing to the bar in another room. They were good.'

Like everyone else in the entourage, Chris was the 'target' of some jolly japes. Ray and Mike Elliott took it into their heads on more than one occasion to dress up as 'Santini's ice-cream ladies' – an affectionate piss-take of Chris' family business – complete with pointed bras, some considerable years pre-Madonna. To wrap the month up, the band headlined the Great British Music Festival at Wembley Empire Pool (now Wembley Arena), on a bill that also included Chris, Mike Elliott, fellow Geordie John Miles and Bandit.

New Zealand and Australia were the first major foreign territories the band visited following their permanent reunion. 'The promoters put together about eight shows in February 1979,' Ray explained. 'There was one, in Auckland, which was designed to make the most money and subsidise the rest,' he went on. However, nature was about to interfere with the arrangements in the shape of a typhoon. 'It was rescheduled for four days later, but unfortunately, the only day they could do it was the equivalent of Independence Day, when everybody in New Zealand traditionally goes to the beach and has a picnic.'

In the days in-between, the band desperately tried to publicise the new date, but instead of the eight thousand expected only about five hundred showed. 'The people that were there had a great time, rose to the occasion and it was a wonderful gig,' Ray recalls. Unfortunately, 'this knocked the bottom out of the tour, so we had to abandon it – then they cancelled the Australian shows in Sydney, Melbourne and Perth.' The withdrawal of financial backing also included their air tickets. 'We had to wheel and deal to get our air fares to Melbourne for some unscheduled TV appearances, then buy back our plane tickets home from the travel company.'

On their return to the UK, the band recorded a version of 'Fog On The Tyne' on board the Tyne ferry for Tyne Tees' *Alright Now* as part of a series of Lindisfarne performances the show would feature when broadcast in May. Also included was a barbershop-style rendition of 'Down' from 'Nicely Out Of Tune' – now ten years old – recorded at Balmbra's Music Hall in Newcastle and 'Marshall Riley's Army'. Other television 'highlights'

round the time included Noel Edmonds' *Swap Shop*, *Magpie*, *Top Of The Pops* (alongside Rose Royce!); *Revolver* in Birmingham with bass player Dave Markee (Rod being unavailable) and *Cheggers Plays Pop*. In June, the band entered the festival season with a headlining appearance at Roskilde in Denmark.

A convenient gap in Lindisfarne activities in June finally saw the release of 'Phantoms', Alan's solo album for Rocket. Preceded by the single 'I Wish You Well', the sleeve of the album showed another Magritte painting which seemed to perfectly reflect its contents and emphasised the fact that Alan regarded the album as the follow-up to 'Pipedream', which had sold 100,000 copies six years previously. Several songs had been added to those used on the Radiator album 'Isn't It Strange' from 1977; an alternative version of 'Make Me Want To Stay' which had also been on 'Back And Fourth'; 'Dancin' On Judgement Day', 'Anywhere Is Everywhere' and 'Somewhere Out There'.

Self-penned and co-produced with Micky Sweeney, 'Phantoms' contained some fine songs, including the mesmerising 'Walk In The Sea' and 'Madmen And Loonies', destined to be regulars in the band's set. Reviewers generally agreed that Alan's quality as a songwriter was undiminished, though some suggested he tried too hard to cover too many styles.

The single 'Easy And Free', released in August, was the first evidence of Lindisfarne's new recording sessions during May and early June. Initial indications were good, with *NME* reckoning the single was what the Eagles 'would sound like if they had been raised on brown ale instead of California sunshine and tequila sunrise.'

The band had been keen to work with Gus Dudgeon again, but the producer was unable to fit into the band's schedule. 'After one album and then mixing the live album with him, it also got to the stage where we were getting a bit claustrophobic,' Ray admitted of their association. 'It was nothing to do with personality; we like him a lot. Mind you, having said that, the move we made was on to someone who worked very much the same way.'

The man to whom he referred was with Hugh Murphy, who faced the task of creating what Ray termed, 'a masterpiece… If you take the songs that Alan writes to their extreme and the songs that Rod writes to theirs, that's like two different bands; so it had to be somebody who was going to pick the songs to make a cohesive album.'

The recording venue was Chipping Norton, where Murphy had previously worked with Gerry Rafferty. 'I'd met the engineer, Steve Lipson, when he was 15 and I started using him a lot at Regent's Park Studio.'

With this album, Rod had returned to the songwriting stakes, supplying 'When Friday Comes Along'; once more the durable combination of Jacka and Charlie came up with another offering in 'This Has Got To End', as well as Si's 'Dedicated Hound', which featured some guitar-picking reminiscent of a certain expatriate Glaswegian who had been to Gosforth Grammar School in Newcastle.

Si's self-confessed Mark Knopfler fixation was understandable for various reasons. One was that drummer Pick Withers had moved on from Bert Jansch and joined Mark's band around the same time that Rod had returned to Lindisfarne and was living in the downstairs flat that was part of Si's house in London. The fledgling Dire Straits used to come round to Pick's – and often Si's – to rehearse, as Si explains. 'I used to sit around with Mark and he'd show me how to go, "dukka, dukka, dukka" and I'd go – "Do that again?" He showed me loads of tricks.' *

To further extend the Knopfler connection, it seemed that Mark had actually approached Rod to join his band. Rab Noakes explains: 'Rod actually said something to the effect of, "I'm not really interested. I've had enough of bands – I'm just happy doing this and that." Knowing Rod, I think he'll never have regretted making that statement.'

One of the most distinctive tracks on the Lindisfarne album was the last, 'Good To Be Here?', a song of Alan's which seemed to capture the same mysterious ambience that had been evident in the title track of 'Dingly Dell'. It employed a tremendous string arrangement by Graham Preskett, as Hugh recalls. 'There's some nice arrangements on that album, but Graham pushed himself so far that he actually did the arrangements upstairs in the office while the musicians were waiting. I was so *angry* that night. All these string musicians sitting around, money ticking away – going into overtime – and he hadn't finished the arrangements!'

For Murphy, relations with the band's members were hugely enjoyable. 'Northumbrians are Celts, really, so there was never any hassle. They were always so smooth. That's why it's difficult to remember a lot; because you went in, did it, had a nice time, mixed it and that was that. Rod always liked the mixing; he loved having some faders to play with!'

The album, 'The News', was released in September and, according to Si, the idea for the title had another Dire Straits connection. 'They were sitting round during that second album thinking about what they'd call it and Pick suggested "The News". Mark said, "Good slant, but 'Communiqué' sounds better" and Pick said, "Nah – 'The News' sounds more direct." When he told me that and I told the lads, they said, "Fuck – let's call ours 'The News'!"

Reviews were positive, *The Stevenage Gazette* being one particularly good example: 'It's good to have a fresh album from this group who are nothing but inventive. The last track, "Good To Be Here?", deserves to become a rock classic… "Log On Your Fire" sees them getting back to the country style of rock, with some telling harmonica from Ray Jackson. There's cutting guitar work on "1983", a protest

* Dire Straits actually formed in Si's house, as he explains: 'Pick Withers – who used to be married to my wife, Regan – lived in a flat in my house between 1976-77. My mate Mike O'Neill from 7:84 also lived in the house at the same time as Mark had his band Café Racers – which also included John Illsley, David Knopfler and a drummer whose name I can't recall. Mark quite often used to borrow my amp and then and go and play in Islington at two or three places and stay the night at my place.

'When the drummer left, I said the drummer living downstairs wasn't doing much and that I would introduce him to the band. Pick got the job and then Mark said they needed a new name. Then Mike said, "I've had a couple of names in the back of my mind for a few years now which I think'd be very good; one's Just Add Water – that didn't get much of a response – and the other one's Dire Straights." Mark went, "Yeah – but with the proper spelling." So they were actually "born" in my living room.'

The NEWS

THIS WEEKS INSIDE STORY... ★★★

24th September 1979 to 23rd December 1979.

HEADLINE TOUR FOR LINDISFARNE

...Who is behind the SHOCK BRIBE THREAT

Welcome to the 1979 Tour which for the first time has been split into two legs (see full details on Page 3). The start of the tour co-incides with the release of "THE NEWS" which is the bands third album since they reunited in 1978. LINDISFARNE are pictured here making News after one of their recent appearances.

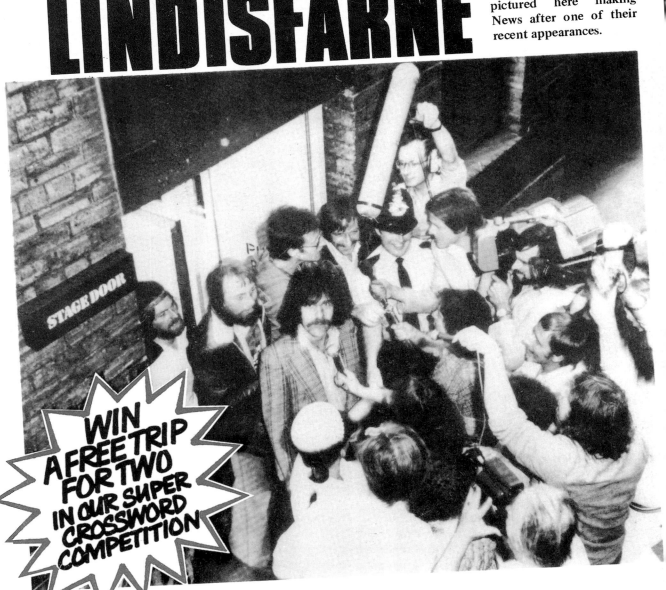

WIN A FREE TRIP FOR TWO IN OUR SUPER CROSSWORD COMPETITION

song, sombre and dark and marked by some excellent drumming.' Much was also made in reviews of Si's 'Dedicated Hound', which – in a touch of irony – was actually a nasty poke at music-press hacks.

Rick Blaskey, now a partner in the Music and Media Partnership, was also involved with 'The News' – but only for a short time before leaving to work at Arista Records. 'I remember an alternative title for the album. Going into the 1980s, we were thinking of "Eight Teas/Eight Tees/Eight Teese…"' he recalls. 'I also remember telling Barry McKay how marketable "The News" was as a title.' However, the eventual album graphics did not lend themselves to the spoof newspaper style of campaign.

The style was eventually used, however, for the tour programme as the band hit the road once again – using Pink Floyd's lights – starting in Belfast. Said Ray of the Floyd connection at the time, 'We've seriously considered an ambitious stage show; with all these lasers and holograms about, we're thinking of investing in a second-hand car battery and a couple of Davy Lamps!'

The video for the next single, 'Call Of The Wild', featured the band 'naked' in a cage directed by Geoff Wonfor, then at Tyne Tees, later of *The Tube* and the Beatles' *Anthology*. 'We had an idea in the back of our minds for ages,' Ray went on. 'A different setting for every line of the song. We just busked it the whole day, stopping along the way. There was Jacka on the footplate of an engine; there's a great shot of Alan singing – extremely nervously – between two elephants…we were all over the bloody place.'

Ultimately, for Ray, 'The News' was rushed. 'We made the classic mistake – again – of pushing an album out too quick, for America.' Although 'Lady Eleanor' had entered well inside the Top 100 there, 'Run For Home' had almost reached the Top 20 and at the time it was looking quite rosy. '"Back And Fourth" had done quite well – good reviews, ready to go and then, the usual way these things turn out some people changed jobs at Atco, our US label, and they rejected "The News". So we cancelled the tour, (which was pencilled in for the third week of July, according to Ray's diary). I wish now that we'd gone anyway.'

Barry had apparently done a great job and quite understandably, as Ray went on, he wanted to do

Top: A hitherto unseen promotional shot from 'The News' period.

Above: Producer Hugh Murphy.

things 'in style'. 'He wanted to go over and stay in the best hotels, travel in a big swanky bus…but once he found the tour support wasn't there from the record company, he said "Right, we'll not go over; we'll wait until support is there." Whereas, we wanted to go anyway and economise; travel in a couple of cars and stay in cheaper hotels – but he talked us out of it; probably for all the right reasons.'

Current co-manager Steve Weltman believes the band should have gone. '"Run For Home" was their biggest hit in America, but they didn't go there. In Britain, because you're not hip, the quality print media is not really going to give a Lindisfarne record any real space because there are 8,000 other young acts or records coming up – but if you have a hit in America, you're cherished for life. At that time – especially when you've got a band that good live – that's the biggest waste of the lot, to me.'

There was a lack of global perspective, 'a fantastic job done in Britain, but what about the rest of the world?' Steve also feels the band should have toured America immediately after 'Fog On The Tyne'. 'They should have been shipped over there and left there to gig for at least a year. The pressure would have then come off Alan in terms of writing another album.'

Below: Rod (left, on guitar) and Ray (obscured) play a charity gig with, from left, Rick Kemp, Maddy Prior and Michael Chapman in March 1980.

However, a definite consideration was a decision the band had made when they first got back together again in 1978: 'We made an unwritten rule,' Ray explained, 'that we would never knowingly lose money. So much money went out the window the first time round – not that we were robbed. The truth of the matter was that we were on a ten dollar a day allowance in the States on our first visit. Time

and time again, people have suggested a promotional tour – "It'll only cost you about thirty grand and you'll re-establish yourselves" – and we've said, "Sorry; we'll break even, but there is no way we'll go on a 'loser'. We've heard that all before." We'll go over on a low budget and play small places; we can easily put that together.'

Following the disappointing performance of 'The News', Lindisfarne and Phonogram parted company. This did not unduly concern the band and, as Lindisfarne began the new decade, they simply didn't worry about recording for a while. 'We were happy touring,' Ray explains, 'doing things our way and gradually getting used to the idea that we could do it the way we wanted; we didn't have to be at the beck and call and in hock to some record company.'

Despite their general optimism, the band also felt a lack of direction, according to Ray: 'Lots of bands of our age and our pedigree were getting nervous in the early 1980s – with good reason. There was lots of new stuff happening in Newcastle as much as anywhere else and you began to wonder where you fitted in the scheme of things.'

There were also news reports that the Christmas shows of 1980 would be Lindisfarne's last. 'I think it was all part and parcel of the same thing; "Do we still carry on doing the same thing for ever? Would people still be interested?" We were going through a bit of an identity crisis. We definitely felt it.' In February, Ray and Rod guested Michael Chapman's album, 'Looking For Eleven', recorded at Fairview Studios in Hull. The session followed a charity gig with Michael in March in the village of Greenhead, Northumberland, where he lived.

Following this, Lindisfarne returned to Tyne-Tees' *Alright Now* and, in April, from a TV date in Germany to Chipping Norton studios for a week of trial recordings with Steve Lipson, who had engineered 'The News'. At the end of the month, Ray was in the studio recording with old colleague Pete Scott. Throughout the intervening months, the band continued to play gigs right across the country, giving the lie to the already growing public and press perception that Lindisfarne only 'came out of hiding' for the Christmas shows.

Meanwhile, Jacka had finally released his first solo album, 'In The Night', with Phonogram. Hugh had been chosen as producer, with Steve Lipson once more engineering. Recording moved to Regent's Park, as well as a couple of sessions at Sarm East, while musically Hugh recalls 'We were trying to go for a "souly" thing. We were pushed by the record company to find a single, so that's why we did Del Shannon's "Little Town Flirt" because it was uptempo.

'The pressure from the record company was a real pain in the arse. I don't think the A&R head at the time – Rodger Bain – liked it that much.' The other tracks, according to Hugh, 'were all quite influenced by Bill Withers.' Other musicians featured on the album included Micky Moody, engineer Lipson who played acoustic and lead guitar and drummer Martin Ditcham, now with Chris Rea. Input came from Jacka's long-time partner, Charlie Harcourt, while Betsy Cook was also on the album. 'She sort of led the band on keyboards and, shortly after that, we started living together,' Hugh went on. 'So it was quite a nice time because of that.'

Featuring six songs written by Jacka and Charlie, other songs included 'Solo Again' from Colin Mason and Les Dodd, who had been part of Harcourt's Heroes – while Gerry Rafferty added guest vocals to a version of the Stealers Wheel hit 'Everything Will Turn Out Fine'. There were also versions of Sam Cooke's 'You Send Me' and an excellent, slow-burning reworking of Wilson Pickett's 'In The Midnight Hour', the album closer – which Micky Moody also recalls playing on.

Jacka's life-long love of soul and blues permeated an album that gave him the chance to play some outstanding harmonica. However, according to Hugh, the record label were going through difficulties at the time and it seemed the spectre that had constantly dogged him since the end of Lindisfarne Mk II had once again appeared. 'Phonogram spent a lot of money on 10CC and the album got lost,' says Hugh Murphy. 'It was a shame that he couldn't get into writing earlier and he got held up in all that and couldn't capitalise on it.'

Steve Lipson, on the other hand, did not like 'In The Night', as he explained. 'That album got on my nerves; it was not stimulating at all – except for one song I really liked. What was he doing recording this album? It was just candy floss. When Ray's singing with the band, it sounds brilliant. I thought he was unbelievably lovely. And talented.'

Harsh comments, perhaps – but it could simply be that, as Steve indicated, he knew Jacka was capable of much more. A television session at Tyne Tees during the end of March followed the release of 'Little Town Flirt' and a band was assembled for it that included the rest of Lindisfarne, plus Alan Clark on keyboards and Bren Laidler on backing vocals. 'That's when we first met Clarky,' Ray recalls. 'Our paths had crossed vaguely before, but he was with the South Shields lot – the other side of the river. We didn't mix much, really. There was us lot over here and John Miles' lot over there.' Then it was back to Lindisfarne.

In June, the band appeared at Knebworth Festival on a bill that included the Beach Boys, Santana, the Blues Band, Elkie Brooks and Mike Oldfield. The following day, they stole the show at Loch Lomond Festival, at Balloch Park – scene of one of Oasis' greatest triumphs many years later. There were a series of festivals throughout that summer, as well as a few shows in Europe and the band took Alan Clark along as guest keyboard player.

Clark remembers the period well: 'It was just before I joined Dire Straits, after I'd been with Gallagher and Lyle and before I worked with Splinter. I remember one time, Mike Oldfield cadged a lift on the Lindisfarne bus, from Belfast to Cork. I was sitting with Alan – who was getting pissed – and Mike was sitting with his girlfriend and I rolled this joint for Alan and he then passed it back to Mike, who said, "Ah, squalor, eh?" He was insinuating we could only afford the one. From that point on, he suffered a load of abuse.

'It got to the point where, because everyone was drinking, we had to pull over. By this point, Mike and his girlfriend were asleep against the window and all of Lindisfarne were lined up against the window, pissing up against it…quite bizarre.' Ray recalls one occasion when the band were rehearsing with Alan when the keyboardist noticed something familiar in a song they were playing. 'We were doing "Run For Home",' Ray recalls, 'when Alan mentioned he recognised something; it took him a few minutes, then he said, "Oh yes – I played this with the Bachelors when we supported the Pope!"'

Two sides of Alan Hull: belting it out at Gateshead's Rock on the Tyne (below) and hamming it up in the photo shoot for 'Sleepless Nights' (top).

In July, a single, 'Friday Girl', was released on the band's own Subterranean label. Produced by Steve Lipson and written by Alan Hull, it was the first product of the April recordings which would eventually result in the next album, 'Sleepless Nights'. The following month, the band appeared at Alnwick Playhouse for 'virtually no fee' at a benefit for the Cheviot Defence Action Group, who opposed the storage of nuclear waste in the hills. Also on the bill was Michael Chapman, who jammed with the band for three songs. This was followed by two festivals in Switzerland, culminating with a TV appearance in Zurich at the end of August.

It seemed the next album was experiencing a long gestation period since the band went into Surrey Sound in October for two more days' recording. As part of the Christmas shows in December, the band included a performance for the Variety Club to 2,500 children, repeating an event Lindisfarne had thoroughly enjoyed the previous year – part of the tenth anniversary shows at Newcastle City Hall, where they played a record-breaking 11 shows to 28,000 people.

In addition to the usual big London date, the decision was made to play a week of London club dates in the New Year. These included the Marquee, the Greyhound in Fulham, the Tramshed in Woolwich, the Half Moon in Putney, the Venue and Dingwalls, from where a review from Robin Denselow in *The Guardian* said, 'By the end, Lindisfarne had the cool Dingwalls crowd joining in. It must have sounded tremendous in Newcastle.' The rest of January and February was taken up with both college and university gigs, as well as larger concert halls.

During the first two weeks of March, the band retired to the familiar surroundings in Devon to rehearse for recording 'proper' at Chipping Norton with Steve, followed by three weeks mixing during April. July saw the band in Ireland at Lisdoonvarna, a festival later immortalised in song by Christy Moore, while the following month saw them special guests at the Gateshead Stadium's first live music event, organised by athlete-turned-promoter Brendan Foster. Also billed were Ian Dury and the Blockheads, Elvis Costello and the Attractions and a young band Irish band by the name of U2.

On the Sunday, Lindisfarne were supported by a line-up that included Rory Gallagher, Dr Feelgood, inger's Nutters featuring Ginger Baker and Fist, a young band signed to Dave Wood's new heavy-etal label Neat. Announcing the City Hall shows for December 1981, the *Sunday Times* had the llowing 'amusing' observation: 'The shows are as much a festive institution in the North-East as panic ⊔ying and being sick and will probably still be going when Toyah has graduated to *Give Us A Clue* or *rossroads*.'

Early 1982 saw the first shows by Pacamax, a loose amalgam of Tyneside musicians that corporated several members of Lindisfarne and who performed only covers of songs by their favourite ⊔tists. Pacamax's repertoire included such gems as Warren Zevon's 'Lawyers, Guns And Money'; ⊔ylan's 'God Gave Names To All The Animals' and Steve Earle's 'Devil's Right Hand'. Marty Craggs ⊔calls his introduction into their ranks – and, as it would turn out, a step closer to his ultimate ⊔stination.

'I had been in London after Harcourt's Heroes and there was no work up here – nothing on the level wanted to work at,' he explained. 'So I started a band down there called the Breakers, with a girl singer ⊔lled Margi Luckley from Hedgehog Pie. We started writing songs, got a contract from Polydor and ⊔ored a national tour supporting Darts.

'They were smashing lads and I got really pally with the guitarist, Rob Davis, who had been in Mud. ⊔e used to put this Sunday morning gig on and the music coming out of that was better than the ⊔reakers, so I used to go up and guest. It was a super band and we used to pack this pub out.'

Marty finally left London 'because I didn't like it; it was too big and I got lost – a lot.' He didn't like ⊔e beer much, either, 'so I came back to North Shields.' Pacamax were playing just up the road at the ⊔ark Hotel in Tynemouth, so he thought he would pop along and see them. The line-up was Ray, Rod, ⊔cka, Mitch and Charlie Harcourt. 'I was confronted by Mr Laidlaw and Billy Mitchell – who I used to ⊔e in Safeways – and he says, "Got your sax?". "Nah". "Well go and *get* it!" I lamely spluttered ⊔mething as Billy jumped in his car and took me to get my sax.'

On Marty's return, he walked into the dressing room, to be faced by Rod. 'Here's the dreaded Mr ⊔ements – whom I'd never met – sitting in the corner. He just looked horrible, frightening… I ⊔member Billy saying, "Marty's getting up with us" and Rod says, "*Is* he?" So I thought, "Oh my ⊔od…" Anyway, I got up with them and it was a great gig; I thoroughly enjoyed it.' Marty was in.

During the summer, Lindisfarne returned to headline Roskilde Festival in Denmark once again, ⊔llowed by Macroom Festival in Eire with Phil Lynott's Grand Slam. A short British tour also went ⊔ead during June, as well as a headlining festival in Vienna, preceded by a gig in Graz. The following ⊔onth, they shared top billing with Joan Baez at the Cambridge Festival, an event broadcast by BBC2 ⊔d which also featured Billy Mitchell in his other guise as part of the hilarious comedy duo Maxie & ⊔itch. *The Definitive History* of the festival, written by Dave Laing and Richard Newman, wondered how ⊔e duo had not become 'huge stars.' Maxie and Mitch no doubt agreed. However, they survive, as busy ⊔ ever, to this day.

Below: Billy Mitchell supplies the instrumental input to long-lasting music/comedy duo Maxie & Mitch.

Meanwhile, Lindisfarne bullied the audience to their feet in the heat of the afternoon, to dance and along with 'We Can Swing Together'. The band then found themselves among old friends at the first Theakston Music Festival in the grounds of Nostell Priory, near Wakefield. Other featured bands were Jethro Tull – by now including Fairport's Dave Pegg on bass – Ralph McTell and the Blues Band. It was here that Peggy received a punch on the nose from Alan Hull.

'It was at the backstage bar,' he recalls. 'No damage was done to the Pegg visage, luckily – and no ill feelings I can assure you – however, I do weights and row now, just in case…' The cause of the fracas is clearly known, but it may have something to do with a curry that Fairport and Lindisfarne enjoyed after the latter opened for the former in Manchester during the early 1970s. 'Fairport – according to Lindisfarne – ran out of the restaurant, leaving them to pay the bill,' recalls Peggy. 'I'm afraid I really don't remember….'

The protracted and fragmented 'Sleepless Nights' sessions had indeed been fraught with difficulties, not least Alan's hospitalisation midway through recording with a punctured lung received while playing football. The album had already taken around a year to complete, before its final release in October 198 'We kept going back and changing songs,' Ray explains.

Steve Lipson had been surprised that he had been asked: 'I got this phone call from Barry, like he w doing me the favour of my life – "We want you to produce the next Lindisfarne album." I have no idea why they wanted me to do it. I thought somebody had made a gross error of judgement!'

Steve has vivid memories of the various sessions: '"Do What I Want" was the first thing I did with them on my own after working with Hugh. Simon had a camera with a motor drive, so I said, "Why do you go out there and just press the shutter in time?" "No problem," he said. I remember that as clear as day. It was one of the tracks we did before the album.' '…Nights' featured some 'great Hammond from Kenny Craddock,' he also recalled.

Another song the band tried to capture on at least four occasions was 'Evergreen', as Ray explains: 'Alan really wanted it on the album, but none of the versions were right…he couldn't put his finger on what was wrong. So we just kept on doing it, until eventually, we thought, "If we don't put this album soon…"' Steve has a clear memory of the track, too: 'That's the song that sticks in my mind. Alan played brilliantly, but the music didn't come out right. The chords are quite complicated, but they didn't "speak well; so we had a melody and just a semblance of how it should come across.'

According to Ray, a version the band cut with Jacka's vocal while Alan was in hospital came closest what they were looking for…but was lost. 'It was like there was a jinx on the song, like the Beach Boys' "Smiley Smile" saga…' Another song of Alan's, 'I Must Stop Going To Parties', was, says Ray, 'the bigg hit single we never had'. 'At the time,' Steve notes, 'I thought it was too lightweight. Now, I think differently. I always liked the "meat and potatoes" stuff – "About You", "Easy And Free" from the prev album – because of the rhythm.'

Rick Blaskey had heard 'I Must Stop Going To Parties' before he left Phonogram. 'It was – and is – a smash song. Nobody has captured the mood we all feel at those party times, but the song was only thre quarters of the way there. I urged, begged and cajoled Barry, Ray and anyone else who'd listen – to spe time crafting it to find the missing "quarter" – and then, and only then, releasing it pre-Christmas. It's a song, but the worst two words in the English language must be applied to this saga: "If only…"'

Steve Lipson was able to observe each of the band's individual personalities and talents at first hand 'Simon and his wife Regan always reminded me of those couples in the 1960s who would both wear Afghan coats and had an Afghan dog to match! It was probably because they both have red hair and th had a red setter dog. They looked like a couple made in heaven…'

For some time, Steve didn't quite understand how Si came to be in the band. 'He seemed completel different to the rest; a totally different type of person.' Rod, as Steve saw him, 'was very dry – incredibl dry – and lovely; he's a great player, as well.' He was also full of praise for Jacka, his faith in his talents clearly restored after 'In The Night': 'He's such a brilliant mandolin and harmonica player – and his voi when it's sunk in there, as part of the harmonies, is great.' There was admiration too, for Ray. 'I think h lovely drummer. He just lays it down how you want it; straight. He's brilliant.'

'The intellectual "ladder" of the group is fascinating,' he continues. 'Simon never struck me in the sa way as Rod, who's a thinker. I have very clear memories of talking with them all around the kitchen tab but not Simon. Perhaps it was because Regan was there and he was more involved with her.'

A financial pecking order was 'so obvious. It was Alan – and then everyone else somewhere,' he reflected. 'It looked like life cost Simon more than it did anyone else. Ray always appeared very careful, did Rod – I can't imagine Rod going berserk. With Jacka, it never occurred to me to think about his circumstances, because his life was like a runaway train and Alan looked like he had loads of money. Simon always looked as if he was in trouble.'

Steve particularly enjoyed talking politics with Alan. 'God, did I argue with him! I always knew his politics stank; what he used to say was such nonsense, one couldn't possibly hold it against him. Comp balderdash… I remember thinking he was a "Red" – I didn't quite know what one was and still don't, really – but if ever there was one, it would be him! Do you remember Dr Zhivago, where Tom Courtena character "switched" half way through? That's fucking Alan Hull! Of course, he's nothing like that at a

His association with Lindisfarne clearly left a lasting impression. 'I learned so much from working w

*Practice makes perfect –
Ray (top), Alan and Rod
in rehearsal, 1979.*

* Steve would later work on many Trevor Horn productions, including Frankie Goes To Hollywood, before gaining much acclaim for his work as producer of Annie Lennox's 'Diva' and 'Medusa', as well as Sophie B Hawkins and Simple Minds.

Top: A wacky video promoted 'I Must Stop Going To Parties'.

Below: Ooh, cheeky! The controversial 'Naked Girl'.

them. There aren't that many artists who are prepared to let people have input and ideas. Out of everyone that I've worked with, I remember them the most fondly. I can't think of anything negative to say about them at all. Even the disagreements were wholesome; there were never any aggressive stances taken.' *

In retrospect, Ray feels that the band were 'a bit overawed' by working with Steve, 'and a bit frightened of him,' he continued. 'The album sounds like a sampler to me now. It wasn't Steve's fault, he was doing the best he could with what was available.' Originally to be called 'Party Policy', 'Sleepless Nights' gained considerable press, with coverage from *The Sun*, *Mirror* and *Star* – perhaps more to do with the very tasteful photograph of a naked model on the back of the sleeve!

Taken at Wallington Hall, a National Trust building in Northumberland, the picture was intended to take a tongue-in-cheek look at the whole rock'n'roll cliché of staying up all night. The Hall was left to the Trust by a family of strict Methodists, who were far from happy with the publicity and rang Rod – who lived not far away – to complain. 'I can't understand what all the fuss is about,' Rod said at the time 'There are paintings of naked ladies hanging up in lots of stately homes.'

US reviews of the album were encouraging and supported Kenny Craddock's view that Americans viewed the band without any preconceptions and despite the array of 1980s technology the band had employed on 'Sleepless Nights'. The Beatles references remained, alongside comparisons with Steely Dan for 'Winning The Game', written by Jacka and Charlie. Much praise was also given to opener 'Nights' and 'I Must Stop Going To Parties' – 'the perfect antidote to all that "let's party" crud of the past several years.' It seemed a shame Britain's press had not given the same consideration to the album – but the 'Naked Girl' story did no harm!

The year did end on a high note, however. A 29-date British tour was announced, starting in Liverpool, plus ten nights at the City Hall. The band got Christmas Eve and Christmas Day off… In addition, November saw Lindisfarne finally receive a platinum disc for 300,000 sales of an album released 11 years previously which had stayed in the charts for an astonishing 43 weeks – 23 in the Top 10. It was, of course, 'Fog On The Tyne' – the best-selling British album of 1972.

Chapter
TEN
AMIGOS

The early 1980s saw Lindisfarne take control of their own destiny as Barry McKay's spell as band manager came to an end. Certainly, as Si pointed out, were it not for Barry's business talents, their career would not have taken off again so successfully. 'From 1983, we worked as a co-op,' Ray explained. 'We used Barry's renowned business acumen, but had regular meetings to decide what we were going to do, what we going to go for – then left him to do it. Occasionally, he came up with something off his own bat, but it was very much a co-operative effort. From there on in, we've continued pretty much the same way.'

Rab Noakes entered the picture again around 1983-84, accompanying Lindisfarne on a small-scale campus tour in a Transit van. The tour was one of the band's regular early-year outings since reforming in 1978, Christmas-type dates later on being altogether a different kettle of fish. Rab recalls that, by the time of this tour, Jacka was perhaps at the peak of his performing powers: 'At one particular point, he actually got the audience to put their hands above their heads and stand on one foot! That takes a certain type of personality – he made people trust him.'

Having enjoyed a close relationship with the band for so many years, Rab was in a unique position to comment. 'Jacka is an exemplary performer when it comes to that; I don't mean in a manipulative sense – it's not as cynical as that – it's actually done with the best of motivations, in a generous and fond-hearted way.'

From something to fill in time while the band tuned up in the early days, Jacka's sonic impressions had developed into a huge repertoire, as Rab continued: 'He'd be walking up to the door of the disco – he'd have this beat-box kind of noise going on quietly – then the door would open and the volume came up. He could also do the noise that comes out of a Walkman when someone's got it on too loud; he could even do a tenor banjo with his mouth…'

One day, Rab and Rod discovered Jacka in the van with a loose piece of metal he'd found on the van's skin: 'He had found a way of getting a tune out of this and was tapping away, the way a finger piano would work. The guy's absolutely *remarkable*!' Such skills tied in with Rab and Jacka's shared love of all things mechanical – and, as Rab laughed, 'the love of things that are slightly off-centre.' This, allied to his performance skills, was what Jacka was all about. *

It was probably inevitable that members of the band would once again be invited to record with Rab, Ray and Rod forming his rhythm section for 'Under The Rain', recorded at Lynx Studios in Newcastle and produced by Rab and Geoff Heslop. It would be his last album for over ten years as he became more involved in radio production.

Shortly after New Year 1983, Ray and Rod also began rehearsing as part of the house band with Mike Elliott for his first TV series for Tyne Tees/Channel 4, *At Last It's Mike Elliott*. Also in the band was keyboard player-vocalist Brendan Healy, ** formerly of Tyneside band the Eastside Torpedoes, Billy Mitchell and Jed Grimes of Hedgehog Pie. 'Pete Scott had written half a dozen songs for it and he needed a band,' Mitch explains. 'So he asked people he knew and then afterwards, someone or other suggested we do some more.' The band, 'just a group of pals, really,' became the previously mentioned Pacamax.

For Ray, much of the first half of the year was spent either rehearsing or performing with Pacamax and Elliott alongside gigs with Bob Fox and Stu Luckley. In May, Lindisfarne reconvened at Rod's house in Rothbury to demo new material and in July, both Ray and Rod were included in Michael Chapman's band for a radio session in Manchester. At Leeds Festival in September, Alan performed as part of Pacamax, as well as playing his own set featuring songs from 'On The Other Side,' his first solo album for almost five years, produced by Alan and Mickey Sweeney.

'Evergreen', the song that proved so difficult to capture during the 'Sleepless Nights' sessions, finally surfaced, though whether this could be considered the definitive version of what Si had called Alan's 'Barry White song' was open to conjecture. With the exception of guitarist Peter Kirtley, the 'Pipedream'/'Phantoms' veterans were absent for the first time, Alan and Peter augmented by drummer Paul Smith and bass player Frank Gibbon.

'On The Other Side' also had the honour (as Alan would no doubt see it) of including his second song to be banned by the BBC – 'Malvinas Melody', performed as part of a live set the band played for Tyne Tees' *Around Midnight* series. During the interview section of the programme, broadcast in October, Alan was seen with a life-size cut-out of his idol, John Lennon, standing next to his piano. Alan's incurably romantic side once again popped up on the album, this time in the shape of 'Inside A Broken Heart' and the plaintive 'Fly Away'.

The venom of old was still apparent on 'American Man' and another classic Hull song, 'Day Of The Jackal' – a distant cousin of 'Poor Old Ireland', this time reflecting on the sad situation in the Middle

Right: Ray Jackson in characteristic pose.

Below right: Band on the Toon – Rod, Jacka and Ray onstage at St James' Park, 1984.

* Jacka also appeared on Rab's 1973 album for Warner Brothers, 'Red Pump Special'; coincidentally, Rab did a short UK tour with Lindisfarne Mk II at Christmas that year.

** The Torpedoes recorded one album, 'Coast To Coast', during the early 1980s and appeared alongside the legendary Ray Charles at the Knebworth Festival. Brendan also presented Tyne Tees Television's *Razzmatazz* music show during the 1970s. He has subsequently made a name for himself as a comedian, being voted Comedian of the Year in 1995 by North East Clubs; as an actor, appearing in many stage productions and the starring role of Tol in Catherine Cookson's Emmy Award-winning *The Black Velvet Gown*, in addition to TV roles in *Auf Wiedersehen Pet*, *Spender* and *Crocodile Shoes*. He's currently writing a musical with good friend Brian Johnson of AC/DC.

ast. 'A Mystery Play' continued Alan's love affair with string arrangements, on this occasion featuring members of the Northern Sinfonia. Sadly, despite the quality of the songs and fine musicianship, it seemed the music press and media at large had forgotten both Alan Hull and Lindisfarne. Nevertheless, the band continued to get on with what they were best at – entertaining people – and in October began a series of dates that would end once again in Newcastle, the day before New Year's Eve.

In the summer of 1984, the band were halfway to fulfilling an ambition when they appeared at St James' Park – home of their beloved and recently promoted Newcastle United – on a bill alongside Bob Dylan and Santana. Before the gig, Ray was almost ecstatic – 'It's going to be great; especially with the lads going up' – while promoter Mel Bush had apparently lobbied hard for Dylan to come to Newcastle. We didn't give his American company much choice,' a spokesman said at the time.

To complete the combination, Lindisfarne returned to Nostell Priory later in the summer on a bill that also included the Band – minus Robbie Robertson and Levon Helm, but still pretty special, as Ray recalled. 'Supporting both Dylan and the Band within a few weeks was a treat for all of us. Having said that, Dylan didn't seem interested and spent most of the gig watching Mick Taylor play endless guitar solos. I would have left halfway through if it hadn't been for my son Jed, then six, who wanted to see the lot.'

Also that summer, Jacka left Tyneside and moved to West Yorkshire to be closer to his wife's mother. Between July and September, the band demoed material for only their second album of the 1980s at the studio in Gosforth, just outside of Newcastle, and operated by musician Steve Daggett, whose girlfriend, Bren had been part of Jacka's band for the BBC session in 1980. Bren and Steve had also been part of a band called Stiletto.

'Steve was a fan,' Ray explained, 'eight or nine years younger than us. He was at school when all of the early albums were about and knew some of it better than we did.' Alan had been demoing songs at Steve's for a while and it was only a matter of time before the band would also gravitate there. Much of the material would not make the finished album, as had been the case with 'Sleepless Nights,' but several tracks later resurfaced on the 'Buried Treasures' collections.

As sessions for the album proper progressed at Impulse (still owned and operated by Dave Wood), with Alan and Steve Daggett sharing the production seat, Britain was consumed with the unrest of the miners' strike. Lindisfarne and Mike Elliott gave as much support as they could – collectively and individually – to the cause. Alan also became involved with the Red Wedge project, appearing live on stage at the City Hall with Paul Weller and Billy Bragg, and the miners' issue seemed to give him the opportunity to flex his political muscles.

Perhaps surprisingly given his oft-displayed views, Alan had not even joined the Labour Party until 1980 but, as he began to get more involved, he was voted on to the executive. 'Then I was nominated to run for the council,' he told *Magic In The Air* magazine. The NUM and T&G then said they would

Below: One man and his Avro Vulcan… The photo session for Alan's 'Another Little Adventure' produced some striking images.

Above: The cast of Geordie Aid included many famous faces. Mike Waller, writer of the single 'Try Giving Everything', is fourth from the left in the front.

sponsor him to run for Parliament. Although he did consider it – and could have had a safe seat – 'I would have been stuck on the back benches.'

A major change in 1984 came with the addition of Marty Craggs to the line-up as 'permanent extra man'. Marty, a very fine sax player and vocalist, could also handle keyboards and several other instruments. Just as importantly, he had a similar background to the rest of the band – something crucial to the essence of Lindisfarne. 'I had to do the audition, of course,' Marty recalls. 'It was at Mattie's Hall in Tynemouth. I didn't know Alan or Si at the time, so this was basically for them. I remember meeting Alan when Pacamax did Leeds Festival. We were in the beer tent before the gig and Alan was talking away…then he looks down at me and says, "So who's this awesome little sax player, then?" Once Alan found out I liked real ale and smoked tabs, we became buddies.'

In August, Lindisfarne made their contribution to supporting the victims of famine in Ethiopia, recording the single 'Try Giving Everything' written by Mike Waller who had played keyboards in Harcourt's Heroes. Under the name of Geordie Aid, Lindisfarne, along with 35 other North East pop and rock musicians including John Miles, AC/DC's Brian Johnson, Irene Hume of Prelude, Mick Whittaker and the Toy Dolls' Olga plus actor Tim Healy, recorded the track at Impulse. The purpose of the project, as Ray pointed out to the *Newcastle Journal*, was that 'we are hopefully going to embarrass governments into realising that things can be done if people want them to.'

Marty Craggs became a full-time member of the band in time for the Winter Tour of 1985, with ex-Byrd Gene Clark in support. 'I'd done two or three tours and lots of festivals and it just seemed to fall into place. The boys just turned around and said, "You're with us all the time – why don't you join?"' Acceptance by the fans was a major worry however, as Marty continues: 'It was weird for me when I walked out for the first gig with them at Leeds University. I was shitting myself. Y'know – it was the original members and all of a sudden, they're dragging this sax player on. I was a bit worried, but no problem.'

The die-hard fans were Marty's biggest concern. 'The musical side was great, it really worked – and the social side was marvellous, we got on great – they were such a great bunch of guys; but I was worried about that other aspect. They just warmed, though. All of a sudden, I had 18,000 friends. Lindisfarne fans, eh?'

Martin Sydney Craggs was born in Pendower, Newcastle, not far away from Alan Hull, in 1950. His first introduction to music came at school, when his music teacher played Ravel's 'Bolero' to the class. 'I just blew my socks off!' He went home, asked his parents to buy a copy of the piece and then proceeded to listen to it 'over and over and over again'.

His parents saw he was getting interested in music, 'so they sent me to piano lessons for three years, where I learned the "dots" – Beethoven, Bach, Brahms, Liszt – all the "business".' A move to Redcar on Teesside followed when Marty was 12 and he began listening to bands like the Stones and Small Faces. He was very happy in Redcar, a seaside town which had a beach and amusement arcades where the music blasted out on to the street. 'They had a disco in the Redcar Bowl and played music in there that blew my head off. I heard Sam and Dave then. That's when I became a frustrated drummer, but my Dad wouldn't buy me a kit.'

Young Marty would sneak into the woodwork room at school and make drumsticks to use on his 'kit' of pots and pans at home, studying every move Charlie Watts made. 'But the tips of the sticks used to snap.' At 16, he moved back to Tyneside and started listening to the blues: 'Buddy Guy, Memphis Slim and Howlin' Wolf – particularly Memphis Slim, because of the horns. "Mmm…*horns*," I thought.'

Then Marty began going to the Club A Go Go and there started getting into the unique sounds of sax. 'The soul sounds – the horns again – Junior Walker, Booker T, all those people. I remember seeing Roger Chapman down there when Family were a soul band. He was the lad, Chapman. Just watching him on stage – he used to blow away on the sax, swing it round his back and then grab the mike…' Marty is embarrassed to say he also went to see Geno Washington and the Ram Jam Band – just to see the two saxophones, though: 'I thought, "That'll do for me…"'

At 18, he asked for and got, a sax. Thirty pounds bought 'a beat-up old thing' but, as he points out, that was a lot of money in those days. Even his best efforts playing along to records in the garage proved that he needed lessons and, having grasped the basics, Marty headed off into outfits that were the very opposite of those his teacher had in mind for him. 'He was a great old guy, actually – a pukka dance-band man with a huge beer gut his alto sax used to rest on!'

At 21, he played with the Talcum Snakes, but it was not until he joined the Georgia Quintet showband around 1971 that Marty felt he had really started on the road to his ambitions. 'They were an eight-piece soul band doing the stuff I really wanted to play,' he recalls. 'They didn't do the clubs, either; they were doing universities and places like that. Neil Perry, the other sax player, was from the Junco Partners.' The Juncos were, of course, the band that had inspired Ray Laidlaw and Rod Clements, and Marty and Neil are still good pals.

He then began listening to people like Captain Beefheart and the Mothers of Invention. 'I think that's where I got screwed up a bit; listening to Beefheart too much!' When the Georgia Quintet split Marty joined a band called Halfbreed, fronted by Mick Whittaker. * 'I suppose that's where the Lindisfarne connection came in,' he points out. 'We masqueraded as the Chosen Few for a few years. We needed a name, so we pinched theirs. They'd split up by then, mind. We were *stormin'* places.' It was following this association with Mick that he then crossed paths with Harcourt's Heroes drummer Colin Mason; from there, London. On his return, Pacamax, which brings us back to where we started: Lindisfarne.

It was 1986 before the next Lindisfarne album, 'Dance Your Life Away', appeared, and the band continued to tour as widely as ever. In many ways, it was a typical 1980s album, embracing new technology – the band had never been afraid to augment their sound to help project the performances. The songs dealt with the same issues as ever and one – 'Heroes' – seemed to be Alan's impassioned rallying call to the miners' cause.

He decided to include the song simply because it had originally been recorded (solo) for the 'Heroes' benefit album and Billy Bragg had also recorded a song for the compilation which he subsequently put on his own album. 'So fair dos…' Alan told *Tracks* magazine.

'Although it doesn't actually mention the miners,' Alan went on, 'it could be about any kind of people who struggle for their rights; the cause that they believe in whether they have a good result or whether they have a bad result. The miners had the forces of evil lined up against them but they still believed and still believe their struggle was correct. "Heroes" turned out to be a fine rock'n'roll song and it's great to do on stage.'

Second time round, the song benefited from a performance of almost E Street Band proportions, hardly surprising given Marty's devotion to Clarence Clemons and Ray's huge admiration for Springsteen's drummer Max Weinberg. 'Ringo re-wrote the book,' Ray explains, 'but some of the drummers on the Chess sessions did the same sort of thing; solid and down the line. Max Weinberg does the same thing. I used to love Levon Helm in a different way. He was sort of a non-drummer – the way he played was great. He went with the flow, very sympathetic to the songs.

'I also like a lot of the reggae drummers,' Ray continued, 'and Hal Blaine, who played on the Spector records; he was on loads of stuff, like the early Byrds records. They were all great players; those records wouldn't have been the same without them.'

The album opener, 'Shine On', was written by Alan and Steve Daggett and its positive sentiments and seasonal vibe made it the obvious choice for the single that preceded the Christmas shows at the City Hall. Rod's 'Love On The Run' combined fiddle and synths and featured one of Jacka's best ever vocals. Another song that would prove a classic was Alan's 'One Hundred Miles To Liverpool', the second single and a heartfelt ode to a city the band have always had such a special affinity with.

'It was inspired by a couple of great girl fans called Sue and Annie,' Alan explained to *Tracks*. 'Every month or so, they write me a huge letter. That's where the first line came from; "Sue and Annie wrote

* Mick is a superb interpreter of songs, with a voice that, at its peak, could evoke Ray Charles, Van Morrison and Bob Marley – and that was on a bad night! Possibly the greatest Tyneside talent not to make it, Mick has had virtually all of Tyneside's musicians through the ranks of his various bands. At one point, he was almost part of Manfred Mann's Earthband; at another, AC/DC. He still performs to this day. During the mid-1990s, he recorded an album, as yet unreleased, for a label run by Ray Laidlaw.

me, they're coming down to quote me, know every word of every song".' The closing, 'Song For A Stranger' was probably the closest the band got during the middle 1980s to contemporising their unique sound; a slice of Hully whimsy wrapped in mandolin, harp, sweet'n'sour vocals with that solid Max Weinberg drum sound.

By now Ray had stepped into the managerial breach, having got more and more involved in the process as the relationship with Barry had progressed: 'I've always taken a big interest in the production of the shows and the liaison between the band, crew, that sort of thing, as well as putting together the tours. I was getting more involved in the business side and it seemed the obvious thing to do.' There is another opinion that says he got the job because he was the only one that owned a Filofax – that 'boon' of the 1980s…

In July, the band headlined Dock Rock in Hartlepool on a bill that also included the Wailers, Doctor and the Medics, Madness, Dr Feelgood and Steeleye Span. Lindisfarne's show climaxed with a laser display during 'Clear White Light' and in the shadow of HMS *Warrior* – the world's first ironclad battleship – the crowd lit dozens of campfires and candles in the darkness. In August, the band returned to the Cambridge Folk Festival, while that same summer saw a live TV special in Switzerland. Lindisfarne's British tour of 47 dates was the biggest undertaken by anyone in 1986.

'Dance Your Life Away's sleeve design – a young ballerina leaping with a backdrop of the Tyneside shipyard cranes – deserves explanation, especially since, for Ray, it didn't quite come off. The concept came from a local photographer called James Taylor. 'He was a real pro. He didn't want a mock-up, he wanted an August evening just before sunset when you get this beautiful-looking sky. Day after day went by with bland, grey weather and eventually we had to get the sleeve printed, so when he took the shots it was just a milky sky. He could have cheated, but he didn't want to compromise… It was still okay, but it wasn't as good as it could have been with a much more moody sky. It summed up this area; "you can't kill the spirit."'

A deal was struck with Priority (part of the RCA/Ariola label at that time) to market and distribute the album, purchasers getting the chance to win holiday accommodation in Britain, Holland, Belgium or America. 'The Priority deal worked a treat,' Ray recalls. 'We didn't want to get saddled with a deal for five years with somebody who might go off you after two – and not bother trying. So we do it project by project.'

Release of the album was slightly delayed when the master tape was sent to the wrong company in Japan to be remastered for CD, resulting in an October rather than September release. Since much of the fuller sound on 'Dance Your Life Away' was down to Steve Daggett's input on keyboards and sequencers, it made sense to have him along on the road. 'He played some guitar, as well as all the computers and stuff us old chaps don't understand!' laughed Ray.

There were other advantages, too: 'Sometimes, when we were rehearsing, we would be thinking out loud, "Who played what on this one?" and he would say, "You played *this* and he played *that*…"'

Around this time in 1986, Rod and Bert Jansch began a major tour of UK folk clubs as a duo, although Bert was in bad shape. 'I was in my heavy drinking days and hadn't actually done any club work for years. I remember the tour started off pretty shaky from my point of view, but as it progressed it got better and better.' The dates were preceded by an album, 'Leather Laundrette', which featured a superb composition of Rod's called 'Sundown Station', a country blues that would resurface regularly.

The title track, also written by Rod, came to him in a dream, while other fine performances came in the shape of a new version of 'Strolling Down The Highway' from Bert's 1965 debut album, 'Ain't No More Cane', and 'Brownsville'. 'I thought, musically, it worked out very well with Rod during that time,' Bert reflected. 'He was very creative in that whatever you actually do with him it will always complement you. He's very sensitive to that; whereas I'm the opposite…'

With each successive year's Christmas shows, the band would spend considerable time discussing ways of doing something different; whether it was the exploding vicar at the City Hall organ, the naughty schoolgirls or the Killingworth Sword Dancers… All had developed from the band's desire in the early days to give people a memorable show. The Zappa/Mothers approach to entertaining an audience was evidenced by the

Right: Steve Daggett's studio abilities translated to the stage, where he became the band's 'sixth man'.

114

clusion of people like Ron Geesin or Roger Ruskin-Spear during the early 1970s or later, people like Mike Elliott or Chas'n'Dave; the other element was the practicality of finishing a tour back at home in time for Christmas.

There have been other artists who have either toured solely on the seasonal aspect of their show, or specifically scheduled annual tours to fall on the run-up to the Christmas season. It could therefore be argued that Lindisfarne were simply the first – and others, seeing success, followed. However, it was Lindisfarne who subsequently found the tag most difficult to shake off.

The atmosphere of these shows could certainly be intimidating, as John Oley – then presenter at Metro Radio – describes. 'I had got in early and I was just preparing for my show that Christmas Eve (1984) on a shift that even the automated system would have turned down when I got a phone call from Metro's promotions manager, Dave Roberts. He was trying to explain, in a nervous, frenetic sort of way, that he needed a very big favour.

'Metro promoted the gigs, allowed the band studio facilities to rehearse and had also agreed to supply a presenter to take care of the announcements. The problem was that the scheduled presenter had gone on holiday and Dave desperately needed a replacement – me.'

Arriving at the stage door, the then-rookie presenter (now an independent producer) was met by Barry McKay. 'It was then that I realised just what I had agreed to do…in front of two and a half thousand people. When I met Barry, he informed me of something Dave Roberts had conveniently forgotten to mention; that I would have to make the announcements dressed in a Santa costume, with sticky-up hat. Surely this couldn't get any worse – *could* it?

'As I watched from side stage, Lindisfarne were on top form, and for a moment I became caught up the music; those classic songs and the amazing atmosphere created by that special annual event. By this time, the nerves had subsided somewhat and I thought, "Sod it! this is one of life's little experiences and, like it or not, I'm going to enjoy myself." I took my cue, but could only see the first couple of rows of people – the rest were obscured by a mixture of cigarette smoke, body heat, atmosphere and low lights. It's a sight I will remember forever.

'As I made my announcement and left the stage, the adrenalin was still pumping and I wanted to stay till the very end. But reality clicked in and I suddenly realised I had to get back to the station for ten o'clock. I walked back to my car as if walking on air…'

Above: Picturesque North Yorkshire was the setting for the Old Peculier Tour photo shoot.

With the 1986 Christmas shows, it was decided to give the entire audience a unique treat. None of the material written since the band reformed in 1978 had been released on a live record so, as Ray explained, 'We pre-sold the album to fans when they bought their concert tickets and got the recording gear in for nearly the whole tour. We said to the people who had ordered the album, send your vouchers in and come to the shows. We'll send you the album back in January – and *you'll* be on it.

'We turned the whole thing round within a month. What it meant we had to do, though, was pick the tracks up front, ready for the sleeve and the labels to be done up front too. The next year, we put out Volume Two, because we had more than enough material left over. We did it basically as a promotional device and then later put it in the shops at a cheaper price. It worked out great.'

Entitled 'Lindisfarntastic!' as a nod to the *Melody Maker* front page of 1972, the recordings were produced by David Batchelor, a Glaswegian who had worked closely with the Sensational Alex Harvey Band as not only co-writer and engineer but also producer. 'It was 1985 when I was first approached to work with Lindisfarne as sound engineer for their UK tour that year,' David recalls. 'The previous engineer had been with them for many years and, of course, the band were a bit precious about who would take over the reins.'

When Dave first saw the band he was a member of Tear Gas, who eventually linked up with Alex Harvey to become the SAHB. 'It was about 1970 , when they headlined a gig at Newcastle Poly, and we were one of the support groups on the bill. Lindisfarne blew everybody away; they had such melody and I remember the fantastic atmosphere they generated.'

Above: Tour rehearsals at Metro Radio, 1984.

After Alex, Dave produced acts such as the Skids, Starjets and Wilko Johnson but returned to live sound around 1981, having lost some of his appetite for studio work. 'When the Lindisfarne tour was offered, I had a gut feeling we would work well together. That first tour culminated in their annual Christmas concerts at the City Hall, ten days of absolute atmosphere. It was an incredible show, playing to packed houses every night with audiences spanning three generations.'

When the Christmas shows the following year were announced, Dave – who had continued to tour with them – was asked to co-produce the live album. 'Lindisfarne have a set-list of evergreens most bands would kill for. Great vocals, a natural harmony blend right up there with the very best, as well as very fine individual musicianship all round. From an engineer's point of view, the band were a real joy to work with as people and performers.

'The live arrangements were totally sussed; all the individual instruments sounds coming from stage were excellent – vocals and harmonies to raise the hairs on your neck, and a duck's arse rhythm section locking the whole thing together. Add to that no small amount of stage presence and wit and you have a concert that touches you with every emotion, like all the great bands were able to do.'

Alan Clark happened to be at one of the City Hall recordings featured on the album and when he was asked if he wanted to 'do a bit' at the end, he readily accepted. 'Then a week after that, Knopfler pinched him!' Ray laughed. 'He's a wonderful piano player; the closest in Britain to Roy Bittan and that's what Mark was looking for. Piano players are born, not made.' *

In 1987, out of the blue, Lindisfarne were approached by a TV-promoted record label to do a 'party' album of cover versions – a project that stood to make them money but put their credibility at risk. 'They were looking for a well-known band to do a party record of famous rock'n'roll stuff,' Ray explains.

He was keen for the band to be involved – for one reason only: 'We did it for the money. We were in a bit of a financial hole at the time and the album represented an opportunity for us to climb out of the shit.' The company wanted a double album containing re-recorded versions of Lindisfarne hits – the rest they left up to the band.

'We could pick 80 per cent of the songs, but what we had to give for that was that they chose the packaging, which turned out to be tacky in the extreme,' Ray went on. 'It was Barry McKay's idea and I just went along with it,' Alan told *Magic In The Air* magazine. 'My idea was to make it like John Lennon's "Rock'n'Roll", which was a labour of love, a beautiful album,' he went on. 'It was a mistake but you don't know at the time, you do what you think is best. It was a great attempt that failed. I don't think it did the band any favours either, it made the media even more anti-Lindisfarne. It was far too cabaret-ish.'

* Interesting to note, then, that on Dire Straits' 'Making Movies' the piano player was indeed, the E Street Band's Roy Bittan. Alan was, however, on board for the next album, 'Love Over Gold'.

The album, 'C'Mon Everybody', was described by one rock reference book as Lindisfarne's 'artistic nadir' and the cover photo – 'Courtesy of Club 18-30', for heaven's sake – was even more tacky than the most devoted retro freak could possibly take.

The fact that Lindisfarne were involved made it even less appetising to the critics. Nonetheless, the public bought it. 'It did remarkably well,' according to Ray. 'It sold about 50 or 60,000, but I reckon it would have done double that if they'd done a better cover, because it was a great record – real good fun to do. People kept saying, "Is this your new direction?"

'It was also a lot of fun to do at the shows that year. We did a lot of the material and hammed it up a bit – suits, hair and everything.' It was also one of the rare occasions a band has 'supported itself', as Alan pointed out, with the band doing around an hour of rock'n'roll before returning as themselves. One of the Newcastle shows was filmed by Tyne Tees Television and transmitted nationally on Christmas Eve.

The band's association with Barry also ended in 1987. Although his original management deal had come to an end in 1982, there was a further agreement that he would promote the Christmas shows for the next five years. 'So from then on we did everything ourselves,' Ray explains. 'I'm not a natural businessman and I must admit it was a big decision to make. I think the whole band is happy with it now; they weren't sure at first.

'It's about keeping everything tight,' he continues. 'There's no secrets among us. It cuts out the middle man. I know if an offer comes in I don't have to ask everybody; I know what they'd want to do and what they'd not because I've known them so long. I know the approach Lindisfarne want to take.' According to Ray, it can be better having a member manage a band. 'It's nothing unusual; Mick Fleetwood used to manage Fleetwood Mac.'

Given Lindisfarne's activities at the time, it says a considerable amount about Rod's abilities that he could also manage to slip into what many Lindisfarne detractors may term more 'acceptable' musical pursuits during at this period. 'I got a call from Bert Jansch to say that Mike Piggot had left Pentangle and would I step in?' Rod recalled. 'Bert wanted me to join because he was looking for someone who could play fiddle as well, but Mike's fiddle-playing was very different to mine – he was more of a Stephane Grappelli, jazz-type player, which I can't do. So I developed my slide playing in that style.'

Rod had depped once before for a member of Bert's band – in 1980, when Jansch was attempting to bring Pentangle together again for the first time in several years. Nigel Portman-Smith had been unable to make a short UK tour which went ahead not as Pentangle but as a double-header consisting of Bert with Rod and Martin Jenkins alongside John Renbourn. The relationship with Bert had never really cooled, nor was there any reason for it to; Lindisfarne was (and is) Rod's priority, but since setting out on his particular path in 1973-74 he's managed to satisfy himself creatively within and beyond Lindisfarne without any conflict.

From Bert Jansch's point of view, Rod was always reliable: 'He's not a soloist. He can create and he can construct – that's his strength. Someone who does a solo doesn't think about it – he just does it – whereas Rod would construct something that does the same thing. He's very good at layering. Plus, he plays his instrument with subtlety and colour.'

During 1987, both Rod and Jacka, along with Bert, Rab, Rory McLeod, Dick Gaughan and Pat Rafferty, recorded an album of Woody Guthrie songs called 'Woody Lives!', the idea coming from good friend and producer Geoff Heslop. Geoff had a long association with Lindisfarne and its members and had a studio near Rod in Northumberland. Geoff was also responsible for the illustrations in Alan's previously-mentioned book of poems *The Mocking Horse*, long since out of print.

The idea of the recordings was to mark the 20th anniversary of Guthrie's death. Naturally, for Rod and Jacka, as much as everyone else, this was a perfect way of celebrating the life and work of someone that had had a profound and inspirational effect on their music from as far back as 'Nicely Out Of Tune's 'Jackhammer Blues'.

It would be almost ten years before Bruce Springsteen would record his love of Guthrie on album and tour – and would even feature 'Tom Joad', a track recorded for 'Woody Lives!', in the album's title. What a tragedy that 'Woody Lives!' – 'A fine tribute packed with skilled musicianship,' as Chris Groom and Ian Taylor wrote in *Magic In The Air* – did not receive the critical plaudits heaped upon Bruce's 'The Ghost Of Tom Joad'.

In October, the BBC studios in Manchester was the location for an historic reunion of Downtown Faction as they recorded a session for Paul Jones' *Rhythm And Blues Show*. The Faction – Jeff Sadler, Ray, Rod, Jacka and Si – performed several songs, including 'Sporting Life Blues' and 'Loving Around The Clock.' The line-up clearly revelled in the occasion, Paul Jones highlighting on air the quality of Jacka's harp-playing. Si has another memory: 'Jeff's saying to me, "Go on – you do a solo, Si" and I'm saying, "I'd much rather *you* did. You've got much better ideas."

'So I'm sitting with the engineer while he overdubs his solo; so he does the first. "Nah. Not that one." Then he does another – the same bit of music, but completely different attitude – he's coming from a different plateau to play exactly the same part of the same tune. Chalk and cheese.' Si, like everyone who knows Jeff, is saddened by how rarely he plays. 'What a waste of talent. His mind's so sharp; it's *instant*. He thinks the music as he does it, I've never known anybody with such capacity for different styles.'

Virgin Records by now owned the Charisma catalogue having, as Ray states, 'bought the whole bloody company because they wanted Phil Collins' contract.' So in the summer of 1988, the band began talking to Virgin about releasing the first three

Right: Lindisfarne returned to Holy Island for this photo shoot to promote the re-recording of 'Lady Eleanor' in 1988.

Charisma albums in compact-disc format. They had been asked two years previously, but there had been a conflict with the 'Dance Your Life Away' album. This time around, the timing was right.

'We were asked if we wanted to remix them,' Ray recalls, 'but we said, "No. That's the way it was done then; that's the way we meant it, so it defeats the purpose".' However, the band did take the opportunity to shoot some new photographs on Holy Island, many of which mimicked the shots used on the original gatefold sleeve of 'Fog On The Tyne'.

The CD reissue of 'Dingly Dell' would sport one of these new pictures and, at long last, the ghost of the grey sleeve could be laid to rest. The issue had been so contentious that following the reunion in 1978, whenever the 'Dingly Dell' sleeve was reproduced for a discography, the American version, issued by Elektra, had been used every time. The band had wanted to use the American sleeve for the new CD, but were unable to persuade Virgin.

Each reissued title added relevant single B-sides and press response was excellent. In a meeting with Jon Webster, Virgin's managing director at the time, Ray also mentioned that the band had been planning to re-record 'Lady Eleanor.' 'They said, "Yes please, let us have it",' Ray went on. The new recording was produced by Steve Daggett and made available as a single in time for that year's Christmas shows.

'Lady Eleanor '88' coincided with the release of Strange Fruit's 'Peel Session' featuring Lindisfarne's recordings for the BBC in May 1972: the songs were 'Poor Old Ireland', 'Mandolin King', 'Lady Eleanor' and 'Road To Kingdom Come'.

While trade paper *Music Week* felt the contemporary 'Eleanor' 'added a new dimension to this unforgettable song,' it was difficult to tell if *Sounds* was just taking the piss: 'Quite frankly, an agoraphobic's nightmare – a vacuous, wide-open space of song…suddenly the chorus swoops down like some prehistoric vulture from the dark ages. *Very* scary.' Another time, another music paper…

Not content with all this activity, the band were then stirred to react to the alarming news that Australian brewery giant Elders – the company responsible for Foster's lager – had put in a hostile £1.6 billion bid for Scottish and Newcastle Breweries. The band feared that jobs would go as a result of any takeover. 'Behind the fun is a serious message,' Alan told the *Daily Mirror*: 'Newcastle could well do without any more job losses.' Thus inspired, Alan came up with 'Save Our Ales'…while sitting on the toilet!

There was no doubt that there was serious message to the protest song – in fact, one of Lindisfarne's finest walkin' blues, in the spirit of 'Meet Me On The Corner' – but the song was light-hearted. 'People have been singing our praises for years,' the S&N spokesman said in *The Star*, 'but this is the first time a famous group has actually put it out on record.'

The cover of the single sported a giant bottle of Newcastle Brown floating down the Tyne – with a lifebelt! George 'Porky' Peckham, the mastering engineer who had been part of the La Chasse Choir in 1970, was brought on board to master the single and was even inspired to etch one of his famous messages on the run-off groove: 'Dog bites Skippy'. Ultimately, Scottish and Newcastle won. It was a long way from the Brown Ale TV advert that Brethren had recorded back in 1970 at Impulse in Wallsend… *

With Lindisfarne's 20th anniversary (1989) in view, the previous year's annual tour was kept nice and compact. This enabled Rod to tour the States as a member of Pentangle, having recorded the album 'So Early In The Spring' (released the following year) with them. ** Lindisfarne's own tour included five nights at the City Hall in addition to shows in Cardiff, Fareham, Worthing, Woolwich, Hull, Sheffield, Bradford, two nights in Nottingham and the Town and Country Club, London. Jacka's plane sketch was left out of the City Hall show in deference to the recent Lockerbie disaster.

While away playing a week of dates in Italy in February 1989, the band found themselves together at a little café in Milan drinking expresso coffee and the occasional beer. 'We'd played four nights in this big club,' Marty explains, 'and up until we went to Italy we'd been scattered all over the place. Milan really brought the band together for a week; drinking together, playing together. It was really romantic, sitting in this little café.'

* 'We were hired to do this Brown Ale advert,' explains Si. At the time, Si was working for Dave Wood, covering speakers in vinyl cloth. 'Jacka had to go to the dentist, so he couldn't do it,' Si went on. 'We were hired as the band, so I ended up singing it. It was done to the tune of the Dave Dee, Dozy, Beaky, Mick and Tich song "Bend It". I think we got 15 quid each and Rod worked out we got paid 12 shillings per note. I think we had to do it in 27 and a half seconds to fit the 30 second slot. All Ray did was the bloody counting, and he got 15 quid as well!' Another thing Brethren and Alan used to do when 'we were idle,' as Si puts it, 'was to put music to lyrics. Dave used to advertise for songwriters: "Why not have your songs realised into music by our affectionate staff?" It was me and Alan, basically…' PS: Newcastle Brown Ale is often referred to as 'Dog'.

** The album included only traditional songs, bar two: 'Lucky Black Cat' and the instrumental 'Eminstra'. Both were written by the band: Bert, Jacqui McShee, Nigel Smith, Gerry Conway and Rod, who played electric guitar and mandolin throughout.

The meeting would prove critical. 'It wasn't like a 30-date tour when everyone would scatter and does their own thing, then meet up later,' Marty went on. The band reflected on where they stood in their career and came to the conclusion that it was time for them to collectively 'pull together' and return to 'songs'. As Alan pointed out some months later, 'Maybe it was the fact that we were in foreign parts, maybe it was the time of year, maybe it was the beer, but through the mist emerged a simple idea. Let's return to our roots. Let's go back to the essentials and make a record for US and the thousands of solid supporters we had back in England.'

As Alan pointed out, this required 'Songs we can happily play on stage without gimmicks. Songs that anybody can sing and everybody can remember. The first three LPs were packed with them. "Back And Fourth" had its fair share and the others a smattering. Okay, let's pack the record with belters.' Si, too, recalls coming out of the meeting in Milan invigorated: 'It was so uplifting and Alan and Rod writing together was all part of that "pulling ourselves up by our bootstraps" thing.'

This wasn't the only writing combination that emerged, although it was perhaps the most surprising. Marty continues: 'Out of that, Alan said, "Marty, if you've got any ideas, give me a nod." So I did. "Everything Changes" was the first, I think.' Once the idea sunk in, the band realised a September release meant getting into the studio in March: 'Everyone was charged up,' Alan pointed out, so it was with this positive frame of mind that Lindisfarne returned to Britain.

Recording for the album took place during the spring and summer of 1989 at Reeltime in the centre of Newcastle. The studio was owned by Steve Daggett, who produced the tracks along with the band and Mickey Sweeney. The new writing combinations came up with songs that proudly stood alongside the best in the Lindisfarne canon. 'Everything Changes', as Marty mentioned, gave him his first chance of writing with Alan.

'That came together in a bar – *quelle surprise*. Angela, the barmaid in the Tap and Spile in North Shields, was talking about her boyfriend, saying how people's eyes change; she was saying, "He's supposed to love me, but when he talked about me his eyes never changed, and that's how I knew he didn't mean it." So I thought, "Everything changes when you talk about someone you love", whether it's your mother, or your baby or your wife – your voice softens and your eyes change.

Below: The 'Amigos' band pictured at Coal Staithes on the River Tyne in 1989 included Marty Craggs and Steve Cunningham (second and third from left).

119

'I ran to the toilet and I'm muttering away, "Everything changes, everything changes…", singing away to me willy! I went back to the bar and sang it in Alan's ear and he went, "My house – tomorrow".' Marty was in a unique position to observe how Alan worked. 'That frightened the life out of me; to write with the great Alan Hull. It was an honour and a privilege to sit in Alan's company and work. I was in awe. The way he works; his big, dangly legs splayed out on the floor with his guitar. I gave him my idea a little nervously, to say the least. I fed him the odd lyric, the odd melody and he banged away on the guitar with those lovely chords…

'Then, the shyness rubbed off me, so I thought, "Right, let's have some more; 'Karen Marie' and all that stuff." That gave me the confidence to approach these two great songwriters, Alan and Rod – who I hold in my heart.' The much-anticipated Alan and Rod combination came up with 'Working For The Man', and Alan explained in that year's tour programme how this collaboration came about.

Right: Three Amigos…an outtake from the album sleeve photo session.

'Clem (the gentleman of the band) said he had a song that needed a middle bit. So, I went back to my attic. The song is there. Typical Clem. To me, the song says it all. Me and Rod over a hot four-track and it's done. Middle bit works fine – off to the pub.' While Si was every bit as enthusiastic with the approach to the album, he admits that writing was not as easy for him.

'I was at least a couple of hours' drive away, so it wasn't practical for me to slip into a similar situation. I had written five or six songs down at Thornton-le-Dale on the edge of the Yorkshire Moors where I lived and found a wonderful place to write, next to a tiny lake. I always like to write near water; so inspiring for writing. I played them all up at the studio, but the lads were all going, "Er – very interesting, Si…" – a question mark on every face. A little too *strange* for Lindisfarne,' he smiles.

Included on both the album and a three-track CD single at the time, 'Roll On That Day' was originally written by Rod for Jacka to sing, but the circumstances surrounding its recording pointed to potential difficulties within the band. Jacka's relocation to London with his new wife following the death of his mother-in-law in 1987 appeared to make it difficult for him to be completely involved in recording of the album.

When it came to 'Roll On That Day,'

Above: Si (far right) is highly amused by the antics of the Killingworth Sword Dancers, Newcastle City Hall.

Marty was presented with the song as Jacka could not make the session. 'Rod did most of the work,' Marty explains, 'but being the gentleman that he is credited me for my contribution to the writing of the song. I was flung in at the deep end…' The song had started life as a tune Marty used to play at soundchecks and Rod had said how much he liked it. 'After Italy, we made a conscious decision to write together. We tried a few things – none of which came to anything – then, just as I was leaving, he said, "Bang that little tune down on the piano." Next thing, I get a phone call and he says, "I think you should hear this."'

The band, meanwhile, showcased some of the new songs at Alnwick Castle during the summer and 'Amigos' was released in September. It seemed that Lindisfarne had been right in their approach to the album, as Ray, at the time, had suspected: 'For me, "Amigos" is probably the most commercial album – from an American point of view – we've ever made because it sounds like our roots, which is the sort of thing they still love. There's the Nitty Gritty Dirt Band, there's the blues, strong vocal performances – all mixed together.

'On the last couple of albums, we've tried to be a bit more self-consciously "modern", but it's gone now. It's completely out of the system. I listened to our album all the way through for the first time today – because I've lived too close to it – and I wound the window down in the car with the wind in my face and I think it hits the nail right on the head. It's a "proper" Lindisfarne album.'

The album's title had come directly from the shots taken for the sleeve, according to Ray. 'When we saw the photographs, we were so pleased with them, it just instantly came to us. One of the working titles was "Bring On The Cheesy Organ"! Rod's got a soft spot for garage-band organs. Them, Hammonds and pianos are the *proper* rock'n'roll noises, y'know?'

Jacka travelled up during November to rehearse at the band's unofficial HQ – the Magnesia Bank pub in North Shields – for the Amigos Tour. Encouraging reviews seemed to prove that the band were once again moving in the right direction, Phil Sutcliffe in *Q* giving the album four stars and praising the 'earthy, main-street USA rock' of Rod's 'When The Night Comes Down'.

Simon Jones in *Folk Roots* was equally impressed, calling the album 'the strongest since "Back And Fourth"…born-again James Alan Hull dominates the set and it's very much his creation', while *Music Week* concluded that 'Alan Hull writes as well as ever, whether it's the "Imagine"-style utopianism of "One World" or friendly love songs like "You're The One".' Alan had written 'One World' for his new grand-daughter, Roxanne, and it seemed fitting that the melody was so naggingly reminiscent of his idol, John Lennon. A beautiful instrumental reprise of the song (titled 'Another World') closed the album and featured Kathryn Tickell on Northumbrian pipes. (Rod had played on Kathryn's first album, 'Borderlands', in 1986.)

Alan's new-found status as a grandparent was obviously a source of great pride, and recognition of this buoyed him considerably as he moved towards the tour. He had also released another solo album, 'Another Little Adventure', recorded live with young Tyneside musician Ian McCallum, whom he had taken under his wing.

Produced once again by Geoff Heslop, the album showed Alan on fine form with an almost perfect selection that combined key Lindisfarne songs like 'Poor Old Ireland' and 'All Fall Down' alongside selections from 'Pipedream' such as 'Money Game' and 'United States Of Mind', as well as 'One More Bottle Of Wine' from 'Squire'. From 'On The Other Side' came 'Fly Away' and 'Malvinas Melody'. Even 'Heroes' turned up again. Alan appeared to be feeling good about himself and his music.

Despite breaking his ankle during the 'Amigos' tour – 'He was sober, too,' Ray laughed – Alan soldiered on and the gigs showcased the band with just the right combination of power and subtlety, thanks largely to the new material. New bass player Steve Cunningham was now looking after Rod's 'old duties', another decision that had come out of the 'bootstraps' meeting in Milan. Rod had always played slide in the studio and in the same capacity with other 'employers'; now he was quite clearly relishing the idea.

Some observers were astounded by the sheer power of Lindisfarne's performances. By the time the tour reached Newcastle, Alan had thrown away his crutch but was still forced to remain behind his piano for most of the performance, hopping to the front when the fancy took him. 'Walk in The Sea' from 'Phantoms', augmented by Si's keyboards and Marty's wistful flute was, without doubt, as one reviewer noted, 'one of the most memorable songs of a remarkable night…it conjured up visions of early Genesis.'

For this tour, Alan's acoustic guitar on 'Winter Song' was supplemented with soft, electric slide from Rod, 'speaking with the same passion as Alan's lyrics,' the reviewer continued. The first night at Newcastle was also Steve Cunningham's City Hall debut…to think he wasn't even born when 'Winter Song' was written!

During 'Clear White Light,' the Boogie Brothers (Billy Mitchell, monitor engineer Ian Byrom and AN Other) were wheeled on stage crouched in a flight case, complete with miners' helmets, lamps and shades. Mitch returned alongside Rod before Lindisfarne's Twentieth Anniversary Tour ended in a blinding flash of light. There were more fireworks to follow…

Chapter ELEVEN

'YOU TALK TOO MUCH, MR HULL'

Conveniently, 1990 was not only the start of a new decade but Lindisfarne's 21st anniversary as a band. Tyne Tees Television planned a three-part series, chronicling the band's story from 1969, including archive footage of the band as well as recollections of the Six Bob Tour from Peter Gabriel. Taking its title from the lyrics of 'Working For The Man', the series – released on video – would be called *Keep The Beacon Burning*.

The year promised a whole host of different Lindisfarne-related projects. As Ray told the *Newcastle Evening Chronicle* in April, 'A lot of long-term projects have come together at the same time.' One was the opening of Hi-Level Studios, where the band would now be able to record to their heart's content. Others flocked, too: Chas Chandler produced the Alligators (later Animals II) featuring former Animals partner Hilton Valentine; Jimmy Nail was another client, while Michael Chapman recorded his 'Navigation' album, co-produced by Steve Cunningham and featuring Ray Laidlaw.

Lindisfarne had attracted sponsorship for the next two years from Theakston's Breweries – a marriage made in heaven – starting with the 21st anniversary dates which, in the brewery's honour, would be called the Old Peculier Tour. Twenty-five dates were scheduled, including two shows at London's Mean Fiddler, two at Nottingham – long a hotbed of support – and five days at Newcastle City Hall.

The Theakston association was launched with a media gig at the White Bear pub in Masham, North Yorkshire, next door to the brewery HQ. Various combinations of Lindisfarne's extended family had already played there, as had the Albion Band – all, no doubt, in search of a convivial atmosphere and a fine pint. Alan had earlier that day performed a solo set at the Labour Party Conference in Blackpool and brought a couple of his companions along with him to the White Bear, as well as his wife Pat.

The question of Jacka's commitment to Lindisfarne had been a growing subject of discussion within the band and Alan felt he had to take up the issue with him as soon as possible. 'About '87 or '88, Jacka was grumbling about not working enough with the band and that he was going to have to do something else,' he told *Magic In The Air* in 1995.

As both Alan and Rod were doing things musically outside of the band, there seemed some justification for Jacka's frustration. 'It was his choice to go and buy a flat in London,' Alan went on. 'We were all okay, the money wasn't fabulous, but we were surviving quite happily, enjoying the work we were doing – getting together, rehearsing, planning things. But he was never there for that; he was in London. Then his wife got him a job as a PR for Guinness, doing these things in the summer.'

More than a little worse for wear, as this writer noted, Alan could not resist grabbing the opportunity at the White Bear. 'I said, "Look, you're playing around, you know? If you don't take the band seriously, why don't you leave?" and he said, "Right. I will".'

Si, who 'knew tensions had been running high,' recalls one occasion in the dressing room when Jacka made a comment about a song he felt wouldn't succeed because, as Si recalls Jacka commenting, 'the BBC won't play it…' As well as a sense of negativity, Si feels outside influences were affecting Jacka at the time: 'His missus got to him, to some extent – and the fact that he was having to come up from London to rehearse'n'stuff.'

According to Si, Jacka claimed 'he couldn't afford to be in the band anymore. He didn't want to be in the band, basically.' Perhaps the seed of discontent had been sown with Marty's full-time membership of the band: Jacka had apparently been opposed to the idea. If true, it was a tragedy, particularly given Marty's involvement with Harcourt's Heroes and the enthusiasm they seemed to share on stage with Lindisfarne. It seemed irrational.

'I walked in to the soundcheck after travelling up with my wife from London and I noted a definite atmosphere, which was unusual,' Jacka recalls of the event. 'Prior to this, I had been unable to take part in a video recording of "Fog On The Tyne (Revisited)" with Gazza because of previous commitments with my other job. Bearing in mind that my second income was crucial for economic survival – not for me large royalties from songwriting – the band were beginning to be unhappy with divided loyalties, although I only missed this and one other event.'

Ray Laidlaw felt Jacka was certainly the injured party on the night, 'predominantly because Alan should never have said what he said, at that time – and in the way he did. I don't disagree with Alan's sentiments, but it was done at the wrong time and at the wrong place. It was in a room full of people who were basically strangers. It was hugely embarrassing for Jacka – and for me, because I was busy trying to "impress" our sponsors.'

Jacka, however, states that Alan had actually been 'designated by the band to give me an ultimatum, but his large consumption of alcohol meant that he actually publicly asked me to leave the band.' It had

Right: The irrepressible Brendan Healy gets down on the City Hall stage.

Opposite: A little-known saxophonist blows his own trumpet.

been an undignified mess, by all accounts. The only reasonable way to go about the issue was to discuss it calmly and rationally – which did subsequently happen, albeit after the event.

Ray had a meeting with Alan first, as he explains: 'The next day, I said to Alan that if he couldn't guarantee to me that he would never, *ever* repeat that behaviour I was going to walk; I was not prepared to manage the band under those circumstances, because I thought he was completely wrong. He apologised, because he knew he was drunk. Having said that, I think it had been building up inside of him for a long time.'

At the meeting, Jacka was asked whether he was prepared to put Lindisfarne before all other considerations. 'He said "No",' Alan told *Magic In The Air*. 'So, fair enough, you don't deserve to be in the band. But it was his decision, you know. He changed. He was great at the beginning, he was great in the early 1980s, but he just drifted; he just lost interest.'

Perhaps Alan had simply brought the issue further forward on the agenda. It had to be dealt with sooner or later, as he had pointed out. Maybe Jacka should have voiced his obvious discontent earlier. Certainly, by his own admission, Jacka had been unhappy with the selection process for deciding which songs were included on albums after Lindisfarne had set up their own label.

'I didn't feel it was as fair a process as it had been previously, and only one song of mine was ever included for release. After this, the band became more and more a vehicle for Alan's songwriting and less and less a musical blend of individual members' styles – resulting in a one-sided approach to arrangements and recording. For me, this was frustrating as I became less a part of the whole thing. This was Alan's choice.'

Jacka's exit took Si, for one, by surprise. 'I didn't know anything about it until he'd left. Not a thing. I drove back to Thornton-le-Dale on the night. It was two weeks later, when Ray Laidlaw rang up and said, "I'll be sending you an agreement about the split with Jacka." *"What* split with Jacka?" I said. "He's left the band." *"When?"* "The night of Masham, y'know." So I said, "I wasn't there – I came straight back, don't you remember?"

'So I spent half an hour on the phone with him; half an hour with Rod. Everybody was apologetic, understandably – to be told two weeks later that Jacka wasn't in the band any more.' An agreement was subsequently made that Jacka would fulfil his commitment to the Old Peculier Tour but then that, as they say, would be that.

Jacka was not present at a show for the brewery staff in Masham Town Hall on New Year's Eve, where Lindisfarne were in subdued mood both on stage and off. It was not until later that this writer realised why the mood had been so uncharacteristically sombre – and, even then, not until the official announcement of Jacka's exit. Recalling the circumstances of his departure from Lindisfarne for this book, Jacka appeared to be firmly resolved: 'I doubt that I would choose to ever play with them again.'

In terms of profile, an association with a rather useful footballer not long before Christmas 1990 put Lindisfarne in the national eye once more. When World Cup hero Paul Gascoigne's management approached the band with a suggestion that they back him on an album of his favourite songs, the 'C'Mon Everybody' episode suggested caution. Instead, Ray proposed they re-record 'Fog On The Tyne', as it had never been released as a single. By 22 December, the song – rewritten by Alan and Marty as 'Fog On The Tyne (Revisited)' – had reached Number 3 – or 2, depending on which chart you're looking at – as Lindisfarne reaped the rewards of Gazzamania.*

* A couple of years later, a legal case arose over the similarity of Whigfield's 'Saturday Night' smash to Alan's song, when it was discovered how successful the Whigfield track had been in Italy – where Gazza was playing at the time. An out-of-court settlement was reached with Alan's publishers.

The video was recorded at Red's Club in Newcastle (owned by Brian Johnson's ex-wife, Carol), but did not, of course, feature Jacka. Steve Wright, then at Radio 1, was even inspired to play the original track on prime-time radio – and though Gazza and Lindisfarne both attracted flak for desecrating a classic, like 'C'Mon Everybody' it sold.

'We did the Gazza thing with the same frame of mind as the whole rock'n'roll thing,' Marty explained. 'We were just having fun. It was no worse than any other rap song on the radio at the time. Nobody questions any other band…didn't Elvis Costello do a country album? Phil Collins dresses up to do "You Can't Hurry Love", and no-one slates him for that. The band lost a bit of its cred, I suppose, in certain people's eyes.'

Despite this well-reasoned argument, it's arguable that the Gazza episode wiped away much of respect the band had worked hard to regain with 'Amigos'. Lindisfarne even made *Melody Maker* again, but this time courtesy of a three-page special on the Boy Wonder. Reporter Steve Sutherland was far from excited at Gazza's new diversion from football, branding 'Fog…(Revisited)' 'a farting, beer-bellied conga set to embarrass us all at wedding receptions and office parties for decades to come.' The single wasn't a new career move for Gazza or Lindisfarne – it was just a laugh. Even the backing track had been lying around from a Bo Diddley-style version of the song the band had been doing live. All in all, 1991 had certainly been some 21st…

Lindisfarne's 22nd year saw the band headlining at such diverse and wonderful locations as Trowbridge Festival in Wiltshire and Newark Castle. However, this year's Christmas tour gained its title – Keeping The Rage – from events that followed a Radio 2 Arts programme performance in December 1990 hosted by MP Austin Mitchell.

Also invited along to Broadcasting Centre were similar forthright individuals such as playwright Alan Plater, Tim Healy, musician Ian Carr and Mike Elliott who, along with Alan, later discussed the

Two Geordies hit Minsk, 1991 – personal tour manager Jimmy Moore and (bottom) Brendan Healy.

state of Newcastle's architecture. Alan, on top form, was able to put forward his long-held views on the damage done to the city earlier expressed by 'All Fall Down'. It was an intriguing evening. Later, Alan had heard the phrase 'keeping the rage' in a play that Mike and Tim were appearing in. Alan turned to Marty with the sudden realisation: 'That's exactly what *we've* been doing all these years.' So was born yet another song collaboration from Messrs Hull and Craggs.

Earlier in the year, the band had begun recording new material at Hi-Level, engineer Steve Cunningham presiding over some fine tracks with an edge not heard for some time. Alan's 'Running Man' was a menacing piece with manic, sneering vocals and a tortured sax solo. One of Rod's new offerings, 'Old Peculiar Feeling', was prompted by the brew, while his contrasting 'Black Rain' was a scathing stab at the state of the world's skies inspired by a newspaper report. The track was driven along by a rhythm and sax that could have been taken straight out of some Booker T session.

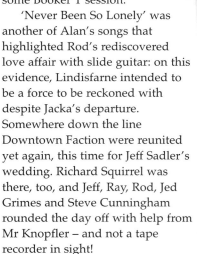

'Never Been So Lonely' was another of Alan's songs that highlighted Rod's rediscovered love affair with slide guitar: on this evidence, Lindisfarne intended to be a force to be reckoned with despite Jacka's departure. Somewhere down the line Downtown Faction were reunited yet again, this time for Jeff Sadler's wedding. Richard Squirrel was there, too, and Jeff, Ray, Rod, Jed Grimes and Steve Cunningham rounded the day off with help from Mr Knopfler – and not a tape recorder in sight!

Also in early 1991, Brendan Healy

t a phone call: 'Ray said, "Do you want to
me and do a few club dates with us?" They
ere in Russia, Hong Kong and Butlins!'
rendan had been to the same school as Ray
d was known to the band from Pacamax
ys. He was a great entertainer, with a
ntastic dry wit, and would be a great asset
the band live.

In November came the visit to Russia –
st mooted a year previously – where 20,000
ng along with the band to 'One World' at
e Minsk Dynamo Stadium. The event was
ganised as a benefit for the child victims of
ernobyl who still suffer the effects of the
tastrophe. There was fun to be had, too,
ch as meeting up with old Quo mate Bob
ung, who was also there as manager of
verpool band Sian – but the visit had a
ofound effect on everyone concerned.

'It was a real eye-opener to see old
omen in the streets, with babies in their
ms,' Marty recalls. 'I just thought, "Christ…" and
ve her everything I had in my pockets. There
ere gangs of gypsies, small children just living
the streets and sleeping in the subway. That
as very sad.' The show itself was a terrific
ccess. 'I remember Alan jumping into the middle
this five-deep row of 17-year-old soldiers with
ry stern faces, taking the cap off one of them and
acing it on his own head. He just had the
ack…he gets away with it. He threw his arms
und this soldier and they just *loved* him. There
ere big smiles on their faces…they couldn't help it.'

Despite the cultural, economic and social divide,
e audience knew enough to know how to react, as
arty went on. 'It was wonderful to see all those
ung kids – especially in Minsk, which had never
d a stadium gig ever before. They were really ready
r it. There were a lot of bands on, but Lindisfarne
ent out and grabbed the audience, where the rest of
em just "played". There were tears from the
owd…it was very moving.'

As expected, the band were tailed all the time during their visit. 'You're not aware of it, because they
ep swapping,' Marty pointed out. 'When we left in the coach to go for the plane, this guy waved
rewell to me; he specifically pointed at me. He put his fists up and went "Yo!", with his thumbs up.
here were people as we left Minsk, crying. Men, soldiers – all crying. A *very* moving experience.'
nother 'shadow' gave Alan the rather unsurprising news: 'Mr Hull, you talk too much…'

The band's next stop couldn't have been more different. Hong Kong still had some time left on its
itish clock and the contrast between the two locations was on everyone's minds. The band were
awn towards Brendan's Bar, which Mr Healy duly made his own. The gig was organised by the Hong
ong Folk Festival and, in such joyous surroundings, everyone felt obliged to 'go for it'.

'One night,' Marty recalls, 'Si had been out drinking and I hadn't, because I'd ginned myself too
uch on the flight. Me and Mr Hull were the only ones who stayed up, and we annoyed everybody on
e Jumbo Jet. I fell in love with one of the air hostesses – he was called "John" – and we kept on
dering gin and tonics. I pestered the life out of Ray Laidlaw and he'll never forgive me for it. Me and
lan going, "Cor, look at that…they look just like mountains" – because they *were*, of course. All the
hers were snoring their heads off with their special socks on, and me and Hully just smoked tabs…we
ere a bit ill when we arrived.'

What was it about Lindisfarne travelling in the East? At least Francis Rossi couldn't be blamed this
me. Marty was rooming with Si when, as a result of over-indulgence, he felt the urge to go to the
athroom. 'Si had fallen asleep on the toilet…I brayed and I brayed and I *begged* him to open the door.
ut nothing. So I took a knife to the lock, opened the door – and there was Si in all his glory. He stayed
ere all night.'

Marty is convinced he was set up, especially as the horror did not end there. 'I love Simon Cowe

*Top: Lindisarne lead their
KGB minder (far right) a
merry dance.*

*Above: Ray and co-manager
Steve Weltman huddle
together for warmth at
Minsk's Dynamo Stadium.*

Above: Quiz night in Hong Kong included comedian Steve Womack (back row, right).

dearly, but if you ever have to share a room with him take a very large pillow and place it above his nose – pressing down with your knee… For seven or eight years, I'd been told about the ferocity of Si's snoring and it all came true that night in Hong Kong. I came close to killing him was set up; they will *all* pay for it – individually

On their return to Britain, the band returned to the studio, this time with producer Nick Tauber (Thin Lizzy, Deep Purple, Marillion, Soup Dragons), continuing to work on tracks for the new album. Remixing duties fell to Walter Turbett, best known for his work with Malcolm McLaren and Wet Wet Wet.

It was around this time that Steve Weltman began to manage the band on a joint basis with Ray. He had enjoyed Alan's respect ever since they had worked together at Charisma, being there every step of the way as Lindisfarne rode that wave between 1970-74. He subsequently became the label's managing director, signing Malcolm McLaren and Julian Lennon.

'Alan and I had always kept up a relationship over the years,' Steve recalls. 'He'd been with Warner seven or eight years and his deal was up. He had appointed a lawyer some six to nine months earlier to secure a new publishing deal. My faith in Alan is such that I feel he is one of the greatest British songwriters since the 1960s – so I went up to see him. I was actually stunned by the lack of interest, the lack of knowledge of the law firm involved, so I went off and struck him a new deal.'

During that six-month period, Steve was around so much that he began seeing the rest of the band. started going to the shows and then Ray said to me, "Why don't you get involved?" So I did. The arrangement was that Ray would continue to look after all the logistics and Steve would deal with all the record-company affairs. As he lived in Surrey, it made a lot of practical sense and Steve's experience and business acumen was second to none.'

His first decision was to impose a strict regime on the band. 'By the time we came out of the fourth meeting,' says Si, 'Steve had kicked so much ass… It was a case of "We'll make a business plan, like proper businessmen." We sat down and made important business decisions that we had to rescue our career – as of *now*!' Steve intended to keep a tight rein on the material for the next album, as Si went on 'Weltman said, "If it doesn't fit within the 'walls' of the album it's out"; specific "designer writing".'

Brendan remained on board for the Christmas tour that year, as well as – for the very first time on stage – two girl singers, Liz Wilson and Amanda Charles-Vincent. Mr Healy's prowess at the keyboard was one of the highlights of the shows, and the sweet sound of Liz and Amanda as they sang the opening words to Si's 'Uncle Sam' seemed perfectly natural to these ears. It was as legitimate to experiment with people as it was different instrumentation – and Lindisfarne had never been afraid to give it a try.

The shows were as good as ever but the changes too radical for some, given that this was the first time many had seen the band after Jacka's departure…indeed, many might have wondered if this was Lindisfarne's last, desperate gasp. One lady at the City Hall walked out in disgust, demanding to know 'where Ray Jackson was'.

If the question of Marty Craggs 'replacing' Jacka crossed anyone's mind, it most certainly had not crossed Marty's, as he insisted: 'Harcourt's Heroes were who they were; Pacamax was Pacamax and Lindisfarne were a totally different kettle of fish. I think I was in the band about five years before Jacka left, so I didn't feel any awkwardness about that at all.'

He was sincere in his feelings about Jacka: 'He's got a wonderful voice – a wonderful melody to it – and nobody can replace Ray Jackson. I would never dream of trying to. I'm just doing what I do in the band and, with him leaving, there needed to be another vocalist; I'd sung certain songs before Jacka left so it just seemed the natural thing for me to pick up more.' People would always draw their own conclusions, as he pointed out: 'The fact I'm singing songs Jacka used to sing – they are the songs I think the Lindisfarne public would like to hear; so I was given the job to do that.'

There were, however, songs that Marty considered out of bounds. 'Songs like "Warm Feeling" and "King's Cross Blues" I would never dream of touching; they are so well suited to Jacka. Nobody could *ever* do what Ray Jackson did. A lot of people will look at me in that way, if only because of the position I stand on stage between Rod Clements and Alan Hull…it's hallowed ground, I suppose. But people leave bands, y'know – it's no big deal.'

During the following year, all energies were put into recording the next album and it was decided there would be no Christmas tour. Virgin were working on a two-volume collection called 'Buried 'reasures' that would round up many of the band's lost tracks, rare live material and previously nissued songs. A unique bonus was that several of the tracks would be linked with interviews with the and, explaining the inspiration or background to many of the tracks.

'Buried Treasures' was meant to be a stop-gap album until the release of their next all-new set, as ay told the *Newcastle Evening Chronicle*, 'It started off as just an idea, but became a Holy Grail as all orts of things started coming out of the woodwork. We were restricting it to only the best quality, but nded up with more than enough for three volumes.'

The timing was fortunate, too; ending one episode efore moving on to the next. The aim for Lindisfarne was ust as it had been after Milan – if anything, even more so. ll energies were to go into getting the new material. There ould be only one show this winter, on Tuesday 22 ecember at Newcastle City Hall – and with none of the raditional decorations on stage it seemed the audience ensed something very different was in store that night.

Lindisfarne walked on as though just off the street. here was never much in the way of 'dressing up,' but to is observer, it was perhaps more to do with their emeanour… The event proved to be truly unique. 'The and were well fired-up,' *Magic In The Air* reported. everal new songs were highlighted in the set, including Elvis Lives On The Moon" and Rod's "Old Peculiar eeling", but one of the real surprises for those lucky nough to be there was the performance of Alan's Tomorrow – If I'm Hungry", which he hadn't played since he day he demoed the track at Impulse way back in 1969.'

Featured on 'Buried Treasures', the song had eventually een recorded as 'January Song' for 'Nicely Out of Tune'. 'n the night, sitting cross-legged on a monitor at the front f the stage with his acoustic guitar, Alan even slipped back to the lyrics of 'January Song' for a moment before pologising and moving on. Marty got to sing an nreleased Rab Noakes song, 'On My Own (I Built A ridge)', performed live by Lindisfarne for the first time, nother song recorded during sessions for the first album nd also included on 'Buried Treasures'. 'It's a great song,' Iarty pointed out. 'It has everything that Lindisfarne were bout in those days. It was a lovely song to sing.'

Finally 'and perfectly' said *Magic In The Air*, 'there was ry Giving Everything"; with Tim Healy, John Miles (fresh om a world tour with Joe Cocker), Mick Whittaker, relude's Irene Hume and even the writer, Mike Waller, mong a cast of dozens to close the first half.'

The band rehearsed the song with the rest of the set – en on the night, according to Marty, 'the rest of the atured vocalists just walked in and did it as though ey'd been singing it all their lives – and it worked.' eturning to the studio shortly after the holiday, the essions with Nick Tauber were not judged a success. eve's remit was harsh, but the band knew it was right. indisfarne were determined the next album should be 'the ne' and they needed someone who not only knew what ey were about, but could steer with a strong hand; they eeded another Gus Dudgeon. The man for the job was enny Craddock.

'When I was approached to do the album, I was in a uandary about how best to approach it,' Kenny explained his interview with Chris Groom. 'I knew everyone cially but hadn't worked with them as a band for some me.' Indeed, since the Mk II band and Alan's solo albums, enny had acted as MD for Gerry Rafferty and Van Iorrison and had also been working with Paul Brady – npressive credentials.

'In the end, I called a meeting in a pub, which turned

Below: The wild and wacky photo shoot for the 'Buried Treasures' compilations.

129

out to be a good move – it gave everyone the chance to put forward their ideas and misgivings about the songs and arrangements, everything was brought out into the open before we actually went into the studio, plus we had a really good drinking session. Needless to say, we didn't go straight into the studio the next day!'

Marty echoes the sentiments of the entire band in his praise of Kenny's work on the album: 'He had such foresight; he plotted the whole album out for us, so it was dead easy when we came in. He knows every member and the way they play. He understands Alan very well and Alan's material. He got vocals out of me I didn't know I had. He was the perfect choice; the man for the job. He's just so experienced – a talented musician and such a wonderful, *wonderful* Hammond player.'

The role of Steve Weltman was also crucial: 'We wrote a load of songs and had them ripped to shreds by Steve; he just tore them apart, because he was our yardstick before they even got to Kenny. Good songs from all of us didn't make it. Steve did a brilliant job.' Alan and Kenny had been writing together before the album sessions and one song was a direct response to Alan's experiences in Russia, as Kenny explained to Chris Groom.

'About two weeks after they got back, Alan called me up and said, "I've written this lyric, but the tune is crap." He couldn't wait to tell me all about his experiences over there; he loved it – apart from the fact he couldn't get a drink on the aeroplane! So he sent me the lyric of "Mother Russia".' Kenny wrote a new tune, recorded a new demo with his vocal on it and sent it back to Alan. 'Alan came down to my place in Hastings, put his vocal on to a new demo and the collaboration went on from there; another new start in our ongoing friendship.'

The two would contribute two further songs to the album – 'Demons' and 'Spoken Like A Man'. Rod's 'Old Peculiar Feeling' had enjoyed a couple of different guises, but it was Marty who came up with the idea that provided the definitive version of the song: 'We were sitting in the Bacchus pub in Newcastle and talking about the way the album was flowing. The way we did the song on stage just didn't seem right; a good song, but it just didn't seem to fit with the way the others were going. They all seemed to have a certain feel about them.

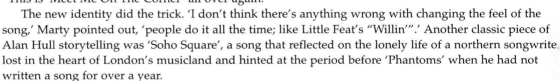

'I turned to Kenny and asked if there was anything we could do to drag it into the album and I suggested it should be something like "When I'm Dead And Gone" by McGuinness Flint. Then Stevie Cunningham – who was engineering the album – suddenly says, "That's *it*!" and we ran back to the studio to "catch" it. Kenny's got his guitar and he's thumping his foot up and down – "Somebody get that timing!" he says.' Rod was at home that day, so Marty excitedly rang him up and told him the idea. 'He just calmly took it in, said "Ta" and put the phone down. Next thing I know, he's got it. He'd obviously gone away, worked on it and there it was. I even dared whisper to myself, "This is 'Meet Me On The Corner' all over again."'

The new identity did the trick. 'I don't think there's anything wrong with changing the feel of the song,' Marty pointed out, 'people do it all the time; like Little Feat's "Willin'".' Another classic piece of Alan Hull storytelling was 'Soho Square', a song that reflected on the lonely life of a northern songwriter lost in the heart of London's musicland and hinted at the period before 'Phantoms' when he had not written a song for over a year.

At the end of the sessions, the band were absolutely delighted with the results of what was now entitled 'Elvis Lives On The Moon'. 'At the playback,' Marty continued, 'we all just sat there – like in the cinema – Kenny just pressed the button and him and Stevie just buggered off to the pub. The two of them worked so hard and so well together on that album.' Marty had been so excited that he couldn't keep away from the studio – even when he wasn't needed; 'The sessions were the most fun month of my life. Even when there was nothing to do, I was finding excuses to go in; "Ee, the lads aren't eating well, I'll make them a curry" – and I'd be taking it in for them just to hear what was coming out of the studio!'

Recording completed, the band headed out for a series of festivals, starting in April with Torquay, Wath on Dearne and Milton Keynes. This was swiftly followed by a week playing shows in the United Arab Emirates. Back in Blighty, the band returned to perform once more at St James' Park on the occasion of the Toon's triumphant return to the Premiership. The rest of the summer saw Si collect many thousands of Air Miles as he wove his way back and forth from Toronto, Canada, where he had finally relocated with his Canadian wife, Regan and his family. Si had at last got the opportunity to fulfil a lifetime ambition to start a brewery over there – poor soul!

In May, the band played at Portsmouth and in June, the first of three Fleadhs; one each in London and Waterford, the first in Glasgow. The shows saw Lindisfarne sharing the bills variously with Van Morrison, Bob Dylan, the Pogues, Runrig and John Martyn. The circumstances around the Glasgow show proved particularly memorable, as this writer wrote at length in *Magic In The Air*:

'Whatever you do, don't say Good Morning to Alan,' Ray Laidlaw had warned me. Gordon, the driver, collected Ray, Rod and myself from Ray's place in Tynemouth at 6:30 that morning, Marty was

ext aboard in North Shields, then Alan who without a word slid into the seat next to Gordon. There
vas no acknowledgement from anyone. I was aware that I could now be involved in some time-
onoured pattern that would unfold as the journey progressed.

From my seat at the back, I quietly – and hopefully unobtrusively – observed proceedings. Rod sat
n my left immersed in his *Guardian*, Ray in front of me with his paper and Marty ahead of him, gazing
ut of the window. Alan lit up the first of many cigarettes as we made our way from the coast to the
ity where we picked up Gary Carverhill, the band's merchandiser, and then Steve Cunningham. As we
nake our way north towards the border Alan curled up on the front seat to sleep, and I was glad that I
ad heeded Ray's warning.

Alan raises his head as we approach a motorway cafe. 'What about some breakfast then, eh?' Ballast
aken on board, everyone seems to liven up considerably. The talk turns to festivals in general…their last
proper' festival in Denmark where Ian McCallum was Si…the Genesis gig in Milton Keynes organised
o bail Peter Gabriel out of his first WOMAD, where the band's invitation to play had been 'blocked by
omeone in their camp'… Before long, we see the perimeter fence of the People's Palace, a massive open
rea that is the venue for the gig.

As we arrive, Rod discusses, rather mock-theatrically, the question of his headgear for the day.
emoving his woolly hat, he delves into his bag periodically to discuss the various options with Ray
nd Marty. The first selection is introduced by its owner as 'very Arnold Palmer', while Marty –
bviously *au fait* with golfing apparel, agrees: 'Very Bing'. Finally, Rod settles on the original woolly hat.
What you see is what you get,' he proclaims. Pretty well sums up the band, I think to myself.

*The Toon are going up!
Lindisfarne at St James'
Park. The keen-eyed may
spot TV sports presenters
Steve Sutton and Roger
Tames, actors Tim Healy,
Alan Meachan and
Sammy Johnson, plus
actor-turned-singer
Robson Green.*

Once inside the perimeter, Gordon drops us behind the stage area. We are met with an endearingly genuine hug by Steve Weltman, the band's co-manager who has flown up from London with Glen Colson. Approaching the stage I notice a familiar bearded face and recognise it as a guitarist and mandolin player of some repute, formerly of North Shields and now of Toronto. It's Si Cowe. He's apparently been there for a couple of hours having flown in directly from Canada and seems in fine fettle for someone who has made several transatlantic trips over the past few weeks.

We return to the Portakabin where Jimmy Moore, the band's road manager, is relaxing in the sun outside, having set up the gear earlier in the day. Jimmy goes back a long way with the band, and has also worked with Judas Priest and Frank Zappa. Although famed for his sense of fun and practical jokes, it was a foolish person who trespassed on his area of responsibility, or as Jimmy put it, 'My stage'.

The weather had held and everyone was in good spirits as the band went on stage. As they played, I took the opportunity to watch from several different vantage points, crossing from side to side behind the backdrop. Glen and Steve watched from the wings where they could observe band, crowd and pressmen. The set included several songs from the new album, and it was also noticeable that the crowd's response was as sincere and warm for the newer songs as for the old. As the band leave the stage there is little to gripe about.

Retiring backstage, the mood soon changes as it transpires that Steve Weltman has arranged for the band to play a second set as compensation for the bringing forward of the first, only notified the night before. Eddi Reader has pulled out and Lindisfarne are to take her place in the acoustic tent. The response from the band is generally positive – if nothing else they can enjoy the sun, catch some of the other bands and get to play to a different audience. However there are at least four hours to kill and they learn that they will be playing at the same time as Runrig are headlining on the main stage.

Alan is not happy. 'We're going to be playing to five fuckin' people while they're on!' This seems not an altogether unfair observation, given the Gaelic band's almost Messianic following in Scotland and the nature of the festival we're at. Jimmy and the crew had agreed to stay, but Alan's reaction had made me, for one, feel slightly awkward. The rest of the band seemed unperturbed, however, and the decision had been made, so it was just a question of how to spend the intervening hours.

I began idly wondering just what the lads had found to do over the years to kill time. Just then I noticed Glen, Si and Alan sitting chatting on the grass. I join them and it quickly becomes apparent that Glen is delighted to be back in the band's company again. In the early days of incredibly intense gigging, they had all shared many, many hours together all over the world. They were clearly comfortable in each others' company. Then in a rash moment I succumbed to Alan's innocent 'Coming with the bad boys, Dave?' Glen, with the look of someone wiser in such matters, declines and we go off, ostensibly to '…have a look around…'

As it turns out, it is far from the Olympian drinking spree I had anticipated. We settle after about ten minutes for the sort of bar that could neither be described as a pub or working men's club, as it is the only place we can find. Alan and Si are immediately at home and we hitch ourselves up on to barstools as they order the first of several shorts. The conversation centres around Si's new life in Canada, as I listen I find it hard to imagine the ill-feeling between the two I had heard was around at the time the band split. The honesty of their recollections made a very big impression on me as I observed two friends reconciled a long time ago with that part of their past. At four-thirty Alan grudgingly acknowledges the time on the pub clock and we get up to leave. The band are due on at five.

As we return it transpires that the band's set has been put back another hour. Alan is immediately fired up again and a row ensues between him and Steve. Both stand their ground and it's over in minutes – as if they had only been going through the motions. I just feel awkward again, and as we reach the Portakabins the rest of the band are assembled and ready to go. Alan, though still seems set on a confrontation, quietly asking Si to 'back him up' like a schoolboy preparing his response to some misdemeanour. Ray, ever the calming influence, quickly takes control. He calls all of the band, plus Steve Weltman, into the Portakabin and the door is ominously closed behind them.

The door opens and it seems all is resolved. Alan, beaming, turns to Ray and gives him a big hug. 'Are you still my friend?' he asks. Rod rolls his eyes to the sky and smiles as he shakes his head in disbelief. These lads know each other inside-out.

The second set takes place in a large tent. Gary and I find a spot on a raised platform at the back, next to the sound desk. Already there is a good crowd in, but would they stay when Runrig were on? We needn't have worried. The band *stormed* it. People continued to file in and, once in, they stayed. There was a definite edge to this show. Alan's Celtic heart was clearly stirred as he announced, 'We're not English, you're not Scots. We're from the North East. We're all Celts!'

The same set is played except that during 'Poor Old Ireland' Alan introduces Scots singer Carol Laula to sing a quickly rehearsed duet. The crowd seem genuinely to love the show and the band look well pleased too. Si later explained the difference between the two sets: 'Same band – different audience.' Fair enough.

After the show we get packed up as quickly as possible as I get the impression that Gordon is none too pleased with the unexpected extension to his day. As I help Ray strip down his kit, I ask him what all the fuss was about earlier. With characteristic honesty he puts things firmly into context. 'It was basically because Alan had to get up early. Simple as that. Then he had timed his alcohol consumption to fit in with the earlier start and just made a fool of himself for an hour and a half.' Ray seems to take it all in his stride.

Everyone is back on the coach apart from Alan and Marty. What a surprise. Engine running and barely disguising his temper, Gordon threatens to leave them if they're not back in five minutes. I volunteer to find them. Only one place to look really, and yep, there they are in the bar. As they stroll leisurely back to the bus, Gordon makes his opinions known while Si, who is coming back with us to see his father, dips into his duty-free bag. Here we go…

We have no sooner left the arena when Alan and Marty begin questioning Gordon as to where we can stop for another drink. Gordon is unmoved, his face set in stony silence. As we drive past more than one imbibing opportunity, Alan and Marty's faces sink and they gaze wistfully out of the window. After an hour or so, Alan convinces Gordon that he needs to go to the toilet and Gordon grudgingly stops at a small caravan site at the side of the road. Alan swiftly disappears into the darkness behind a brick wall.

Now I'm no expert, but I reckon that to do what Alan had to do, even with a 'full tank', shouldn't take more than a couple of minutes. Alan has been gone for ten. A combination of realisation and blind fury had registered on Gordon's face. 'If he's not back in two minutes I'm going without him.' Marty, playing the good guy, springs to his feet and goes off to find him. Five minutes passes. Gordon is almost catatonic. Then Marty emerges into the headlight beam – clutching a pint of Guinness!

It transpires there's a club on the site where Marty had found Alan and he'd '…just got this while I was waiting'. A couple of minutes later, Alan jumps in next to Gordon, apparently oblivious to the driver's imminent tirade. Its only effect is Gordon's sworn oath never to drive for the band again, and there is an uneasy silence for some time afterwards. Meanwhile, Rod suggests a word game to pass the time, and they get well into it for an hour or so.

It's called 'Backwards and Forwards' and is clearly a long-established tradition, and if I only just got a grasp of it then, I buggered if I can explain it now. Suffice to say that it concludes with Rod saying 'Squareless'. Confused? You should have been there.

As we near home, Alan, who has been asleep next to Gordon, is heard talking to the driver about children. Bloody hell! Sensing he has re-ingratiated himself into Gordon's good books, he gradually resumes an upright position and they continue on one of Alan's favourite subjects until we are almost home. He's a wily bugger.

So was it a significant gig? Well it must have been. The band got their picture in the *Sunday Post* next day and, said Ray, that must mean they've cracked it!

Another unique landmark in the band's career occurred when, at Skagen Festival in Denmark, Lindisfarne actually shared the bill with Jack the Lad – who had reformed for fun following the CD release of their Charisma albums around the time of 'Buried Treasures'. Jack's line-up included Mitch, Phil and Walter, accompanied this time round by Jed Grimes and Ian McCallum's drummer, Simon Ferry.

The combination of the two line-ups was a potentially lethal concoction, both on stage and off. 'I was only at Skagen one night,' explained Si 'because Lindisfarne had to be back for Glastonbury the next day and I went to bed, like a good boy, about half one – because I had to be up at five – so I missed all the good bits.' However subsequent reports confirmed events, as Si went on.

'The festival was on a fish quay, just like North Shields, but with loads of beer. There was a wonderful atmosphere. About a thousand people, just chilling out down there. This went on until seven o'clock in the morning, apparently. There was another band on called Toss the Feathers, who were renamed Toss the Furniture and whoever was still up – crew, Jack the Lads – all went down to the fish quay after I'd gone to bed. When they came back, that's when Toss the Feathers started Tossing the Furniture.

Below: The Skagen Festival, Denmark. From left, Marty, Phil Murray, Mitch, Jed Grimes and Steve Cunningham.

'Basically, they just stripped the hotel corridors of all the furniture and paintings, lamp standards – anything they could find. Then they waited outside the White Bear pub, knocked on the door, then threw in the contents of the hotel. Apparently, they did this four times.' It was comforting to note that Jack's 'sense of fun' – or is that 'chaos'? – was in good hands…

Lindisfarne attacked the gigs in support of 'Elvis…' with huge enthusiasm and Glastonbury was another appearance that proved the point. Skagen though, had not gone well, according to Si: 'They didn't know who the fuck we were or what we were about. Glastonbury – totally the opposite.

"Whoosh!" – brilliant. To see 3,000 people giving it "that" with their arms during "Run For Home" was *great*.'

The comparison illustrated Lindisfarne's approach to performing, as Si continued. 'Ray said, "Why couldn't we be like we were at Glastonbury at Skagen?" So I said, "If you're the centre-forward at Newcastle United and there's nobody in the stand – or they're all Sunderland supporters – what do you expect?" It's definitely a two-way thing. Ray's attitude is that is doesn't matter what the size of crowd,' Si went on, 'or where the event is or what it is – it's business as usual, every time.'

At Glastonbury – where the band were, unbelievably, appearing for the first time – representatives of two major booking agencies were in attendance who, according to Si, had specifically come along because they had heard the buzz on Lindisfarne; the band were coming 'out of the dark'. Back on Tyneside, several members of the extended family performed on a stage designed as a masted ship alongside Newcastle's Quayside as part of the Tall Ships Festival that August.

There was Maxie and Mitch: the Doonans (featuring Phil Murray); Hedgehog Pie (featuring Phil Murray) and Jack the Lad (featuring, er, Phil Murray!) with the rest of the Skagen line-up. Also along was Rab Noakes, with an all-too rare live performance in support of his new album, 'Standing Up'. Sadly – and somewhat ironically, at a festival celebrating the sea – things were not going as well further up the Tyne at Swan Hunter shipyard.

Though he was already hugely committed to his consultancy role at the Tall Ships, Ray had no hesitation in saying he would help when the call came through from the union rep. The principle was exactly the same as the attempt to take over Scottish & Newcastle, and Ray is a man of high principles. He felt it personally, too; his father had been at Swan's.

The 'Sailing Home' event was the response to the union's call. Named after the album released to celebrate the Tall Ships Festival, it was a perfect banner under which to perform. Many of the artists who had appeared at the Quayside activities gladly agreed to participate; there was poet John Hegley, writer Tom Pickard – the man behind the inspiration of Alan's 'Squire' album – Mike Elliott…

The icing on the cake was the last-minute decision of Mark Knopfler to bring his Notting Hillbillies – including Alan Clark – to open the night's entertainment. Mark had heard of the of the yard's plight and immediately pledged his help. Phil Murray got the 'I'm Already Very Confused' award, on the night; being part of every band on the day, or so it seemed, he couldn't figure out if he was playing electric or acoustic bass, squeeze box or centre-back for the Toon!

Stiff Little Fingers' Jake Burns did an impressive acoustic set with Ian McCallum and during Lindisfarne's closing set, the Felling Male Voice Choir accompanied the band for 'Run For Home'. This writer's abiding memory is of waiting behind the curtains for the song's finale, leading the be-suited and be-dickie-bowed 50-piece choir for the 'arms in the air' bit. They were revelling in the excitement of a truly remarkable evening.

To top off the Tall Ships Festival, Lindisfarne played from a stage on the cliffs high above Tynemouth later in the week as the magnificent ships sailed out of the mouth of the Tyne and the band played Alan's 'Tynemouth Song' from the 'Sailing Home' album. * Si was moved to note that, as a lad, he used to climb the trees just near the stage.

Newark Castle in August was Si's last gig with Lindisfarne. He'd spent the last two months flying back and forth across the Atlantic but, despite his fatigue, he judged every moment worthwhile; he was proud of 'Elvis Lives On The Moon' and was happy to support it. Now was the time for a sabbatical. Opening a brewery had been his dream; now all he had to do, apparently, was figure out how to weaken his own beer a little bit for the wimpy Canucks. Still, a big part of him would miss music: 'I've got about 30 songs either half-finished or finished. One day, when I make my album…' he smiled.

It was logical that Kenny would join the band for live work in Si's place. 'Having produced and played on the album, when it was time to take it on the road, I played Hammond, piano and guitar.' Kenny pointed out in the Chris Groom interview. Obviously, Simon's vocal would have been missing from their wonderful choruses, so I helped out there too.'

The album had been well supported by Essential/Castle – the band's new label – with poster sites across the capital and a single, while a new version of 'Day Of The Jackal' served its purpose, waking up several people in radio with its provocative lyric. The sleeve of the album was a different matter. An inside-sleeve shot – by famed Island Records and Bob Marley photographer Adrian Boot – had been taken of the band, but, rather unfortunately, in a scrap yard. The intention was perhaps to suggest a certain sense of determination that personified the album's contents. It didn't, especially as the front cover sported a shot of scrap cars with a black border.

The remit for the album had been followed to the letter; the songs were great and several were linked by musical 'interludes', which made fascinating listening. Alan was very upbeat when he spoke to *The Biz* magazine: 'I'd like to think "Elvis Lives On The Moon" is one of the first albums to define what the 1990s are about.' Apart from the support of Johnnie Walker – then back at Radio 1 – critical response was almost nil.

For the tour, the band were coupled by promoters Flying Music with the Strawbs, who opened, but the two bands did not sit comfortably together, neither outfit drawing any more people than they would have solo. Flying's reputation was built on 1960s revival-type packages; most certainly not what

* The song had been performed publicly only once before, on John Peel's show, broadcast on 18 January 73, at the time of 'Pipedream'. The album also included specially recorded songs from Martin Stephenson, Hedgehog Pie, Billy Mitchell, Mick Whittaker, the Doonan Family and Tim Healy – who was a very useful singer in the clubs at one time.

Lindisfarne were about. The new songs sounded better all the time and Alan was obviously in his element with Kenny on stage.

Below: Rod, in solo mode, celebrates the release of 'One Track Mind'.

The set itself was memorable, too, suggesting something far more intimate than Lindisfarne had attempted before. Designed by Gary Carverhill – the man behind the band's merchandise and several of their CD sleeves, as well as the Tall Ships Festival stage set – was a pub interior planned to replicate those operated by the tour's sponsors, Tap & Spile. Naturally, it also included its own bar, dartboard and crackling fire. 'I suggested the idea when the band said that they wanted a more subtle approach than the whole "Christmas thing",' Gary explained.

'This way, the set could be folded up after each show and the majority of the stage lighting came from, or was suggested by, the set itself. This meant that production and transport costs were kept down.' The concept was a big hit with both band and audience. With no need to sneak off for a 'quick one', any member not participating in a particular song could simply sit at the bar and have a drink, served by roadie Woody – and, if they needed to, leave stage via the door marked 'Exit' and nip off to do their ablutions. Brilliant.

The ongoing gag for the tour was the addition of various comments chalked on the reverse of the Guest Beers board propped up on stage every night. This was the side the audience couldn't see and, according to Gary, most comments were aimed at Marty. However, Alan was the recipient one night. 'He had gone into one of these walk-in cash dispensers in Rhyl, wearing a kagoul. As he went in he'd either knocked the door, or it had got stuck and he'd kicked it – either way, the door was automatically locked with Alan still in the lobby as a crowd gathered outside. So the message chalked up that night was, "Kagoul Man Robs Bank In Rhyl"!'

The new set made its debut as part of the launch of the tour for BBC-TV North at the only convenient location that could be found – the theatre within St Nicholas' Hospital. The same hospital that Alan had worked at, all those years ago. Fate is funny, sometimes…

'Once the tour had ended, Alan decided to keep the momentum going and we went off on an acoustic tour with Miller Anderson,' Kenny told Chris Groom. Miller had been part of the Keef Hartley Band, Savoy Brown and, for a short period, was with Mountain before joining the final line-up of Marc Bolan's T Rex. Alan's tour produced an album, 'Back To Basics', taken from shows at Blackheath and the Mean Fiddler in January and reviews were very good indeed, with long-overdue reinforcement given to Alan's writing talents and the performances from both men.

Kenny contributed accordion, keyboards and acoustic slide, as well as his sweet vocal support of Alan's more acidic vocals. Even better than 'Another Little Adventure', 'Back To Basics' was yet more evidence that Alan's creative fire had been stoked again, given the impetus of 'Elvis…' creative success and the re-establishment of his relationship with Kenny. 'Mother Russia' and 'Day Of The Jackal' were included from 'Elvis…', as well as selections from each of Lindisfarne's Charisma albums, including a rare airing of 'Oh, No, Not Again' from 'Dingly Dell'.

There was also 'Mr Inbetween' – an old song that hadn't surfaced until after the '78 reunion – 'Run For Home' and 'This Heart Of Mine', a song originally written by someone else, as Alan explained to *Magic In The Air* in the spring of 1994. 'I rewrote it. A guy called Kevin Phillipson wrote it and I heard it about ten years ago and started playing it – I've always wanted to record it.'

Alan admitted he'd neglected his solo career over the last decade and that he 'has a lot of catching up to do on people like Roy Harper and Ralph McTell.' The signs were very good indeed, if 'Back To Basics' was anything to go by. What was needed now was new songs.

May and June saw the very first Rod Clements solo tour and album, 'One Track Mind' – something he'd wanted to do for years. This activity gave him the opportunity, both in the studio and on tour, to mine the rich seam of acoustic and electric slide blues he'd always loved. As Rod told *Magic In The Air*: 'My idea was to combine some of my own songs with examples of the folk and blues material which had always been a source of inspiration to me.'

'One Track Mind' had begun life as a solo acoustic project a couple of years before, at Redesdale Studio in Northumberland, with Geoff Heslop at the controls. Apart from reworkings of his own songs – including 'Train In G Major' and 'Road To Kingdom Come' – Dylan's 'Down In The Flood' was a highlight; Woody Guthrie's 'Hard Travelling' was another. 'One Track Mind' also included tracks first heard on Bert and Rod's 'Leather Laundrette' as well as a solo take on 'Meet Me On The Corner' that had an almost Dylanesque quality in feel and simplicity.

Several reviews likened the instrumental closer, 'No Turning Back' – originally written for a Hull Street Freaks video – to the work of Ry Cooder. Fine praise indeed, and also a pointer to things to come… Rod thoroughly enjoyed the project, as he concluded at the time: 'The next one is already in preparation – in my head, anyway!' Several dates were performed as a trio with Ray and Steve Cunningham as the rhythm section and one, at the Kings Head, Allendale – billed as the Rough Riders – with the addition of Fraser Spiers, a superb harmonica player fresh from recording Del Amitri's 'Twisted' album.

Fraser and Rod had also been gigging as part of Rab Noakes' new band, the Varaflames, who set out on tour following Rab's departure from the BBC into the land of independent radio production. Some months later, an album – featuring Rab, Rod, Fraser and Pick Withers – was recorded, but has yet to be released.

Lindisfarne continued to tour hard following Kenny's departure to join Mary Black's band for her US tour, finally arriving at Fairport's annual Cropredy hootenanny in the Oxfordshire countryside. Lindisfarne were on storming form and Ian Burgess, from Fairport fanzine *The Ledge* was moved to say, 'Lindisfarne delivered the goods, the audience soaked it all in. Old favourites like "Meet Me On The Corner" to the new album's title track, "Elvis Lives On The Moon". For around 90 minutes, all that existed was that stage in the field…*we* were on that corner, *we* were on that moon.'

It was surprising that it had taken so long for Lindisfarne to make their debut at Cropredy, given their long association with Fairport, but as Ray pointed out in the subsequent sleeve notes for the CD and video, 'It was inevitable that, when the time was right (ie when Pegg could be persuaded to part with the lolly) that Lindisfarne would be invited as special guests.' As the same notes also indicated, it was important that Lindisfarne 'were appreciated for what they have always been; a bloody tremendous live band' and Cropredy was one of the most critical audiences around.

Castle, who by now had control of much of the Lindisfarne catalogue barring the Charisma albums, decided the time was right to put out a new 'Best Of'. The title put out by Virgin's budget label some years previously had done extremely well, but the band were not happy with the 'old geezers supping pints' illustration on the sleeve, as Ray pointed out. More importantly, Castle wanted to push the newly acquired catalogue and the band were keen to include post-reunion material.

The band set out on tour to support the resulting album, 'Lindisfarne On Tap' – a title which fitted the bill perfectly, not the least due to the fact that the band were still sponsored by Tap and Spile. 'We Can Make It', a song co-written by Alan and Ian McCallum, was released as a single in time for the tour, backed by 'Running Man' from the Nick Tauber sessions in 1991. The same stage set would be employed but, for the first time since the early days, there would be no keyboards. The band also announced that there would be no Christmas shows at the City Hall and it seemed that Lindisfarne had made a conscious decision to have their music taken seriously. They also promised a number of songs from the early 1970s, 'rediscovered' and given new arrangements.

Meanwhile, the Jack the Lad gigs during the summer (Ray had guested on the drum stool at Leeds) had been so well received that the band went out again during November. Whoever still thought Lindisfarne or its component members simply sat around until December was obviously well out of touch.

Alan had returned from his holiday home in Cyprus with a throat infection so bad that, for possibly the first time in their career, Lindisfarne had to postpone a show; in this case, at Ulverston. When his voice failed to improve over the next few shows, the band were forced to change arrangements to accommodate his temporarily limited range. Other songs were dropped altogether, replacing them with others that Rod or Marty could handle. Diverse circumstances often bring about surprising results and, in the case of the early shows, these came in the form of a solo set from Rod, including Leadbelly's 'Bourgeois Blues' and 'Hard Travelling' from 'One Track Mind', as well as 'Train In G Major'. When Alan's voice improved the spot was left in as it had gone down so well.

Another innovation was the introduction of guitar tech Dave Denholm – another 'sixth man' – who started off playing guitar on 'We Can Make It' and 'Lady Eleanor' to allow Rod to play fiddle and mandolin respectively. At Ray's instigation, Dave stayed on stage one night after 'Eleanor' and played on 'Evening' from 'The News' – to the great surprise of everyone else and a delightful bonus.

As ever, it seemed, the band had stumbled on another musical partner who shared much of the collective and individual background. Dave was born in 1967 in Willington Quay, near Wallsend, moving to Cullercoats where he lived until he was 17 or 18 years old, spending much of his time listening to Springsteen and playing drums – 'badly'. A succession of local punk bands followed after his attentions turned to guitar and in the early 1990s he spent three years with Newcastle band This Is This.

'When I was 13, I nicked the money for my first guitar from my mate – we've already met him on our once. It didn't work out well…' Dave laughs. 'It was a Kay SG guitar. I just missed punk, but at the me, I was really into the Jam and Paul Weller. I remember frantically trying to learn the D chord, just so could play the start to "In The City" or whatever it was.'

It was a fascination with songs that spurred Dave on: 'Definitely Springsteen. I played "The River" l the time; particularly "The Price You Pay" – the sound of that. That semi-Phil Spector production. I ways liked the "dark" songs. That's probably why I liked the Jam – a songs band.'

It was mutual acquaintance at art school that put Ray Laidlaw in touch with Dave when the band as looking for a roadie and guitar technician in 1994. 'Lindisfarne was my first guitar tech job. At the ne I was studying art – as I still am – at Newcastle College. I'd been there a year when I got the call om Ray. I remember saying "Is this for real?".' Dave believes the initial connection came through This This, who had contributed one track to 'The Playhouse Album', produced by Steve Daggett.

This was the year he was asked to go 'out front' to play guitar on 'Lady Eleanor' while Rod handled andolin duties. 'That was the warm-up gig before Cropredy. It was great to go from a club gig to mething like that.' By the spring tour of 1995, he was contributing guitar and backing harmonies on rtually every number. 'By then I'd established a relationship with Alan. I think he was pretty strumental in getting me in. Whether he had another agenda, I don't know… Alan was certainly strumental in bumping up my wages – but then, he'd always get me to buy the beers!'

In March, the band set off on a British tour but discovered that, no matter how much they tried to fuse, they would still have to return to the 'squalor' of the Middle East to play yet more lucrative ows. This time, the shows were in hotels and country clubs in Muscat, Abu Dhabi, Bahrain and Qatar. ews had filtered through that last time, in 1993, the lads pulled crowds which had broken audience cords previously held by Duran Duran!

Steve Cunningham would not be able to make the dates due to his wife's impending pregnancy, so e band invited Ian Thomson, formerly of Dust on the Needle, along for the trip. Dust were another fshoot who had recorded a session for BBC Radio Manchester during 1984 and had variously included embers of Hedgehog Pie, the Doonan Family and Lindisfarne, as well as Kathryn Tickell in its line-up. ltimately, Steve Cunningham left to concentrate on his other musical interests – his band with Lee oud, the Proud Ones, eventually signing to Ritz Records – and Ian was immediately up for the ndisfarne job.

Ian was born in 1961 in Wallsend, the son of a local GP. After quitting art school, he picked the bass uitar and never looked back. His parents wouldn't buy him a bass, 'So they bought me what they lled a *proper* guitar; a nylon-string semi-acoustic, which was good because it meant I learned chords.' nce the former choirboy's voice had broken, 'I went more off the wall in my tastes. I was very into ade and T Rex as well, but that led into Bowie and the Spiders From Mars – which led into more aughty" stuff – MC5 and early Blue Oyster Cult, which I'm not embarrassed to say because it was all ree-chord thrashes. Basically, it had to be simple, loud and raucous.'

When punk came along, Ian was 'overjoyed', frequenting all the w-wave venues around Newcastle like the Cooperage on the uayside while studying fine art. His first band, a nine-piece called rthur 2 Stroke, entertained North East audiences with their 'mental »st-punk'. 'They didn't have a bass player, just two guitars and a ummer. I was 19 and I'd just bought my first bass with my first udent grant. At one of their gigs I just said, "You need a bass player" d they said, "Yeah, but we just haven't found the right one." So I id, "I'll do it".'

Around the same time, he decided to study music theory at llege, 'but it was really stuff I knew already.' In 1983, Ian joined the uring line-up of the Kane Gang, another of the successful groups to me out of Newcastle's Kitchenware Records along with Prefab »rout and Martin Stephenson and the Daintees. Following this, he ce again linked up with former 2 Stroke colleague Pat Rafferty, who d played accordion on 'Woody Lives!' alongside Jacka, Rod, Rab »akes and Bert Jansch. This was Dust on the Needle.

The line-up developed from its beginnings as a showcase for athryn Tickell to yet another version of Pacamax, which included ast guitarist/vocalist Jed Grimes, Marty Craggs, Ray Laidlaw and lly Mitchell. Ian's real break came when he answered a *Melody Maker* l placed by former Long Ryders frontman Sid Griffin. 'I'd got sick of ewcastle by then,' Ian recalls. 'The ad said that the person must be epared to relocate, so I said, "That'll do for me." So I sold everything ad; my Cortina, my stereo, my amps.'

Around Christmas 1987, the Long Ryders had broken up and Sid ready had the basis of his new band, the Coal Porters. 'I'd got a

Opposite: Doin' that scrapyard thing…an unused 'Elvis' shot.

Below: Dust on the Needle. From left, Ian Thomson, Marty, Ray, Ross Winning (front), Jed Grimes and Pat Rafferty.

friend in London to place the ad for me, just for a laugh,' Sid recalls. Ian sent his photograph and letter and Sid replied, saying 'If you can get yourself to LA, we'll consider you for the band – thinking we'd never hear from him again…about four weeks later, he turned up on my doorstep. I just couldn't believe it.' Thinking it was cheaper to fly to New York, Ian had planned to buy a car and then drive to Los Angeles. 'I really didn't have much money; about three hundred quid – thinking back, I must have been completely mad!'

Sid uses a quote from the movie *Casablanca* to describe his relationship with Ian; 'It was the start of a beautiful friendship. We're real close. I only have that with two or three people.' Sid also recalls that, in the period before taking off for LA, Ian had met up with broadcasters Liz and Andy Kershaw when they came up to Newcastle. 'Ian mentioned to them that he was going over to link up with this guy Sid Griffin and both Liz and Andy said that he had to go for it. That was kinda cool.'

Ian had seen the Long Ryders on TV's *Old Grey Whistle Test*; 'I just took one look at them – the sound was down – and thought, "Yeah, they look really great!".' For the next five years, Ian and Sid took the Coal Porters across the States and then relocated to London in 1991. 'We weren't successful with Ian in the band – not that we're successful now – but it got me into the Lindisfarne picture.'

Sid's initial introduction to the North East music scene came through the music of Kathryn Tickell, 'through the record collector-cum folk-circles in Los Angeles, California. I can also remember in 1981, 1982 buying a cut-out (deleted) vinyl album of Lindisfarne's for one dollar. At that time, I didn't quite "get" it. The tracks I liked I loved, and I knew the other stuff was pretty good.'

Around 1985, Sid had also had a house in Los Angeles and Eric Burdon had been a room-mate, as he was friend of Sid's roadie. Also sharing the house, according to Sid, were the Bangles and Rockpile guitarist Billy Bremner. 'Every once in a while, someone would mention Sting, or the Junco Partners, Bryan Ferry or Lindisfarne. So I was not unaware of Lindisfarne when Ian Thompson walked into my life.'

Ian moved back to the North East in 1992 and once again took up with Rafferty, who was by this time part of Archie Brown and the Young Bucks, a very fine, hardworking band. The local base suited Ian's personal circumstances as a single parent of two pre-teenage children, so when the opportunity came with Lindisfarne he grabbed it with both hands – while still remaining a member of the Young Bucks.

Ian's sense of humour proved to be a real asset to a band he remembers listening to at his 'Aunty Doreen's house' when he was ten. 'What struck me was "Meet Me On The Corner". I thought, "What's that thunderous sound coming out of that dirty old radiogram?" It was Rod's bass. I remember being struck by that, thinking, "Phwoah – what a *great* sound!"' There is an actual photo in existence of the young Thomson sitting in his bedroom, surrounded by posters of Slade, Alice Cooper, Argent and…Lindisfarne. It is strongly rumoured that this photograph is under lock and key in a security vault. Another little-known fact outside of his native North East is that Ian was a star of *Viz*…

On Lindisfarne's return from the Middle East, Rod swiftly set off on more solo dates supporting multi-instrumentalist and raconteur Robin Williamson of Incredible String Band fame, while Alan announced plans for a new solo studio album as well as a nationwide tour during April and May. Alan was still obviously 'on a roll', having 18 new compositions from which to select. The musicians lined up included Dave Denholm on lead guitar, Frankie Gibbon on bass and drummer Paul Smith, both of whom had played on 'On The Other Side' in 1983.

Dave regarded it a natural development of his contribution to the band that he went on to collaborate closely with Alan in all aspects of his solo work: 'Alan had not pushed to get me in the band or anything, but we did get on well and he invited me to help him out on his solo stuff.' The album was to be released by the Grapevine label, home of Mary Black, Sharon Shannon, Christy Moore and Emmylou Harris and a label whose reputation was built on the effort and resources it was prepared to put behind its artists nationally.

Just as crucially, Tyne Tees had confirmed that they would be recording the 25th Anniversary show at Newcastle City Hall on 2 July 1995. A CD and video would be released later in the year. Shurely shome mishtake? The first time Lindisfarne played the City Hall supporting Jackson Heights was actually…2 July…er…1970. Where the bloody hell did all that time go?

Chapter
TWELVE
CAN'T KILL THE SPIRIT...

The Quarter Century Concert was a resounding success. The presence of the Tyne Tees Television crew was barely noticed, such was the unobtrusive way they went about their job, while the pub stage set worked brilliantly as a televisual treat. Friends and family filled the tiers up to the organ loft behind the band, special guests along for the night including Tim Healy, his wife Denise Welch (now a firm favourite on *Coronation Street* as Natalie Horrocks) and a strangely-bearded Kevin Whately.

Other 'names' in the hall included Newcastle United supremo Sir John Hall, along with fellow director Freddy Shepherd. Woody, 'barman' for the evening, was well-pushed to keep up with demand, having to send out for more supplies to assist the transition between full glass and empty jug (hidden below the bar – the beer was meant to look hand-pulled).

The show was opened by Mike Elliott, very much part of the Lindisfarne family since Phil Murray and Walter Fairbairn had suggested him as MC for a Jack the Lad tour. Mike and Alan had become close, particularly in shared political beliefs discussed in the convivial atmosphere of the Maggie Bank. Neither man was shy of forthright speaking, either – a talent Elliott was to put to use (as Mike the Mouth) on his popular Century Radio phone-in programme.

Rab Noakes, the only possible choice to open the night's proceedings at the City Hall, was in fine fettle, having stirred his creative juices with the recording of his 'Standing Up' album a year before. His performance was as assured as ever, highlights including several covers on the album such as Talking Head's 'Psycho Killer' and 'Downtown Lights', the latter from fellow Scots the Blue Nile and whispered to be writer Paul Buchanan's favourite interpretation.

Lindisfarne performed a superbly assured set. There was a musical smoothness that managed to wrap itself around every facet of their repertoire – not tonight the 'ragged mess' Michael Chapman had experienced over 25 years ago in Belgium. To quote Geoff Wall in *Folk On Tap* magazine, the band were 'Still fresh, still a long way from blasé about their repertoire or their position in the world of music. The are still a great gust of fresh air…'

Though the live recording was released as both a CD and video (ironically titled 'Another Fine Mess'), one highlight not included in the package was Tim Healy's fantastic rendition of 'January Song' – introduced as one of the first songs he can remember playing – which he accompanied himself on Alan's acoustic guitar. 'Evening' from 'The News,' was given a rare outing, while co-writer Ian McCallum joined the band on stage for 'We Can Make It'. 'Squire' was brought out and dusted up, sounding fresher than it ever did.

Throughout, Dave Denholm's contributions on acoustic and electric guitar were understated, the arrangement working better all the time. Ian Thompson, too, looked and sounded supremely at home on bass, particularly accompanying Alan on 'Winter Song'. 'This Heart Of Mine' from 'Back To Basics' was another highlight, as was 'Money' – a classic Alan rant unveiled on a recent Radio 2 broadcast on National Music Day.

Alan appeared more at ease on stage than he had been for some time, bolstered by the solo performances he and Dave Denholm had been giving since the spring. As Dave recalls of their shows, 'The two-guitar thing really helped his performances. It really seemed to gel. You feel very exposed in the sort of intimate venues we used to play, but it worked well.'

By 'Fog On The Tyne', Tim, Kevin and Ian had joined in for the chorus, with a verse thrown in by Billy Mitchell for good measure. If the band was frustrated that they would be forever tagged as 'daft lads at Christmas' – or tarred by the party album/Gazza episodes – then this performance was a kick in the proverbial knackers to their detractors. Here was a band regularly capable of remarkable performances that could measure up to – and often surpass – their peers.

Four months after the Quarter Century Concert, Alan Hull was dead.

It was Rod Clements' birthday, 17 November 1995. Alan was in fantastic spirits, talking excitedly about his new solo album he was recording with Dave Denholm as sparring partner. He had enjoyed a meal with Pat and then complained of chest pains. Pat called for an ambulance. By the time it arrived, Alan was gone.

He and Dave had been recording at Frank Gibbon's studio, situated in a beautiful location in the midst of the Lambton Estate in Durham. As they drove home the previous night, the pair were listening to some rough mixes of a song called 'Walk A Crooked Mile' and a new version of '100 Miles To Liverpool' and, to quote Dave Denholm, 'We realised something special had occurred during that first week of recording.' The plan was to include several old songs, including '100 Miles To Liverpool'; 'Drug Song', 'This Heart Of Mine' and 'Treat Me Kindly'. 'Poignantly, as it turned out, Alan said that in a way, this record would sound autobiographical; a life story.'

The shock waves of Alan's death from a heart attack reverberated around the music industry. Elvis Costello, who had long acknowledged Alan's talents, commented, 'He was a wonderful songwriter who will be remembered for his dark and thoughtful compositions, as well as his humour.' In Parliament, several MPs tabled their acknowledgement of Alan's commitment to both the Unions and the Labour Party, while letters of sympathy were posted on the Internet from as far away as Canada and Japan.

Singer-songwriter Chris Rea has already indicated the respect with which Alan was regarded by his peers. Perhaps the emotions were best illustrated by a note received from fellow songwriter Martin Stephenson, which read: 'Another beautiful head in the beautiful lights of heaven; my love to Alan's family and that beautiful democracy of a band.' He then went on, in verse:

Right: Lindisfarne 1995. From left: Rod Clements, Dave Denholm, Ian Thomson, Marty Craggs, Alan Hull and Ray Laidlaw.

Keep starting up the van,
'til the last one can,
Yes a band's a little village
and this one's lost one of
its men
But if it keeps on singing
He'll always be there,
again and again!

IN MEMORIAM
ALAN HULL

H FEBRUARY 1945 - 17TH NOVEMBER 1995

During Alan's funeral in Tynemouth – a non-religious occasion, in keeping with his wishes – Rod, Kenny Craddock, Marty, Dave and Si performed three specially selected songs: 'One World', for Alan's optimism following the birth of grand-daughter Roxanne; 'Fog On The Tyne', the 'throwaway' forever associated with both Alan and Lindisfarne, and 'Alright On The Night' in recognition of good company, good beer and good crack – one of Alan's greatest pleasures.

Ray Laidlaw read two of Alan's poems from *The Mocking Horse*; 'The Slipway' – describing the launch of another ship from the banks of the Tyne, with the final line, 'And the ship stayed where it was...' and 'Love Part 383' that so simply put into words what Alan and Pat shared. Each showed just one element of the complex character that was Alan Hull. We can only allude to those complexities here. Another book, perhaps; another time.

Writing in *Folk Roots*, Simon Jones got very close to what Alan was about: 'His world was concerned, sociable, caring, environmental, proud, historic, incurably romantic. A place where having a drink meant party time, where authority was often ridiculous, where people came first, where honesty was celebrated, where magnanimous failure could be immortalised kindly and above all – where hope and romance were never trivialised or forgotten.'

Mike Elliott's eulogy generated huge laughter with some personal tales of Alan's company, finally ending with a choked, 'T'ra, bonny lad'. We all sang 'Imagine' and, finally, 'Clear White Light' as the music was relayed out into the packed cemetery where members of the public mixed with others who had come to pay their respects; Chris Rea and former manager John McCoy; Jacka; Terry Morgan; Mickey Sweeney; Brendan Healy, Tim Healy; long-time friend and BBC (now Tyne Tees) anchorman Mike Neville and John Anthony, producer of 'Nicely Out Of Tune'.

UNITED STATES OF MIND (HULL)

THE RAINDROPS FEEL LIKE LIQUID DIAMONDS
FALLING FROM A CLOUD WHO HAS A SILVER LINING
MADE BY PASSING TIME
AND THOUGH I'VE NOT JUST HAD A SMOKE
I'VE NOT BEEN STRUCK BY LIGHTNING STROKE
OH LET IT THUNDER LET IT WHISTLE
LET IT BLOW LIKE HELL I'M NOT REALLY CARING
AND MY STATE OF MIND NEEDS NO REPAIRING

YESTERDAY WAS PAINTED GREY
AND I'VE FOUND OUT NO RELIABLE WAY
OF KNOWING WHAT TOMORROW'S COLOURS MIGHT SAY
WHILE HEADS AROUND ME TURN AND TWIST
AT SITUATIONS THAT DON'T EXIST
OH LET IT THUNDER LET IT WHISTLE
LET IT BLOW LIKE HELL I'M NOT REALLY MINDING
AND MY STATE OF MIND NEEDS NO DEFINING

I'M WANDERING THROUGH A FAIRY STORY
LOST IN LOVE AND SEEKING GLORY
LISTENING TO THE MUSIC, CHILDREN SMILE
WHILE OTHERS WITH MORE COMPLEX CLAIMS
PROTECT THEMSELVES AGAINST THE RAIN
OH LET IT THUNDER LET IT WHISTLE
LET IT BLOW LIKE HELL I'M NOT REALLY BOTHERED
AND MY STATE OF MIND HAS FINALLY BEEN DISCOVERED
OH LET IT THUNDER LET IT WHISTLE
LET IT BLOW LIKE HELL I'M NOT REALLY BOTHERED
AND MY STATE OF MIND HAS FINALLY BEEN DISCOVERED

IMAGINE (LENNON)

IMAGINE THERE'S NO HEAVEN
IT'S EASY IF YOU TRY
NO HELL BELOW US
ABOVE US ONLY SKY

IMAGINE ALL THE PEOPLE
LIVING FOR TODAY...

IMAGINE THERE'S NO COUNTRIES
IT ISN'T HARD TO DO
NOTHING TO KILL OR DIE FOR
AND NO RELIGION TOO

IMAGINE ALL THE PEOPLE
LIVING LIFE IN PEACE...

YOU MAY SAY I'M A DREAMER
BUT I'M NOT THE ONLY ONE
I HOPE SOMEDAY YOU'LL JOIN US
AND THE WORLD WILL BE AS ONE

IMAGINE NO POSSESSIONS
I WONDER IF YOU CAN
NO NEED FOR GREED OR HUNGER
A BROTHERHOOD OF MAN

IMAGINE ALL THE PEOPLE
SHARING ALL THE WORLD...

YOU MAY SAY I'M A DREAMER
BUT I'M NOT THE ONLY ONE
I HOPE SOMEDAY YOU'LL JOIN US
AND THE WORLD WILL LIVE AS ONE

A EULOGY

BY MIKE ELLIOTT

There was no doubt in the minds of the remaining members of Lindisfarne that the band should stay together. If anyone was entitled to play Alan's songs, then it was them. It was also felt that this would be the best way to keep those songs alive – and, for Ray Laidlaw, 'the best way we could deal with Alan's death…' Pat Hull gave her blessing and, in a very short space of time, the decision to continue was made.

As Ray told *Magic In The Air* at the time; 'We've been making music together for most of our lives and treasure the relationship we have built with our audience. Alan has left us a fantastic musical legacy and the most positive thing we can do for him is to ensure that his songs are performed, recorded and enjoyed.' Ray confirmed that Alan in particular had felt the most recent line-up of the band was Lindisfarne's most musically successful and artistically credible since early days.

Right: Mitch refuses to throw in the towel, 1997.

'We intend to build upon last year's solid musical foundation,' Ray continued. 'To do this, we need another great singer. Harmony is an important aspect of Lindisfarne, from both a musical and personal point of view. With both of these considerations in mind, there was really only one candidate.' Twenty-three years after first being asked, re-enter Billy Mitchell.

Mitch was not there to replace Alan but, as he put it, 'In my heart I've always been part of Lindisfarne; I've celebrated their successes and shared their despair during difficult times. Now I'll just play my part to help Lindisfarne continue.'

Rod clearly supported Ray when he said, 'In some ways we're only now beginning to fully appreciate Alan's songwriting ability. We were perhaps too close to it before. He is irreplaceable in the band, but Mitch's status as a performer and a friend qualify him uniquely for the task in hand.'

In January 1996, the newly constituted band reconvened in Rothbury – minus Ray – to work out songs for the rescheduled November dates, which would now be happening during March. It was a sign of each promoter's faith in the band that, almost without exception, all the original venues agreed to the band's return. Inside Rod's aunt's house, the scene was reminiscent of a backwoods shack in Arkansas – or somewhere like that – as a TV news crew came to take a peek.

This acoustic format proved to be an interesting pointer for things to come. Rehearsals then moved to the Maggie Bank, to be knocked into shape with the full band, adding electric instruments. The format was the same as that which proved so effective during 1994-95 although, as work progressed, it was clear that there was more breadth instrumentally.

The first visit by this writer found the band launching into a storming version of Jack the Lad's 'Rocking Chair' – Mitch's DMs pumping up and down as Dave, Marty and Ian added harmonies. On another occasion, it was hairs-stand-up-on-the-back-of-the-neck time as Dave sang 'One World' alone. Within the perimeter marked by these two songs, something fascinating was occurring.

The first show by the new line-up and the first date on the tour came at Hartlepool Town Hall. There was a sense of nervousness; uncertainty. And, as Steve Weltman drove up from London to introduce the band on stage, there would undoubtedly have been a whole host of questions and emotions going through his mind.

As Judith Watson wrote of the occasion in *Magic In The Air*, 'There was a great deal of trepidation mixed in with our anticipation. How would we feel as they walked on stage for the first time without Alan? More to the point, how would they be feeling? Would it be as if Alan had never been there – just like *Fawlty Towers* – "Don't mention Alan!" Would Billy try to take over? Would it all be just too much?'

As this writer reported: 'As the band moved on to the stage, they began to play a waltz-like introduction – reminiscent of the "Theme From The Last Waltz" by the Band – it is as if the band were trying to throw the audience, who seemed confused. They didn't recognise this. "Oh Jesus," you could almost hear everyone whisper, "they've lost it..." They were expecting the Grand Statement – a Message of Intent from this new line-up, not *this*... Then – BOOM! – "Alright On The Night". Bloody brilliant. A masterstroke of rearrangement.'

The edge to the night brought some remarkable performances despite – or perhaps, because of – nerves. Dave's 'One World' was a highlight, as was 'Log On Your Fire' from 'The News' – never before played live and specially chosen by Mitch as one of Alan's finest. Mitch also pulled out a spellbinding 'United States Of Mind', willed along by the audience who immediately latched on to the sense of respect and commitment in his performance of the 'Pipedream' classic.

Rod's electric slide guitar solo on 'Road To Kingdom Come' ripped through the hall, a 'clearly liberated and delighted' Mr Clements receiving a standing ovation. As Judith Watson explained, the band struck the right balance in acknowledging their departed friend: 'Alan was talked about with just the right amount of affection and humour, without any sentimentality.'

A later date at South Shields saw the band return to Tyneside for the first time since Alan's death. The sense of nervousness was discernible to this writer, but outwardly they seemed relaxed. Alan's widow Pat was in the audience, and how difficult this was for her may never be known. After a short set from Mitch and Marty's sons Scott and Andrew, there seemed a sense of reticence from the audience – understandable, really.

Meanwhile, the band just got on with the job in hand. This time, there were some really choking moments: 'One World' was astounding, the cracked emotion of Dave's vocal delivery reflecting a depth of recollection that was very special indeed. Dave, who got a tremendous response from everyone, band included, had quickly become aware of other people's tendency to see much of Alan's delivery and vocal frailty in his singing.

'I have no problem in singing Alan's songs or having a voice that can be likened to him,' he said recently. 'I don't understand what that is; I don't hear it like that. When I hear my voice, I don't hear Alan. I think I'm partly to blame for people thinking that, by choosing his songs to do.' Ian recalls one person coming into the dressing room once and telling Dave, 'That was really great; but you haven't quite got the voice right...' 'Walk A Crooked Mile' was a song Alan and Dave had recorded for Alan's yet-to-be-released solo album and it fitted like a glove into the set.

For the second half of the show, Pat took her place in the balcony with Mitch's wife Sue. Maybe Pat couldn't face all of this at first. Mitch turned in a quite remarkable performance of 'Passing Ghosts' from 'Fog On The Tyne'; yet another song to resurface after a long absence. Lindisfarne had clearly taken the opportunity to go back across the whole breadth of their catalogue – just to see what would be great to play again, with *this* band.

Rod's 'leaving gift' to Jack the Lad, 'Why Can't I Be Satisfied', was another, and it lifted the mood considerably. Intriguingly, the song had come full circle, having been in the running all those years ago for 'Dingly Dell', while wrapping the night up once again was 'Jackhammer Blues'. Pat came backstage after the show and there were tearful hugs all round. Much was unspoken. But much, this writer suspected, was understood. Tyneside's band had returned home safely.

The team of Dave, Rod, Marty, Ian and Mitch had thoroughly enjoyed the dozens of live radio sessions that had promoted the tour; Alan had apparently never been keen on this aspect of the 'game'. More significantly, there was the realisation that it would be great to do the gigs in the same format, too. It seemed to make so much sense. As Michael Chapman would later comment, 'This is the way people *think* Lindisfarne sound.'

The decision was made that, depending on venue, the shows would be in both electric and acoustic formats – 'Untapped', as they were christened in a nod to the 'Best Of' collection. The first Untapped show was on 18 May at Ede Tower in Sunderland and figured very well indeed. The band were all seated in a semi-circle, Ray off to the right, using a simple three-piece kit plus hi-hat. Mitch had a prior commitment to Maxi and Mitch gigs in Canada, and in his absence Marty, Dave and Rod simply shared the vocals.

Below: Lighting up Blackpool for Radio 2, 30 August 1997.

To quote *Magic In The Air* contributor Geoff Mallin, 'That's the way it is with Lindisfarne; no edge, no egos – just a collection of mates having a great time.' The situation threw up some rare delights, including Rod's take on Woody Guthrie's 'Hard Travellin'' from 'One Track Mind'; he and Marty also contributed a wonderful version of 'Train In G Major' before a radical and successful reworking of 'Run For Home', *sans* big intro, *sans* 'big' anything except that fine slab of a chorus.

The first mention of 'Jimmy Alan Hull' after 'All Fall Down' brought a spontaneous burst of applause from the audience, while a new song, Rod's 'Refugees' – originally in the running for the 'Elvis…' album – was also premiered. 'Jackhammer Blues' once again came complete with original gibberish introduction from Rod, and at the same point in the Carlisle show a few days later Steeleye's Maddy Prior could not contain herself, joining the hoedown with her celebrated gusto.

May also saw Untapped gigs at the Maggie Bank as part of the 'unofficial' element of the North Shields Fish Quay Festival, * while at Harvey's in Stockton Dave's solo version of 'Winter Song' mesmerised everyone: there seemed to be magic afoot. As Chris Groom noted of the Farnham show: 'The hard work the band have been forced to put into rearranging their set was obvious right from the start…they passed their own strict test with flying colours; *we* were enjoying it, *they* were enjoying it, thankfully it was pretty much business as usual.'

June found Lindisfarne headlining a highly emotionally charged show for the opening of the Eurofest '96 in the centre of Newcastle – just over the road from St James' Park. Earlier that day, Alan's family and friends had been joined by the band for the scattering of his ashes at the mouth of the Tyne. Despite there being none forecast, fog did, indeed, roll in…

In the evening, the band were joined on the bill by a clearly distraught Ian McCallum ** – who presented the new 'Song For Alan' – Archie Brown and the Young Bucks (featuring Ian Thomson on bass); Andrew Craggs and the Junco Partners, whose rhythm section had so inspired Ray and Rod all those years ago and tonight featured Charlie Harcourt on rhythm guitar. Beginning a little shakily, Lindisfarne – in individual international football shirts – soon hit their stride.

A show of this size (6,000 people in a huge marquee) was a very different animal, but the band rose to the occasion, their power and confidence growing progressively with each song. They were back in 'electric' mode. A simple reference from Mitch that 'We said goodbye to a friend today' proved sufficient and, by the close of the show – with two junior Mitchells on stage along with Andrew Craggs and Ian McCallum – everywhere you looked, every type of person you could imagine, was singing.

Lindisfarne continued through the summer with more split-format gigs, including a co-headlining spot with the Holmes Brothers at Glasgow International Festival. While there, they took part in a one-hour radio special for BBC Radio Scotland.

In August, work was also finally completed on Alan's album, entitled 'Statues And Liberties' – to be released in November. Lindisfarne meanwhile, prepared for another tour the same month, this time as a fully-fledged Untapped series of shows. Further dates were planned for February 1997, including Europe. The band continued to work hard, putting in the hours and the miles, gradually adjusting to their new form. Slowly, but most certainly surely, promoters, press and audiences were coming to the conclusion that here was a very viable band.

As Rod explained to Dick Godfrey in the *Newcastle Journal* in 1997, it was difficult at first: 'To an extent, in the early days after Alan's death we probably didn't mind being considered a tribute band because a lot of what we did was a rebuilding, reassurance exercise to prove to audiences we were still in business and weren't going to drop all the old stuff and move off in a totally new direction.'

'Statues And Liberties' was finally released as the band prepared to tour the UK again. Faced with two options, to leave the recordings alone or complete the album as Alan would have wanted, Dave and Frankie Gibbon chose the latter – and when it came to promoting the album, the pair shouldered the burden of press and radio activity with enthusiasm.

'We had incredible support from Pat and Alan's daughters,' Dave told Simon Evans in the *Birmingham Post*. This was not a simple task. Fortunately, Alan had discussed in quite some detail with both Frankie and Dave a 'feel' or direction for certain songs; others he saw augmented by certain instrumentation. As fortune would have it, Alan had recorded final vocals for almost all the material, which was unusual in that instrumentation was generally laid down first.

Two songs that weren't already recorded were 'This Heart Of Mine' and 'Drug Song', 'so we had to use vocals from demos he and I had done previously and then arrange some instrumentation around what we thought he would have wanted,' Dave continued. Frankie and Dave had the job of completing a massive puzzle, and emotionally it was a huge struggle.

When Alan had entered the studio in October 1995, he truly believed this album was to be his finest solo effort since those hazy days in Soho. He was armed with a handful of songs co-written with Dave – many during a stay in the Lake District, near Penrith. Among these was 'Walk A Crooked Mile'. 'Dave had shared Alan's innermost thoughts and outlooks,' said *Magic In The Air*, 'and knew how positive, optimistic and enthusiastic he was feeling about life.' Alan's family wanted them to complete the album and, as Dave explained, 'Me and Frankie just had to do the best we could for Alan.'

'Statues And Liberties' was ultimately released by the resuscitated Transatlantic label (which had released his 'We Can Swing Together' single in 1969) just over a year after Alan's death. Reviews acknowledged the sad loss to the music industry of probably one of its most under-rated songwriters. There was a sense, however, that the compliments heaped on both Alan and Dave, along with Frankie Gibbon, would have been the same had Alan lived.

This was not always the case when an artist passed away, opinions often tainted by the glow of past glories or simply regret for creativity lost. *Folk Roots* acknowledged as much, stating: 'We should all feel ashamed to confess that, quite probably, Alan Hull did not realise what a top-grade songwriter critics in particular felt him to be.' There was still a sense of anger that the praise could not have come sooner.

Dave Denholm was angry – as he said after Alan's service – that they didn't get to take the album out on the road. More than one source had indicated that Alan was, in fact, ready to leave Lindisfarne behind, once and for all, such were his spirits around the time of his death. A cruel irony, then, that there could have been two very fine sets of performers split from the same seed...

Q said that the album stood 'proudly beside the best of his solo efforts, capturing the qualities which earned the respect of his peers. A hostage to sentiment and an unashamed romantic, his tender love songs ("This Heart Of Mine", "Treat Me Kindly"), nestle beside his focused anti-establishment rants which savage the iniquities of corrupt political systems, grinding poverty (the title track, "Hoi Polloi")... poignant tribute to a raw talent.' Mike Ollier in the *Northern Echo* acknowledged the renaissance in Lindisfarne's material over their last two albums, 'and this comes in where they left off'.

Ross Fortune in *Time Out* noted that the album was '...pithy, political and good-natured, articulate, energetic and at times very beautiful. Although hardly hip, Hull was a much-loved and respected figure. These 12 songs, distinguished by a simple, eloquent humanity and his distinctively husky, tender and emotive voice, show powerfully why.' This time around, Alan had written 'Save Yourself' for grand-daughter Roxanne and Simon Evans was particularly struck by the line, 'Don't make haste, time is free, save your precious self for me...'

Ultimately, like so many of the reviews, Evans felt that 'Statues And Liberties' was 'the finest showcase of the man's talents since "Pipedream".' Michael White attempted to wrap it all up with his review in *Folk On Tap*: 'No-one is likely to erect a statue to Alan Hull. It is difficult to imagine that he would have felt comfortable with the notion in any case, given his self-effacing nature and habit of deflating such pomposity. Statues were for pillars of the establishment; the kind who give orders that hurt people, scar the country and cripple minds. However, it would be a liberty to ignore this album.'

In December, during the course of a 29-date British tour, Lindisfarne recorded both nights of their 'Untapped And Acoustic' performances at Marden High School, Tynemouth. The venue was significant: Dave Denholm was an 'old boy' and Ray's son, Jed went to the school, as did Mitch's son Tom. Engineered by old mate Steve Daggett, the album was initially only available via mail order.

Finally to be given a worldwide release by Park Records in 1999, the album clearly showed where Lindisfarne now stood; assured and confident in the marriage of their past and their future. Copies that fell into the hands of the music press found an enthusiastic reception. 'This record exudes a depth and sophistication you don't hear in folk anymore,' wrote one critic. 'Lindisfarne perform acoustically with a conviction that comes only with the best practitioners of an art which demands enormous subtlety,' said another.

In an interview with Dick Godfrey in November 1997, Rod explained how this was achieved: 'A lot of bands have tried to go acoustic and found they have to make compromises especially at the raunchy end of things and it comes out sounding twee and soppy or whatever. With us, it come out quite the opposite, which was very gratifying.' As Rod further explained recently, 'The acoustic thing was a great way of re-establishing the band after Alan, leaving a very firm calling-card wherever we went that this is the band now. "Look at us, we're doing something completely different." No pretence. That's what was valuable about that.'

The next stage was the writing and recording of new material, and this aspect could not be underestimated. They had gone a long way to developing their own character so fa and interest was growing. To quote Rod in his Dick Godfrey interview, the gigs had 'forged the band and the newer members together…the work made us a genuine group rather than just a touring band.'

What was clear was that not only were the long-time fans staying with the 'new' Lindisfarne, but due to the profile gained via constant gigging plus dozens of radio sessions alongside very positive press, new and lapsed fans were coming on board all the time. A short stay was booked during early 1997 at an isolated, though idyllic, studio on the West Coast of Scotland – Watercolour Music in Ardgour.

'One of the main things about those sessions was that we didn't have a producer, as such,' explaine Dave. 'As a consequence, we didn't have any time management, it was still all so new – everyone was fumbling around. When you hear those tracks now, it's the way the band *doesn't* play at the right moments.'

As Rod points out, 'I think it's very difficult for a band to produce itself. It fell to Dave and me a lot of the time…but because the function in this band is based on mutual respect – receptive to each other positiveness and playing off each other – it's very hard for somebody to say, "I can do that better". When a producer's there, that's their job and nobody's going to get upset.'

The result of the recordings was a four-track EP, 'Blues From The Bothy'. The lead cut, Rod's 'Coming Home To You', was a wonderful brew of country blues that immediately hit several radio playlists across the country, clearly catching many stations on the hop with its rolling rhythm. Intriguingly, and for the first time, the EP earned a chart position from satellite static Country Music Radio.

There was terrific support too, from Radio 2 – now home to Lindisfarne and many of their peers. Another of Rod's songs, 'Refugees', finally made it to the EF having become a firm live favourite. Rod explained its inspiration to Dick Godfrey: was straight out of the paper, two articles I read the same day. One was about mistreatment of refugees when they arrive in Europe and the other a quote about how the poor don't do any damage to the earth they pass through, don't leave any footprints and move on.'

Godfrey acknowledged that. while Alan Hull was 'an unreformed 1960s protest singer, continuing to write against injustice and war long after Dylan and others

Below: Soundchecking at the City Hall with guest Kathryn Tickell, November 1997.

abandoned the genre,' his legacy was 'alive and kicking' in 'Refugees'. Despite the fact that the only originals left were Rod and Ray, Rod was unperturbed: 'There's only me and him at the back and to the side. And we are still to the back and to the side. It's a bit like the joke about George Washington's axe. The handle has been changed six times and the head ten, but it's *still* the original...'

After another summer of festivals, the band took off again in support of 'Blues From The Bothy', playing 33 dates between 16 October and 29 November. Before that, on August Bank Holiday weekend, the band were invited to mark the switching-on of the Blackpool Illuminations, an event broadcast live across the country by BBC Radio 2. Several old friends were there to announce the artists on stage, including Andy Peebles, Alan Freeman and Bob Harris.

Happily, it fell to Bob to announce Lindisfarne, and his infectious enthusiasm for the current line-up – having remained loyal to each subsequent twist and turn in the band's evolution since the early 1970s – was a source of great satisfaction to all. It was encouraging to learn he'd caught the band performing at the Tall Ships Festival in Aberdeen – which Radio 2 were also broadcasting – and had gone along to see them with no great expectations only to be blown away.

The Newcastle City Hall date on 29 November was somewhat awkward, being the first time they had played there since the Quarter Century Concert with Alan. Lindisfarne were a little nervous, but otherwise now completely comfortable with the current line-up.

As Rod had said in a major interview with David White in *Rock'n'Reel* in 1996, 'Lindisfarne was always a democracy. If anybody was ever higher up the pecking order, it was earned on work done. Alan wrote the majority of the songs, therefore he had a big role in the band as a result. By the same token, Ray's a very important person in the band apart from being the drummer. We *all* are. It kind of evens out, and Mitch has slotted into that.'

As a special treat, the very first Lindisfarne fan convention was organised to coincide with the City Hall date. Apart from the usual goings-on at these type of things, a large collection of band-related photographs was auctioned for the North East Young Musicians Fund, promoted by Kathryn Tickell – Lindisfarne's guest on stage that night. The event was a huge success and another bridge had been crossed.

In May 1998, the band were asked to appear live as part of Mike Harding's new Radio 2 *Folk And Roots Show* from the Newcastle Arts Centre. The other guests were Chris While and Julie Matthews, along with Brendan Croker and Steve Phillips. The running order for the night was a little curious for programming purposes, but the venue was terrific.

Lindisfarne opened and closed the show, while in-between came fine sets from Chris and Julie – with some harmonica from Marty – and the ever-idiosyncratic blues and banter of Steve and Brendan. The audience was even treated to a jam of 'Gonna Tear Your Stillhouse Down', featuring the entire cast on stage, after Steve and Brendan's set. Two new songs, Mitch's 'Born At The Right Time' and an instrumental from Dave, had been showcased in Lindisfarne's set, and both fitted like a glove.

Lindisfarne had returned to Watercolour in Ardgour – a studio they had all fallen in love with, and where they chose to record their first album of new material since Alan's death. There were a dozen songs for consideration, and Rod was now perceived as the main songwriter – though, as he'd admitted in his *Journal* interview with Dick Godfrey, he'd experienced some frustration when Alan had that role. And possibly envy. But I had no business to be, because he was just far more prolific and successful than I was. We'd get together after some time off to play each other our new songs: I'd produce my tape of two things I'd sweated buckets over and he had about 15. And ten of them would be *brilliant*.'

Already in the running in demo form from Ardgour were Rod's 'Can't Do Right For Doing Wrong'; 'Devil Of The North'; 'Jubilee Corner' and 'Born At The Right Time'. Marty also had 'Drifting Through' ready and Dave had an as-yet unnamed instrumental.

'I'd got the growing feeling that the band was waiting for songs from me,' said Rod recently. 'The more I had this feeling, the more reluctant the songs were to emerge. I had various attempts at writing during 1996-97, which weren't entirely unsuccessful – there were bits here and there with Jimmy Barrett, with Billy and with Dave. We got something out of all of them, but it was a time-consuming process.

'There weren't enough three-quarters-formed ideas. There was a lot of tenth ideas: none of us had what it took to see it through.' Both 'Coming Home To You' from the EP and 'Jubilee Corner' were successful, the latter 'popping out' when Rod was attempting to write something else. But he was concerned that, with time already booked at Watercolour, there would not be enough material ready.

He then contacted Nigel Stonier, with whom he had discussed songwriting collaborations while working on sessions for Ron Lister. 'We spoke each other's language,' he says. 'I'm not saying it wouldn't have worked otherwise – with Dave, for example – but it would have been a long, slogging exercise.' Nigel's approach was different, too, as Rod went on: 'He would say, "Right; we've got an afternoon, so let's see if we can get two songs done." It meant we used up a lot of loose ends.'

On 'Unmarked Car', Dave knew there was something there – he had the title, some of the melody and the riff. After a visit from Jimmy Barrett one afternoon, Rod and Dave managed to give the song some form and once again, after taking it to Nigel, it finally came together. On the album, the song seems to be part of the whole but somehow out on its own, with Dave's frail, cracked vocal reminiscent of Neil Young. 'It was originally very celebratory; eventually it became very dark – it seemed the obvious way to go,' recalls Dave.

It had also been decided to approach Sid Griffin to produce the album. Following the Coal Porters, his most recent album, 'Little Victories', had gained fantastic reviews and he was now also a much-respected music journalist and historian, having just completed work on a retrospective album of Gene Clark – the same ex-Byrd that had toured with Lindisfarne during the 1980s. My, how fate turns sometimes.

Sid – like the band – was acutely aware of just how good the songs had to be. As it turns out, the invitation to produce Lindisfarne was not from Ian, as Sid explains: 'Ian insists he didn't think of it. He swears he had nothing to do with it. To an extent, I still don't believe him!'

Griffin had sent Ian a copy of 'Little Victories', as he was in the habit of doing with each of his new albums, to see what he might have to say: 'Like most men, I don't show my emotions well, but I would like Ian to express some approval about what I'm doing; he's a brother who just happened to have a different mother and father. I know for a fact that he played it for Rod and he played it for Ray – and they liked it, which is pleasing to hear. Ian maintains those two desperados put my name on a short-list to produce the album.'

Sid talked to Ray at length before going ahead. 'When he rang, I thought it was a joke. Y'know Lindisfarne are a respectable, active band. I've produced many bands before, but they're usually indie bands when I usually had to chose which one of 28 takes was best. With Lindisfarne you ask them to do something once: it's usually correct and certainly the second time it's correct, because the level of musicianship is that high.'

He clearly enjoyed the association: 'It's been a joy. There's no pricks in the band, which you can hardly say about some.' Crucially, Sid also realised there was still a misconception of the band among the British music press: 'When I spoke to the people at Rykodisc when I was trying to get the guys involved with a Nick Drake tribute album they just couldn't believe it. Are Lindisfarne still together and why would those lager louts want to do something as sensitive as Nick Drake?

'I realise that as an American, an outsider, I have a completely different perspective from Geordies, Scousers, Londoners – whatever. I would be the first person to admit that that's bad. I don't understand some of the Geordie-isms you guys might laugh about in a pub, when I'm thinking, "What are they laughing about…and why is it so funny?" On the other hand, I don't have the emotional and cultural hang-ups some Englishmen have.

'I don't know – or give a fuck – about Christmas shows, the scarf-waving, the drinking…also, I'm incredibly aware of the talent of Alan Hull and what a loss it is to the world, much less Lindisfarne. So he's not here any more, and we have to make do with what tools are at hand.'

The band completed the album during the last two weeks of June. John Dagnell, head of Park Records, Lindisfarne's new label, was, like Sid, enthusiastic about the new material from the early stages, his commitment beyond question. An individual who has the luxury of enjoying all the artists on his roster, he's a throwback to an earlier generation of label bosses – like Strat at Charisma, or Chris Blackwell at Island – who were into the music.

The look and the title of the album would be crucial…and coming up with the title was not easy. Several had been in the pot: 'Breakfast In Bedlam', 'North By North East', 'Senile Delinquence', 'Ghost To Ghost'. Headlining Brigg Folk Festival in North Lincolnshire in July, the band met after soundchecking to nail it once and for all.

No-one wanted to give the press any opportunity to take pot-shots at them, and some of the titles already mooted would certainly give them the ammunition. The title would also suggest the cover painting, which Dave Denholm would be creating. The virtue of taking one song as the title was discarded as the option of choosing Dave's instrumental was thrown into the ring.

The track was now christened 'Uncle Henry', as the piece reminded Sid of a relation of that name. The final decision, Ray stressed, would have to be made by the end of that night's show – and by the time the band returned for the second half, the album title had only progressed as far as 'Songs For Uncle Henry'. The gig itself was a triumph. Over half the set was songs from the new album like Rod's 'Working My Way Back Home', 'Ghost In Blue Suede Shoes' – the album version of which featured Mitch's son, Scott, on piano – 'Devil Of The North' and 'One Day'.

Introducing 'Unmarked Car', Mitch nonchalantly announced the guitarist and singer as 'Dave Hull Denholm'. It was a reference most of the audience missed, but it was telling nonetheless. What they were unaware of was that, following the first day of routining with Sid at the Maggie Bank and unbeknownst to the band, Dave had gone away to Berwick to marry Alan's daughter, Francesca. Pat was there too, along with Dave's mother and, in a simple wedding ceremony, Dave and Francesca swapped names. The knowledge that Alan had wanted this to happen made the occasion all the more poignant. 'Dave was the son he never had,' Pat pointed out recently.

The 800-plus Brigg show crystallised much about the 1998 Lindisfarne; 95 per cent of the audience had not seen the band for 20-plus years, and almost all said that the show was great. To them, nothing seemed to have changed. It was the *music* that mattered.

A week after Brigg, another suggestion had been settled on for the title of the new album. Housed in

LINDISFARNE

here comes the neighbourhood

Born At The Right Time (Mitchell)
Ghost In Blue Suede Shoes (Clements / Stonier)
Jubilee Corner (Clements)
Can't Do Right For Doing Wrong (Clements / Stonier)
...king My Way Back Home (Clements / Barrett / Stonier)
Unmarked Car (Clements / Denholm / Stonier)
Devil Of The North (Clements / Stonier)
Uncle Henry (Denholm)
One Day (Clements / Denholm / Stonier)
Driftin' Through (Craggs)
All tracks published by BDM Music

Lindisfarne - Here Comes The Neighbourhood
Produced by Sid Griffin • Engineered by Nick Turner
...ed by Sid Griffin and Nick Turner • Mastered by Dennis Blackham at Country Masters
Recorded and mixed at Watercolour Music, Ardgour, Scotland during Spring and Summer 1998

*As well as bringing the first all-new
album from the current Lindisfarne
line-up, 1998 saw classic BBC
material reissued courtesy of New
Millennium Communications.*

lindisfarnecitysongs

ALAN HULL

THE BBC RECORDINGS 1973 & 1975

WHEN WAR IS OVER

149

a vibrant, evocative sleeve, 'Here Comes The Neighbourhood' looked like a very different Lindisfarne album. Gone was the Celtic imagery of 'Untapped And Acoustic'; instead, here was a package that had no photos of the band – another conscious decision – but came complete with inner shots of the instruments used, taken by Ian.

There was no doubt that this was very much a group album, and this showed in the songwriting credits; both Rod and Dave had brought songs to each other to see what would happen, while there were also several fine examples of Rod's partnership with Nigel Stonier. This was the spirit in which the songs came to the table.

The opener, Mitch's 'Born At The Right Time', was as much a statement of intent; upbeat, positive – not always the easiest type of song to write. Marty, too, had come up with goods on 'Driftin' Through', the album closer. 'Workin' My Way Back Home' was credited to Rod, Nigel and the previously mentioned Jimmy Barrett, a Liverpudlian friend of Steve Weltman's who had written with the band before.

One song which went beyond the usual remit was Rod's 'Can't Do Right For Doing Wrong', a song with a universal lyric that showed huge potential. Basically, there was a thread; one which duly acknowledged the importance of where the band came from – but, this time, not one which would have Lindisfarne hamstrung beyond the North East. It was now apparent that the perceived notion that Lindisfarne were best received in their native Tyneside was no longer true.

Indeed, it was possibly only the North East that seemed unwilling to allow them to shake off the spectre of the Christmas shows. With all the hard work of the last two and a half years, the rest of Britain could see that Lindisfarne was a living, breathing entity. On their forays to the Continent, Europe could see the same thing, too. In 1999, there would be the United States.

Looking back over nearly 30 years, Rod is able to see Lindisfarne in musical perspective now that the first 'real' product of this band is available: 'I would say the standard of musicianship is a lot higher now than it was then. This band, like that band, is very ingenious. Anything anyone can do, even if it's only a little bit, gets used. In the old days, for example, even though some of us played piano, there wasn't a keyboard player as such, so if there was a Hammond about we thought "Let's give that a try…"

'Nowadays, even the dreaded banjo rears its ugly head on odd tracks! It's all very much part of creative brainstorming; it's not as though so-and-so is the writer, so you have to stick to what they want. Somebody said the new album was the best since "Nicely Out Of Tune"; I think that's fair, because they've picked up on that sense of everyone chipping in.'

Lindisfarne   **Contact: 0191 297-1806**

Rod's prouder of 'Here Comes The Neighbourhood' than any other album he's been associated with. 'I would hesitate to say it's better album than x or y, but it's certainly up there with "Nicely Out Of Tune" and "Fog On The Tyne".' Much of this comes down to the collective feel: 'It's less centred on one person's songs, one person's voice or a set way of playing.

'It really is a collective, group album in the way that "Nicely Out Of Tune" was, before – and I don't mean this in a negative sense – it got centred round Alan's songs being produced as Alan's songs, with accompaniment; however good people's contributions were. That's what they became, for better or for worse. This an album by a living organism – which is the band. All the parts of it are alive and contributing to that.'

Throughout the lifetime of Lindisfarne, what has occurred has often happened organically, not by cynical or calculated means. For example, when Ian joined he was originally a 'hired hand' – just like Dave, 'and he's found a place for himself in the band, as everyone has,' Rod points out. 'Not replaced anybody, but hacked out or grown a new place for themselves in it.

'One of the reasons it still works, I'm sure, is because of the new input that people like Ian and Dave represent. They come from different generations, with new sets of ideas. That's incredibly valuable to the way the band sounds now.' Dave has his own view on this: 'I think it's quite a unique sound – but with classic instrumentation, the minimum. Everyone's looking for that *feel*, and you know when you get that. How it happens I don't know. It's that organic thing – that *balance*.'

Inevitably, today's Lindisfarne will be judged against what has gone before; certainly in the comparison with Alan's songs. 'I feel particularly strongly about this,' explains Ian. 'Enough time has gone by now, and there really had to be statement that said, "This is these six people. Take it or leave it. If you don't like it – fine." If there *is* to be a future, then it has to be these *six* people. We could

Top: New bass player Ian Thomson.

Left: Rod Clements, slide guitarist.

Bottom: Lindisfarne onstage in Gravesend.

have gone back to some of Alan's unrecorded songs, but I think that would be a backward step.'

Dave agrees – and his perspective is tremendously valid, given his circumstances. 'We would be getting into the realms of "tribute", and that's not really what the whole thing's about. There are, obviously, aspects of paying homage – within the songs and the way that they are presented.' Rod feels that probably, about 18 months into this version of the band, 'There were sounds we were starting to make that were linkable to the old Lindisfarne – but different and new.'

Dave also knew that, when it became clear that so much new material would have to go in the set, he could no longer rely on singing those songs of Alan's he had sung previously. 'Even though I loved doing the songs – they were tremendous and I felt I could get inside them – I just thought, to make a definite statement, we can't rely on those songs anymore. I knew the writing was coming together, but I would have no problem singing those songs again – in the right places. Most important is to push what we're doing now.'

The combination of all of these factors – the return to acoustic roots to discover the potential of their future; hard, long gigging that never automatically assumed a certain level of audience, adjusting along the way to the legacy left by Alan Hull; the writing skills hinted at by Rod in particular; a new working relationship shared by everyone and the guidance, faith and skills of Sid Griffin -– all led to 'Here Comes The Neighbourhood'.

Sid is quite clear about what he feels he brought to the album: 'Malcolm McLaren said recently that he likes Americans; they have a built-in bullshit detector. What I bring to the project is that, by not hurting anyone's feelings, I can politely, if not metaphorically, say "You're talking bullshit." That's something Americans are uniquely equipped to do.'

This was not the only asset he felt he brought along, as Sid went on: 'Oddly enough, North East music – or any Celtic music – is the music of America, 200 years earlier. What Lindisfarne play is not that far away from what their grandfathers and their grandfathers before them played. They have the rock'n'roll technology of the new era and the rock'n'roll instrumentation and attitude to go with it.

That's a hell of a lot different if you gave people like me – from Kentucky – those same instruments.

'I'm not producing people from Peru; I'm not producing people from South Korea – I'm producing people who, 200 years ago, gave America the music that evolved into folk music; that evolved into country and western. So the secondary thing I bring, is that I grew up on a music that's a distant musical cousin of the North East of England. It isn't as though I'm a stranger; I'm one of the boys.' What Sid was trying to focus on with 'Here Comes The Neighbourhood' was that the band needed to be reminded of what they are.

'Sing about and write about what you know about,' is what Griffin wanted to get across. He highlights 'Devil Of The North' as one of the songs that really stands out, and it is this type of song the producer feels is what Lindisfarne are all about. 'I want the album to focus on those regionalisms, as well as on acoustic, unplugged sounds. What the Lindisfarne guys are best at is being *themselves*.'

Rod appreciates what Sid was trying to achieve: 'He wanted an album that was a product of a particular group of people at a particular time. I think he's done very well at keeping a rein on some of the ideas, but being very alert and responsive to sudden flashes of inspiration – like trying different instruments.'

Sid has tremendous faith in 'Here Comes The Neighbourhood' and, despite his clear understanding of the current downward swing of the industry – 'no matter who you are, you're selling fewer units than you were a few years ago' – his commitment is total. Lindisfarne, he believes, could come again 'if they get a chance with the media. I do think there is an element of the boys down there in London set against them.

'There's a false image of the band that really doesn't exist any more – Lindisfarne are going to blow some minds with this album. I really think it's *that* good, whether my name's on it or not. When I went into this project, I thought the biggest problem's going to be they don't have the songs. The *fuck* they don't!'

'We've got such a great spirit within the band at the moment,' Ray Laidlaw stresses. 'The gigs we've done since we finished the album have been absolute dynamite. We're doing over half of the new stuff and it's "Lindisfarne" again – just with another shuffle. The same, but different – every time it happens. I feel extremely gratified I'm getting another opportunity for Lindisfarne to make an impression. The current band has exceeded my wildest dreams of what I thought we could do after Alan died. I knew we could have a good band and, at the worst, do a couple of more years reiterating what we'd already done.

'I don't want this to sound insensitive – because I am extremely sensitive about Alan's legacy and what he meant to me. At the same time, I can't stop enjoying my music because Alan's not here. So it goes on. The creativity within the new band is every bit as good as anything I've ever experienced over the years and, at last now, the newer members are in a position where their confidence is sky-high.

'They are creating music which they're a part of; not just playing other people's parts – although they've never had any problem about doing that. The obvious enthusiasm for the new material is extremely exhilarating for me. I see this as the first of a long line of new Lindisfarne records; I don't see it as an end to it. Time will tell.'

> I want no part of being young, don't want the wisdom of a sage
> While there are songs still to be sung, new words to grace the page
> A better age I'll never find
> 'Cos I was born at the right time
>
> And so while wishing that we'll all see better days
> My secret feeling is I'm happy in my ways
> An inner smile comes on me thinking of the past
> But I won't sigh for days gone by
> Now is where I'm at.
>
> 'Born At The Right Time'
> (W Mitchell, BDM Music)

Discography

While original release details (dates, catalogue numbers) are given, most Lindisfarne titles have since been reissued on compact disc and tracklistings may reflect any bonus cuts associated with these. Compilations etc are listed by title only, while reissued singles have been omitted.

LINDISFARNE ALBUMS

Nicely Out Of Tune
Released 1970
Charisma Records CAS 1025
Lady Eleanor – Road To Kingdom Come – Winter Song – Turn A Deaf Ear – Clear White Light – We Can Swing Together – Alan In The River With Flowers – Down – The Things I Should Have Said – Jackhammer Blues – Scarecrow Song – Knacker's Yard Blues – Nothing But The Marvellous Is Beautiful

Fog On The Tyne
Released 1971
Charisma Records CAS 1050
Meet Me On The Corner – Alright On The Night – Uncle Sam – Together Forever – January Song – Peter Brophy Don't Care – City Song – Passing Ghosts – Train In G Major – Fog On The Tyne – Scotch Mist – No Time To Lose

Dingly Dell
Released 1972
Charisma Records CAS 1057
All Fall Down – Plankton's Lament – Bring Down The Government – Poor Old Ireland – Don't Ask Me – Oh, No, Not Again – Dingle Regatta – Wake Up Little Sister – Go Back – Caught In The Act – Mandolin King – Dingly Dell

Lindisfarne Live
Released 1973
Charisma Records CLASS 2
No Time To Lose – Meet Me On The Corner – Alright On The Night – Train In G Major – Fog On The Tyne – We Can Swing Together – Jackhammer Blues

Roll On Ruby
Released 1973
Charisma CAS 1076
Taking Care Of Business – North Country Boy – Steppenwolf – Nobody Loves You Anymore – When The War Is Over – Moonshine – Lazy – Roll On River – Tow The Line – Goodbye

Happy Daze
Released 1974
Warner Brothers K 56070
Tonight – In My Head – River – You Put The Laff On Me – No Need To Tell Me – Juiced Up To Lose – Dealer's Choice – Nellie – The Man Down There – Gin And Tonics All Round – Tomorrow

Lindisfarne's Finest Hour (Compilation)
Released 1975
Charisma Records CAS 1108

Lady Eleanor (Compilation)
Released 1977
Hallmark Records SHM 919

Back And Fourth
Released 1978
Phonogram / Mercury Records 9106 609
Juke Box Gypsy – Warm Feeling – Woman – Only Alone – Run For Home – King's Cross Blues – Get Wise – You And Me – Marshall Riley's Army – Angels At Eleven – Make Me Want To Stay

Magic In The Air
Released 1978
Phonogram / Mercury Records 6641 877
Lady Eleanor – Road To Kingdom Come – Turn A Deaf Ear – January Song – Court in The Act – No Time To Lose – Winter Song – Uncle Sam – Wake Up Little Sister – All Fall Down – Meet Me On The Corner – Bye Bye Birdie – Train In G Major – Scarecrow Song – Dingly Dell – Scotch Mist – We Can Swing Together – Fog On The Tyne – Clear White Light

The News
Released 1979
Phonogram / Mercury Records 9109 626
Call Of The Wild – People Say – 1983 – Log On Your Fire – Evening – Easy And Free – Miracles – When Friday Come Along – Dedicated Hound – This Has Got To End – Good To Be Here?

Lindisfarne Singles Album (Compilation)
Released July 1981
Charisma Records BG5

Sleepless Nights
Released 1982
LMP Records GET1
*Nights – Start Again – Cruising To Disaster
– Same Way Down – Winning The Game –
About You – Sunderland Boys – Love Is A
Pain – Do What I Want – Never Miss The
Water – I Must Stop Going To Parties –
Stormy Weather*

Lindisfarntastic Live
Released 1983
PRT/LMP Records GET2
*I Must Stop Going To Parties – Marshall Riley's
Army – Down (featuring the Fartonium) – We Can
Swing Together – Fog On The Tyne – Engine Trouble
– Meet Me On The Corner – Clear White Light Part 2*

Lindisfarntastic II
Released 1984
PRT/LMP Records GET3
*Moving House – Taxman – Lady Eleanor – Nights –
Mr Inbetween – Brand New Day – Mystery Play –
Lover Not A Fighter – Day Of The Jackal – Stormy
Weather*

Dance Your Life Away
Released 1986
River City Records LINDLP1
*Shine On – Love On The Run – Heroes – All
In The Same Boat – Dance Your Life Away –
Beautiful Day – Broken Doll – One Hundred
Miles To Liverpool – Take Your Time – Song
For A Stranger*

C'Mon Everybody
Released 1987
Stylus SMR738
*Let's Dance – New Orleans – Splish Splash – Party
Doll – You Never Can Tell – Little Bitty Pretty One –
Running Bear – Mr Bassman – Sea Cruise – Let's Go
– Wooly Bully – C'Mon Everybody – Do You Wanna
Dance? – Twist And Shout – Do You Love Me? –
Runaround Sue – Shake Rattle And Roll – See You
Later Alligator – It'll Be Me – You Keep A Knockin' –
Love You More Than I Can Say – Oh Donna – Keep
Your Hands Off My Baby – Rhythm Of The Rain –
Speedy Gonzales – Little Darlin' – Dreamin' – La
Bamba – Meet Me On The Corner – Lady Eleanor –
Fog On The Tyne – Run For Home – Warm Feeling –
Clear White Light*

The Peel Sessions
Released 1988
Strange Fruit SFPS 059
*Poor Old Ireland – Mandolin King – Lady Eleanor –
Road To Kingdom Come*

Best Of Lindisfarne (Compilation)
Released 1989
Virgin VIP VVIPD103

Amigos
Released 1989
Black Crow Records CROCD224
*One World – Everything Changes – Working For The
Man – Roll On That Day – You're The One – Wish
You Were Here – Do It Like This – Anyway the Wind
Blows – Strange Affair – When The Night Comes
Down – Don't Say Goodnight – Another World*

Caught In The Act Live (Compilation)
Released 1992
Castle CCCSD346

Buried Treasures Volume 1
Released 1992
Virgin CDVM9012
*Red Square Dance – Finest Hour – Together Forever
(Live) – Together Crack – Happy Or Sad – Way
Behind You – Behind Crack – Old Peculiar Feeling –
True Love – Love Crack – City Song (Live) –
Rock'n'Roll Town – Swiss Maid (Live) – Sporting Life
Blues (Demo) – Karen Marie (Live) – From My
Window – Window Crack – Run Jimmy Run –
Malvinas Melody (Live) – Let's Dance (Live).*

Buried Treasures Volume 2
Released 1992
Virgin CDVM9013
*Save Our Ales – Ale Crack – Golden Apples – Try
Giving Everything – Nothing's Gonna Break Us Now
– January Song (Live) – Living On The Baseline – On
My Own I Built A Bridge – Bridge Crack – Roll On
That Day (Live) – Loving Around The Clock –
Reunion – Reunion (2) – Friday Girl – Tomorrow If
I'm Hungry – Hungry Crack – Fog On The Tyne
(Pudding Mix) – Peter Gunn Theme (Live) – Winning
The Game – Run For Home (Live)*

Elvis Lives On The Moon
Released 1993
Castle/Essential ESSCD197
*Day Of The Jackal – Soho Square – Old Peculiar
Feeling – Mother Russia – Demons – Don't Leave Me
Tonight – Elvis Lives On The Moon – Keeping The
Rage – Heaven Waits – Spoken Like A Man – Think*

Live
Released 1993
Demon Code 90 NINETY 5
*Court In The Act – Everything Changes – Anyway
The Wind Blows – Roll On That Day – Walk In the
Sea – Lady Eleanor – Knacker's Yard Blues – I Want
You To Be My Baby – Winning The Game – Meet Me
On The Corner – Fog On The Tyne – Clear
White Light*

Lindisfarne On Tap (A Barrel Full Of Hits) (Compilation)
Released 1994
Essential ESSCD214

Another Fine Mess
Grapevine GRAVCD211
Released 1996
Clear White Light – Squire – Lady Eleanor – Meet Me On The Corner – Evening – City Song – One World – All Fall Down – Winter Song – This Heart Of Mine – We Can Make It – Road To Kingdom Come – Money – Run For Home – Fog On The Tyne

The Other Side Of Lindisfarne
(Abridged version of C'Mon Everybody, also reissued as 'Archive' by Rialto/Trojan)
Released 1996
Mooncrest CRESTCD020

Blues From The Bothy EP
Released 1997
River City Records RCR 9702
Coming Home To You – Refugees – Knacker's Yard Blues (Revisited) – Ardnamurchan

Untapped And Acoustic
Released 1997
River City Records CDRCR 9701
No Time To Lose – Why Can't I Be Satisfied – Sundown Station – Uncle Sam – Run For Home – Walk A Crooked Mile – Scotch Mist – ...ing Down The Government – Call Of The Wild – ...ssing Ghosts – United States Of Mind – Lady ...eanor – Winter Song – Dingle Regatta – We Can ...ing Together – Clear White Light

...e Cropredy Concert
...leased 1997
...ooncrest CRESTCD34
...ad To Kingdom Come – All Fall Down – Elvis Lives ... The Moon – City Song – Lady Eleanor – Evening ...Day Of The Jackal – We Can Make It – Train In G ...jor – Walk In The Sea – Drinking Song – Meet Me ... The Corner – Run For Home – Clear White Light ...rt 2

...n For Home (Compilation)
...leased 1997
...usic Club MCCD 305

...y Songs
...leased 1998
...MC Pilot 34
...y Eleanor – City Song – Train In G Major – Fog ... The Tyne – Scotch Mist – Mandolin King – Poor ... Ireland – Road To Kingdom Come – Lady Eleanor ...rug Song – Country Gentleman's Wife – Passing ...sts – Turn A Deaf Ear – Lady Eleanor – Scarecrow ...g – Meet Me On The Corner

Lady Eleanor (Compilation)
Released 1998
Snapper Music SMD CD 159

Here Comes The Neighbourhood
Released 1998
Park Records PRKCD47
Born At The Right Time – Ghost In Blue Suede Shoes – Jubilee Corner – Can't Do Right For Doing Wrong – Working My Way Back Home – Wejibileng – Unmarked Car – Devil Of The North – Uncle Henry – One Day – Driftin' Through

**We Can Swing Together
(The BBC Concerts 1971)**
Released 1998
NMC Pilot 35

Dealer's Choice (Lindisfarne Mk II)
Released 1998
NMC Pilot 36

LINDISFARNE SINGLES
Clear White Light Part 2/Knacker's Yard Blues
Released 1970
Charisma Records CB 137

Lady Eleanor/Nothing But The Marvellous Is Beautiful
Released 1971
Charisma Records CB 153

**Meet Me On The Corner/ Scotch Mist/
No Time To Lose**
Released 1972
Charisma Records CB 173

All Fall Down/We Can Swing Together (Live)
Released 1972
Charisma Records CB191

Court In The Act/Don't Ask Me
Released 1972
Charisma Records CB 199

FOG ON THE TYNE

Taking Care Of Business/North Country Boy
Released 1974
Charisma Records CB 228

Fog On The Tyne/Mandolin King
Released 1974
Charisma Records CB 232

Tonight/No Need To Tell Me
Released 1975
Warner Brothers Records K16489

Run For Home/Stick Together
Released 1978
Phonogram/Mercury Records 6007 177

Juke Box Gypsy/When It Gets The Hardest
Released 1978
Phonogram/Mercury Records 6007 187

Brand New Day/Winter Song
Released 1978
Phonogram/Mercury Records 6007 195

Warm Feeling/Clear White Light (Live)
Released 1979
Phonogram/Mercury Records 6007 205

Call Of The Wild/Dedicated Hound
Released 1979
Phonogram/Mercury Records 6007 241

Easy And Free/When Friday Comes Along
Released 1979
Phonogram/Mercury Records NEWS 1

Friday Girl/1983
Released 1980
Subterranean SUB 1

Red Square Dance/Dance Of The Dissidents
Released 1980 (as the Defectors)
KGB 1

I Must Stop Going To Parties/See How They Run
Released 1981
Hangover HANG 9

Sunderland Boys/Cruising To Disaster
Released 1982
LMP LM 1

Nights/Dog Ruff
Released 1982
LMP FOG 1

Do What I Want/Same Way Down
Released 1983
LMP FOG 2

I Remember The Nights/Day Of The Jackal
Released 1985
LMP FOG 3

Christmas EP
Released 1985
LMP FOG 4
Warm Feeling (Live) – Red Square Dance – Run For Home (Live) – Nights (Acappella)

Shine On/Heroes/Dance Your Life Away
Released 1986
Priority Records LIND 1

Love On The Run/One Hundred Miles To Liverpool
Released 1987
LMP LIND 2

Party Doll/C'Mon Everybody
Released 1987
Stylus Music Records HONEY 3

Save Our Ales/Save Our Ales (Sub Mix)
Released 1988
River City Records LIND 2 A

Lady Eleanor 88/Meet Me On The Corner
Released 1988
Virgin Records LADY1

Fog On The Tyne (Revisited)/Fog On The Tyne (Revisited) (Instrumental)
Released 1990
Best ZB44083

Geordie Boys/Fog On The Tyne (Revisited)
Released 1991

ALAN HULL ALBUMS

Pipedream
Released 1973
Charisma Records CAS 1069
*Breakfast – Money Game – Country Gentleman's Wife
– Just Another Sad Song – Numbers (Travelling Band)
– For The Bairns – Drinking Song – Song For A
Windmill – United States Of Mind – I Hate To See
You Cry – Blue Murder*

Squire
Released 1975
Warner Brothers Records D56121
*Squire – Dan The Plan – Picture A Little Girl – Ain't
Nuthin' Shakin' (But The Leaves On The Trees) – One
More Bottle Of Wine – Golden Oldies – I'm Sorry –
Squire – Waiting – Bad Side Of Town – Mr Inbetween*

Phantoms
Released 1979
Rocket Records TRAIN 6
*Anywhere In Everywhere – Corporation Rock –
Dancin' (On The Judgement Day) – I Wish You Well –
Love Is An Alibi – Love Is The Answer – Madman
And Loonies – Make Me Want To Stay – Somewhere
Out There – A Walk In The Sea*

On The Other Side
Released 1983
Black Crow Records CRO206
*On The Other Side – Evergreen – Inside A Broken
Heart – Malvinas Melody – American Man – A
Mystery Play – Day Of The Jackal – Love In A Cage –
Fly Away*

Another Little Adventure
Released 1990
Black Crow Records CRO219
*Drinking Song – Money Game – United States Of
Mind – Dan The Plan – Treat Me Kindly – Fly Away
– Malvinas Melody – One More Bottle Of Wine –
Poor Old Ireland – Evening – January Song – All Fall
Down – Marshall Riley's Army – Heroes*

Back To Basics
Released 1994
Mooncrest CRESTCD017
*United States Of Mind – Poor Old Ireland – All Fall
Down – Lady Eleanor – Winter Song – Walk In The
Sea – Mother Russia – This Heart Of Mine –
Mr Inbetween – January Song – Breakfast – Day Of
The Jackal – Oh No Not Again – Run For Home – Fog
On The Tyne*

Statues And Liberties
Released 1996
Transatlantic TRACD246
*Statues And Liberties – Walk A Crooked Mile –
Cardboard Christmas Boxes – Treat Me Kindly – One
Hundred Miles To Liverpool – Money – This Heart Of
Mine – Long Way From Home – When The Sun Goes
Down – Hoi Poloi – Save Yourself – Drug Song*

When War Is Over
Released 1998
NMC Pilot 037
*Drug Song – Numbers – United States Of Mind –
When War Is Over – Down On The Underground –
Gin And Tonics All Round – One More Bottle Of
Wine – Dan The Plan – Dealer's Choice – Winter
Song – Peter Brophy Don't Care – Squire – City
Song – Dan The Plan (Live) – Money Song – Gin
And Tonics All Round – Golden Oldies – Alright
On The Night – One More Bottle Of Wine*

ALAN HULL SINGLES

We Can Swing Together/Obidiah's Grave
Released 1970
Transatlantic Records/Big T BIG 129

Numbers/Drinking Song/One Off Pat
Released 1973
Charisma Records CB 208

Justanothersadsong/Waiting
Released 1973
Charisma Records CB 211

Dan The Plan/One More Bottle Of Wine
Released 1975
Warner Brothers K16561

Squire/One More Bottle Of Wine
Released 1975
Warner Brothers K16599

Crazy Woman/Golden Oldies
Released 1975
Warner Brothers K16643

I Wish You Well/Love Is The Answer
Released 1979
Rocket Records XPRES 12

A Walk In The Sea/Corporation Rock
Released 1979
Rocket Records XPRES 19

Malvinas Melody/Ode To A Taxman
Released 1983
Black Crow CRS 2

RAY JACKSON – SOLO ALBUM
In The Night
Released 1980
Phonogram / Mercury Records 9109 831
Everything Will Turn Out Fine – Make It Last – In The Night – Another Lovely Day – Stick Around Joe – Waiting For The Time – Little Town Flirt – Tread On A Good Thing – You Send Me – Easy Love – Solo Again – In The Midnight Hour

RAY JACKSON – SOLO SINGLE
Take Some Time/Working On
Released 1976
EMI 2514

ROD CLEMENTS SOLO ALBUM
One Track Mind
Released 1994
Batsville Music BAT 1 (Cassette only)
Hard Travellin' – Train That Took My Girl From Town – Bourgois Blues – Train In G Major – Ain't No More Cane – Down In The Flood – Road To Kingdom Come – Evil Hearted Woman – Meet Me On The Corner – Leather Launderette – No Turning Back

JACK THE LAD ALBUMS
It's Jack The Lad
Released 1974
Charisma Records CAS 1085
Boilermaker Blues – Back On The Road Again – Plain Dealing – Fast Lane Driver – Turning Into Winter – Why I Can't I Be Satisfied – Song Without A Band – Rosalie – Promised Land – Corny Pastiche – Black Cock Of Wickham – Chief O'Neill's Favourite – Golden Rivet – Staten Island – The Cook In The Kitchen – Lying In The Water – One More Dance – Make Me Happy

The Old Straight Track
Released 1974
Charisma Records CAS 1094
Oakey Strike Evictions – Jolly Beggar – Third Millenium – Weary Whaling Grounds – Fingal The Giant – King's Favourites – The Marquis Of Tullybardine – Peggy (Overseas With A Soldier) – Buy Broom Besoms – De Havilland's Mistake – Old Straight Track – Wurm – Home Sweet Home – Big Ocean Liner

Rough Diamonds
Released 1975
Charisma Records CAS 1110
Rocking Chair – Smokers Coughin' – My Friend, The Drink – Letter From France – Gentlemen Soldier – Gardener Of Eden – One For The Boy – Beachcomber – Ballad Of Winston O'Flaherty – Jackie Lusive – Draught Genius – Baby Let Me Take You Home

Jackpot
Released 1976
United Artists Records UAS 29999
Eight Ton Crazy – Amsterdam – Steamboat Whistle Blues – Walter's Drop – We'll Give You The Roll – Trinidad – You, You, You – Let It Be Me – The Tender – Take Some Time

Back On The Road Again (Live)
Released 1993
Mah Mah MM1 (cassette only)
Peggy (Overseas With A Soldier) – Rocking Chair – Buy Broom Besoms – The Jolly Beggar – Steamboat Whistle Blues – From A Jack To A King – Weary Wailing Grounds – Ballad Of Winston O'Flaherty – Captain Grant – Why Can't I Be Satisfied – The Tender – The Gentleman Soldier – Walter's Drop

JACK THE LAD SINGLES
One More Dance/Draught Genius (Polka)
Released 1973
Charisma Records CB 206

Why Can't I Be Satisfied/Make Me Happy
Released 1973
Charisma Records CB218

Home Sweet Home/Big Ocean Liner
Released 1975
Charisma Records CB 242

Eight Ton Crazy/Walter's Drop
Released 1976
United Artists Records UP 36162

RADIATOR ALBUM
Isn't It Strange
Released 1977
Rocket Records ROLL 14
Spittin' In The Wind – I Wish You Well – A Walk In The Sea – Madmen And Loonies – Corporation Rock – Isn't It Strange – Lay Back And Dream – Something Got The Better Of You – Love Is The Alibi – Love Is The Answer

SOLO DISCOGRAPHIES/GUEST APPEARANCES
(Not including previously listed Lindisfarne/Alan Hull releases)

MARTY CRAGGS

ARTIST	TITLE	SINGLE/ALBUM	YEAR
Landgale	The Millenium	Single	c1975
Five Hand Reel	Reel Reggae	Single	1976
The Breakers	Headline News	Single	1980
Jimmy Nail	Night For Day	Single B-side	1985
Warfare	A Conflict Of Hatred	Album	1988
Pacamax	Live At The Magnesia Bank	Album	1990
Ron Lister	Spun From A Silken Web *	Album	c1992
Ted Grimes/Stewart Hardy	The Rocky Shore	Album	1995

IAN THOMSON

ARTIST	TITLE	SINGLE/ALBUM	YEAR
Arthur 2 Stroke	The Wondersea World Of Jacques Cousteau	Single	1979
Arthur 2 Stroke	The Who Who Song/I'm Not Sorry	Single	1980
Arthur 2 Stroke	Hawaii 5-0 Theme/Heart Of Stone	Single	1981
Arthur 2 Stroke	Live At Banwells	Album	1981
Watt Government	Working My Fingers To The Bone/Waiting For A Phone Call	Single	c1982
Archie Brown and the Young Bucks	Bring Me The Head Of Jerry Garcia *	Album	c1989
Archie Brown/YB	Rafferty, Rafferty, Fists	Album	1990
Archie Brown/YB	Dirt And Romance	Album	1995
Archie Brown/YB	Prisoner Of Fender	Album	1997
The Coal Porters	Rebels Without Applause	Album	1991
The Coal Porters	A Town South Of Bakersfield – Vol 3	Compilation Album	1992
The Coal Porters	Los London	Album	c1995
The Coal Porters	Woah Big Fella	Official Bootleg Cassette	1997
Sid Griffin	Little Victories	Album	1997

DAVE HULL DENHOLM

ARTIST	TITLE	SINGLE/ALBUM	YEAR
This Is This	'Several locally released singles'		c1991
W/Steve Cunningham, Lee Proud	Cunningham, Proud, Denholm	Cassette	c1993

Left: The band with manager Barry McKay (centre), 1984.

Above: With Status Quo in Australia, 1973. From left, Mickey Sweeney, Si, Rick Parfitt, Jacka and Charlie Cameron.

BILLY MITCHELL

The Callies	Remember Laddie/Whip Jamboree	Single	1969
The Callies	Peggy Gordon (Take Off Your Head...)	Single	1969
The Callies	On Your Side	Album	1970
Pete Scott	Don't Panic	Album	1970
Pete Scott	Jimmy The Moonlight	Album	1971
Maxie & Mitch	Double Trouble	Album	1982
Alan Taylor	The Traveller	Album	1983
Mike Elliott	At Last! It's Mike Elliott *	Album	1983
Alan Taylor	Circle Round Again	Album	1984
Pacamax	Live At The Magnesia Bank *	Cassette	1990
Various Artists	Sailing Home *	Compilation album	1993
Maxie & Mitch	Unplugged, Undressed & Unrehearsed Live	Cassette	1993
Billy Mitchell	Almost Grown	Album	1993
Jed Grimes/Stewart Hardy	The Rocky Shore	Album	1995

RAY JACKSON GUEST APPEARANCES

Various Artists	Take Off Your Head And Listen	Compilation Album	1969
Rod Stewart	Every Picture Tells A Story	Album	1971
Long John Baldry	It Ain't Easy	Album	1971
Peter Hamill	Fool's Mate	Album	1971
Rab Noakes	Red Pump Special	Album	1974
Rod Stewart	Smiler	Album	1974
Chris De Burgh	Far Beyond These Castle Walls	Album	1974
Bob Barton	Benwell Lad	Single	1975
Mike Harding	My Brother Sylvest	Single	1976
Derek Brimstone	Derek Brimstone	Album	1976
Pete Scott	Jimmy The Moonlight	Album	1976
Various Artists	Woody Lives! (Tribute)	Album	1987
Breathe	Peace Of Mind	Album	1990
Grethe Svensen	The Love Of A Woman	Album	1993
Grethe Svensen	Your Beauty	Album	1995

ALAN HULL GUEST APPEARANCES

Chosen Few	I Won't Be Around You Anymore	Single	1965
Chosen Few	So Much To Look Forward To	Single	1965
Various Artists	Take Off Your Head And Listen	Compilation Album	1969
Colin Scott	Colin Scott	Album	1970
Bob Barton	Benwell Lad	Single	1975
Maxie & Mitch	Double Trouble	Album	1982
Various Artists	Heroes	Compilation Album	1985
Pacamax	Live At The Magnesia Bank	Cassette	1990
Various Artists	Sailing Home *	Compilation album	1993

ROD CLEMENTS GUEST APPEARANCES

Prelude	Owlcreek Incident	Album	1975
Ralph McTell	Streets	Album	1975
Ralph McTell	Right Side Up	Album	1976
Wiz Jones	Happiness Was Free	Album	1976
Michael Chapman	The Man Who Hated Mornings	Album	1977
Michael Chapman	Looking For Eleven *	Album	1980
Rab Noakes	Rab Noakes	Album	1980
Rab Noakes	Under The Rain *	Album	1983
Kathryn Tickell	Borderlands	Album	1986
Various Artists	Woody Lives! (Tribute)	Album	1987
Ian McCallum	Left Handed	Album	c1988
Pentangle	So Early In The Spring	Album	1989
Nigel Stonier	Golden Coins For The Holy Kid	Album	1993
Rick Kemp	Escape	Album	1997

SIMON COWE GUEST APPEARANCES

7:84 Theatre Group	The Life And Times Of Joe England	Single	c1976

* *Titles also feature Ray Laidlaw, as does Ralph McTell's 'Songs From Alphabet Zoo' (album, 1983) and Michael Chapman's 'Navigation' (album, 1985).*